The Best Of Fine WoodWorking

Power Saws
and Planers

The Best Of Fine WoodWorking

Power Saws
and Planers

The Taunton Press

Cover photo by Sandor Nagyszalanczy

Taunton
BOOKS & VIDEOS

for fellow enthusiasts

First printing: September 1990
Second printing: September 1993
Printed in the United States of America

A FINE WOODWORKING Book

FINE WOODWORKING® is a trademark of The Taunton Press, Inc.,
registered in the U.S. Patent and Trademark Office.

The Taunton Press, Inc.
63 South Main Street
Box 5506
Newtown, Connecticut 06470-5506

Library of Congress Cataloging-in-Publication Data

The Best of Fine woodworking. Power saws and planers : 26 articles /
   selected by the editors of Fine woodworking magazine.
     p. cm.
    "A Fine woodworking book"—T.p. verso.
    Includes index.
    ISBN 0-942391-83-7
    1. Woodworking tools. 2. Saws. 3. Planing-machines
I. Fine woodworking   II. Title: Power Saws and planers.
TT186.B474   1990
684'.083–dc20   90-39700
                                   CIP

Contents

Introduction

Despite our romantic notions, building with wood is hard work. And the drudgery in converting this humble, recalcitrant material into beautiful objects sometimes detracts from the real pleasures of woodworking. Fortunately, modern workers have an entire arsenal of power tools—a variety of saws, thickness planers and jointers—for getting the wood into shape.

These machine tools are fast and efficient, but skill is not always built into them. Each machine must be properly tuned and set up, and that takes time and knowledge. You quickly discover that the operator must do more than just feed stock into whirring cutters.

Even learning how to use the machines doesn't guarantee good results. You still must sort through a bewildering array of blades, fences and other devices, as well as figure out how to set up your shop so your work can move smoothly from operation to operation.

In this collection of 26 articles reprinted from *Fine Woodworking* magazine, experienced woodworkers show you how to evaluate power tools and accessories. They also offer expert guidance in making accurate rip fences, in building your own bandsaw and scroll saw, and in tuning both commercial and shop-built models for best performance. And finally, there's crucially important advice on eye and ear safety, and on clearing dust and chips from the air in your shop.

—*Dick Burrows, editor*

*The *Best of Fine Woodworking* series spans issues 46 through 80 of *Fine Woodworking* magazine, originally published between mid-1984 and the beginning of 1990. There is no duplication between these books and the popular *Fine Woodworking on...* series. A footnote with each article gives the date of first publication; product availability, suppliers' addresses and prices may have changed since then.

Over the years, *Fine Woodworking* has received a steady stream of complaints from readers about bandsaws. Heading the list are troubles with resawing, blade tracking, vibration, breaking blades and lack of power. It turns out that some of the problems are due to compromises in machine design or sloppy manufacturing, others stem from lack of knowledge on the part of the operator—either in misusing the bandsaw or in not recognizing a problem for what it is and fixing it.

In this article I'll talk about what to expect from home-shop bandsaws of various sizes. I'll also list some principles

Home-Shop Bandsaws

Selecting and tuning a mid-size machine

by Jim Cummins

many bandsaws on the market for me to test them all. But having looked at a good number, I've concluded that differences from brand to brand are less important than I had once thought. The fact is, the bandsaw is a pretty stone-simple machine—which is one reason everybody and his brother makes one—and if you tune it properly, almost any kind can be made to work. Fences, miter gauges and other accessories probably don't amount to a hill of beans—when you need a special set-up, it's probably best to make it yourself.

There's no denying that an expensive machine is more pleasant to use than a junky one. But as long as a bandsaw turns that blade, it can be made to do 95% of the jobs that the small shop asks of it. Remember the cowboy in the old song, with a $10 horse and a $40 saddle. Skimp on the machine if you must; in the long run you can get used to, or fix, any bandsaw's ornery qualities. But no bandsaw is worth a dime running a bum blade.

What is important is choosing a machine in the right size category. The bandsaw is close to being the all-purpose woodworking machine. Its virtues, in a sense, are its biggest vice, because they tempt the user to push a machine beyond its limits. Industrial-quality machines in the 20-in. and bigger sizes have relatively few problems because they are rigid and powerful enough to gobble up whatever is fed into them. But few basement shops boast 20-in. machines; they are just too big, too hungry for electrical power, too costly for the part-time budget. Recognizing this, manufacturers have come out with a slew of bandsaws meant for home-shop and light-industrial use.

To make sense of the variety, let's first get some nomenclature out of the way. A bandsaw's throat capacity is the distance from the blade to the column that supports the upper wheel. On two-wheel machines, the throat capacity is typically about ¼ in. less than the diameter of the wheels. Three-wheel machines were developed strictly to increase throat capacity by utilizing a triangular frame shape.

Depth capacity is the height the guides can be raised above the table, and it depends on the distance between the wheels. Many two-wheel bandsaws have the option of adding an extension to the column to increase the depth of cut. The nominal guide height can be deceptive, however, because if the frame isn't rigid enough, and the wheels not round enough, a bandsaw may have trouble sawing wood that's only half its stated height capacity.

If you need a bandsaw purely for scroll work on large panels, by all means consider a light, three-wheel machine. But I'll take it as a main part of my argument that what the home-shop woodworker really wants is a machine that can resaw veneers, cut logs into bowl blanks for the lathe, shape cabriole legs and carving blanks, and do any of these jobs accurately and reliably—without shudder, screech and smoke.

With those requirements in mind, my best advice is that you absolutely ignore the $100 hardware-store-specials such as the little Black & Deckers and Skils. This advice applies to two- and three-wheel machines both.

Two of the large three-wheelers, the Inca and the Wood-Mizer, are compared head-to-head on p. 12. But if you plan to have just one bandsaw, I'll go out on a limb and recommend that you ignore any three-wheeler, unless you really need the throat capacity. Why? Because three-wheel design sacrifices column rigidity. When blades are brought up to proper tension, the weaker column invites blade tracking problems and column vibration that contributes to ragged cutting. A three-wheeler's small wheels also mean shorter blade life, because the blade must bend abruptly with every revolution. If you want a three-wheel saw, stick to blades under 0.020-in. thick. Your best bet for respectable blade life are the 0.014-in.- to 0.018-in.-thick blades pioneered by Olson (Box 262, Bethel, Conn. 06801).

To help you evaluate bandsaw trouble spots, the following is a list of important general considerations. I'll take up some of these in more detail on p. 13, in comparing three of the most popular machines—the 12-in. Sears Craftsman, the 14-in. Delta, and an AMT, one of the imported clones based on the Delta design.

Motor: The less vibration there is, the better a bandsaw will cut. A cheap, unbalanced motor, such as those found on many Taiwanese machines, should be replaced. A decent farm-grade or industrial motor with an honest ½ HP should be enough for any bandsaw with a 6-in. height capacity. You can just get by with the same motor on a 12-in. capacity machine, provided that you change the drive pulleys to slow down the blade speed, thereby increasing the motor's effective torque. A ¾-HP or 1-HP motor isn't too much for a bandsaw, but until you've checked through the rest of this trouble list, keep your money in your wallet.

Pulleys, belts and speeds: As just mentioned, gearing down a saw increases the available torque from the motor and also promotes smoother resawing. For this reason, I recommend a multi-speed machine, or at least equipping your bandsaw with a three-

Bandsaw math

Shifting speeds makes the bandsaw more versatile. The Inca has three speeds, selected by moving the belt and retensioning it. You can accomplish much the same result on any bandsaw by installing new pulleys.

To figure the blade speed in surface feet per minute (sfm), determine the motor RPM (R), and, in inches, the diameter of the motor pulley (P1), the diameter of the wheel pulley (P2), and the diameter of the driven bandsaw wheel (D). Then,

$$\frac{R \times P1}{P2} \times 3.14 \times D = \text{inches per minute.}$$

Divide by 12 to get sfm.

If you don't know the size blade a two-wheel bandsaw takes, and it is inconvenient to measure around the wheels, apply the following formula:

With the wheels in working position, measure the radius of one wheel (R1), the radius of the second wheel (R2), and the distance between the axles (D). Then, (R1 × 3.1416) + (R2 × 3.1416) + (2 × D) = Length.

step pulley on the motor and a 7-in. or 8-in. pulley on the driven wheel. The standard bandsaw blade speed is about 3,000 sfm (surface-feet per minute). You could use 1,500 sfm or 1,000 sfm for resawing, and a variety of speeds in the 100-sfm to 700-sfm range for metal cutting. Many inexpensive imports have this feature.

It's very possible that cheap pulleys are out-of-round or bored off-center and that cheap belts are lumpy. These conditions cause vibration. Small pulleys rob power. If your machine came with 2-in. and 4-in. pulleys, switching to 3-in. and 6-in. (better yet, 4-in. and 8-in.) will improve the saw's performance.

Wheels and tires: Wheels should be round and balanced, and don't take it for granted that they are. Check for roundness as shown in the photo on following page, top left. To check balance, remove the blade and the drive belt and spin the wheels by hand. Unless your bearings are very tight, the heavy spot on a wheel will end up stopped at the bottom every time. You can balance a wheel by drilling holes near the rim or by adding weight (wrapped solder, auto wheel weights, etc.). Just as with a car wheel, a bandsaw wheel can be statically balanced, but dynamically not, so don't add or remove weight all in one spot.

Keep tires clean, because buildup of chips and other gunk can change blade tension and throw tracking off. From time to time, rub the turning wheel with a hardwood block, or whatever, to scrape it clean. It's not a bad idea to mount stiff brushes inside the wheel covers to make the machine self-cleaning. If tires are

You can check wheels for roundness by resting a chisel against a convenient part of the machine while spinning the wheels. The same chisel, used as a scraping tool, can true the tires.

The tension gauge on the author's Rockwell/Delta bandsaw was, as with most such gadgets, a poor indicator of proper blade tension. With the indicator set to the ¼-in. mark, blade tension is about 2,500 psi, or one-tenth what it should be (left). Getting the blade up to 25,000 psi required turning the indicator washer way above the ¾-in. mark (right). The washer position is not reliable because the spring in the gauge fatigues with use—the text explains how to tension the blade by its musical pitch.

stretched onto the wheels unevenly, they'll have high spots that change blade tension with every revolution, producing a whip-lash effect that reduces blade life and promotes ragged cutting. You can true the lower tire by holding a sanding block, file or scraper against it while the machine is running (devise some sort of tool rest, as if turning on the lathe, and, of course, without a blade on the machine). On some machines, you can true the upper tire by mounting the wheel on the bottom; otherwise have someone rotate the top wheel by hand for truing. Retain the shape of any crowning. Check top and bottom wheel alignment with a straightedge.

Make-do tires can be made from crowned layers of masking tape, electrical tape and small bicycle inner tubes or whatever. Wheels on top-notch bandsaws generally get sent to the factory for re-tireing and balancing. Typical cost is $100-plus per wheel.

Tension gauges: Bandsaws tension blades by moving one of the wheels to stretch the blade. This is usually the same wheel that tilts to adjust tracking. Sometimes the movable wheel rides

on a spring, sometimes not. It doesn't make much difference. What's important here is that springs fatigue, and tension indicators dependent on them become inaccurate. For example, my Rockwell/Delta's spring measured 2¼ in. long when I checked it recently; a new spring measured 2⅞ in., a difference, at the ¼-in. scale setting, of 2,500 psi for the old spring versus 12,000 psi for the new. Both these tensions, incidentally, are too low.

My bandsaw's tensioning screw had too few threads to properly tension the standard blade. I buy blades 1 in. shorter than recommended (measure: blade must fit with the saw's top wheel in its lowest position). Other choices: replace the tension spring with a solid length of pipe; shim up the tension screw.

Briefly, if you have a 14-in., two-wheel bandsaw that takes a 104-in. blade—the Rockwell/Delta with height extension, or any of its imported clones—and provided you're using the ¼-in. bimetal blade described on the facing page, tension the blade to produce the same musical pitch found on the lowest string of a guitar. You don't need a guitar, of course, you can keep a pitch pipe or harmonica handy instead. This note, E, corresponds to 15,000 psi and is adequate for all-around work; a G# is 27,500 psi—my choice for serious resawing. On 14-in. saws without the riser block, G# is about 15,000 psi. Please note that this pitch test will work on carbon steel blades as well, but *only* if they're ¼-in., with 6 tpi and 0.025-in. thick—any variation from these specs will change the pitch, just as heavier and lighter guitar strings sound different notes. For an accurate pitch, be sure the blade vibrates freely, without interference from the guides (on most machines, you can pluck the blade at the column side). Don't worry too much about breaking the blade—its recommended tension on an industrial bandsaw is 30,000 psi.

There is one caution here—on the Sears saw I tested (p. 14), the wheels were so far out-of-round that blade tension varied wildly with every revolution. I could play a little tune by rotating the wheels by hand and plucking the blade at the same time, which is how I'd advise you to check your bandsaw's wheels (the gauge varied between 8,000 and 25,000 psi with every revolution). If your saw is much off, there will be no way in the world to get a blade to run right without truing the wheels.

Guides: A bandsaw blade needs to be supported at the sides and back. The various guide systems all work, and I wouldn't make a big point of choosing one over another. It is important, however, that guides should not touch the blade while it's free-running, only under the pressure of the cut. Also, they must not impart, or allow, any twist or deflection of the blade.

Guides set too far from the work allow deflection. This shortens blade life and greatly reduces cutting accuracy. The top guides should be adjusted up or down to the thickness of the work with every cut. In theory, this should be a painless procedure, accomplished by sliding the guide post up or down and tightening its lock. On most cheap bandsaws, however, the guide post twists or slants, mis-aligning the guides. The cause is cheap castings that warp, sloppy workmanship, or bad design. It would be worth reboring the casting and inserting a bushing, or whatever sort of shims it takes, to true the guide post's travel.

To run ¹⁄₁₆-in.-wide blades, you can replace solid-block side guides with pieces of oily hardwood (lignum vitae, rosewood, etc.) notched to suit. The notch will act as side-to-side support and backup bearing at the same time.

Frame and stand type: If your stand wobbles, brace it, add a reinforcing shelf, underlay the top with plywood—whatever it takes. If the factory stand is really flimsy, throw it out and build one of wood. The frame of the saw might be cast-iron, welded

The little blade that could

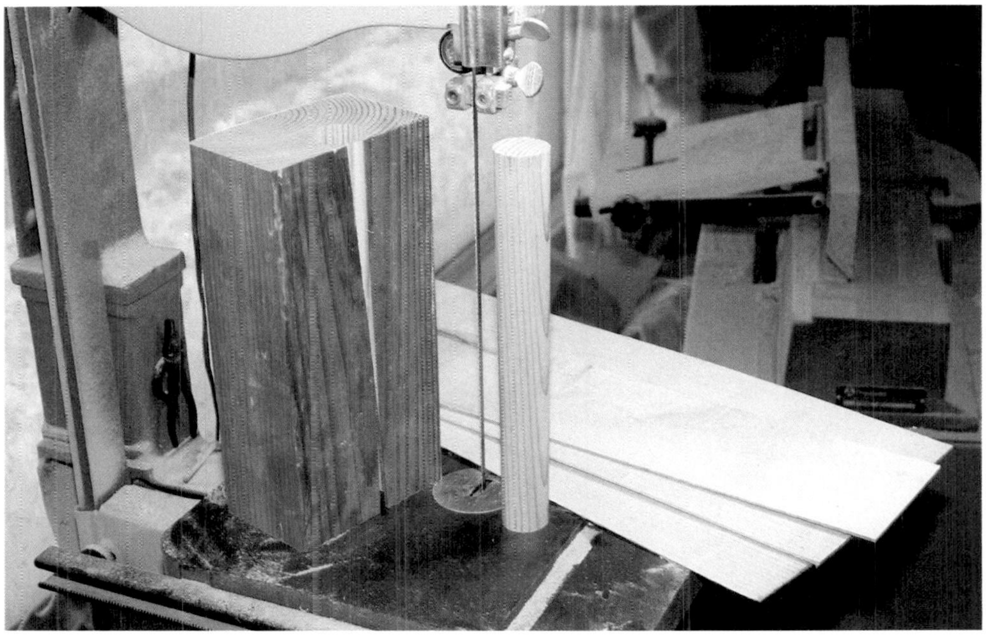

Bimetal blades may do for the bandsaw what carbide did for the tablesaw. This ¼-in. blade, at 25,000 psi tension, can both resaw without bowing and cut tight circles.

The real breakthrough in getting my bandsaw to work came when I visited a blade factory—American Saw Co., in West Springfield, Mass., the home of Lenox brand blades. Engineers Bob Candiano and Marty Kane were wrapping up a year-long research project on what happens as a bandsaw blade cuts.

As a result of what I learned that day, I started a six-month blade testing program, both in my own shop and with the help of several volunteers around the country. The results fly in the face of anything you may have read or seen before: If you own a 14-in., Rockwell/Delta bandsaw, or a copy, I suggest that you fit it with a hook-tooth, ¼-in.-wide bimetal blade, 0.025 in. thick, with 6 tpi for all your bandsaw work. Properly tensioning this blade may use up all the threads in your tension gauge, so order a blade 1 in. shorter than recommended (see p. 10), or plan to shim up the tension screw. This blade will zip through 4/4 walnut as fast as I can feed it, cut clean circles down to about 1¼ in. diameter and huff-and-puff its way through 12-in.-thick oak. It costs about $20, or double the price of a carbon-steel blade, but should last between ten and twenty times longer.

Fig. 1: Bimetal blade anatomy

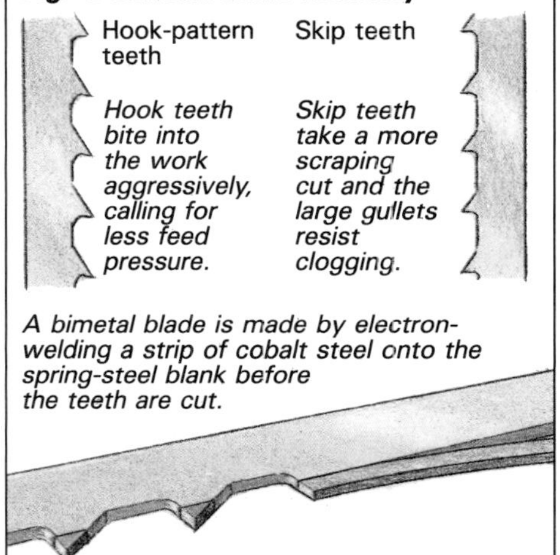
Hook-pattern teeth
Skip teeth
Hook teeth bite into the work aggressively, calling for less feed pressure.
Skip teeth take a more scraping cut and the large gullets resist clogging.
A bimetal blade is made by electron-welding a strip of cobalt steel onto the spring-steel blank before the teeth are cut.

Fig. 2: Why a blade bows

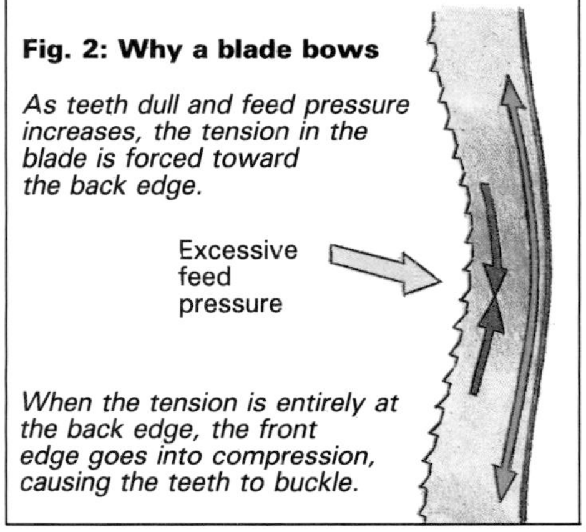
As teeth dull and feed pressure increases, the tension in the blade is forced toward the back edge.
Excessive feed pressure
When the tension is entirely at the back edge, the front edge goes into compression, causing the teeth to buckle.

Why bimetal? Ordinary bandsaw blades are carbon steel, with teeth and backs tempered to a variety of tooth-and-back hardnesses. If the teeth produce dust rather than chips, friction-generated heat anneals the tips of the teeth and, suddenly, the blade stops cutting straight. A bimetal blade has a strip of cobalt steel welded along its leading edge to form the tips of the teeth. The cobalt steel is capable of resisting temperatures of up to 1,200°, whereas carbon steel begins to anneal and dull at about 400°.

Why so narrow? A bowed cut results from transfer of tension to the back of the blade, as shown in the drawing. Unless a blade is properly tensioned, it will bow at even moderate feed pressures.

The reason to choose a ¼-in. blade is simply because the average home-shop bandsaw is incapable of fully tensioning a much wider blade.

As a general rule, if you have been experiencing bowing problems with a ¾-in. blade, they will probably disappear if you run this ¼-in. blade at your saw's ¾-in. tension setting. See the main article for more details about proper tensioning.

Why hooked teeth? Skip-tooth blades are often recommended for resawing—they cut smoothly and have large gullets to carry away chips. I can't disagree with this, and would probably recommend skip-tooth blades to an experienced bandsawyer who is on top of his work at all times. But as a part-timer myself, I prefer a hook-tooth pattern. Hooked teeth cut aggressively. This requires less feed pressure, reducing the chance of bowing. As a disadvantage, hooked teeth alternately pull the blade to one side of the cut, then the other, which sets up vibration that contributes to the bandsaw's typically rough cut. I'll settle for a little washboarding rather than the possible bowed cut of a skip-tooth blade.

Why six teeth? As discussed in the main article, I recommend that you slow down your bandsaw for resawing, mostly to avoid heat buildup. At slow speeds, a blade with four hooked teeth may self-feed so aggressively that it becomes difficult to control. The six-tooth blade takes smaller bites and behaves better.

Where to get? Lenox blades are sold only through industrial hardware stores and the like. Check the Yellow Pages, or call (800) 628-3030 to get the name of your nearest distributor (in Mass., call (413) 525-3961). One mail-order source that will ship UPS, C.O.D., is Viking Machinery and Tool Supply, 2915 Newpark Dr., Barberton, Ohio 44203; call (800) 223-3487, or, in Ohio, (800) 362-0585.

You don't have to buy bimetal from Lenox; almost every major blade manufacturer (except Olson) makes a virtually indistinguishable blade, and intense competition has kept quality and prices uniform from one manufacturer to the next. Just ask for a blade with the specs listed above, and I can practically guarantee that you'll be tickled pink with it. *—J.C.*

steel, or cast-aluminum. There's not much practical difference, just watch out for a warped frame that would affect wheel alignment. Also, if adding a riser block, check that it doesn't throw wheel alignment off—a problem with some Taiwanese saws.

Table and trunnion design: Every bandsaw I looked at had trunnions strong enough that I couldn't shift the table by hand. Most bandsaw tables tilt 45° in one direction and 10° or 15° in the other. This small amount of left-hand-tilt is important if you plan to bandsaw dovetails, although I wouldn't rule out buying a bandsaw without it—to get the job done, you could always fit a plywood table with the requisite tilt atop the one that's there.

An excellent book put out by Delta is *Getting the Most out of Your Bandsaw,* at $8 from Delta distributors, or call Delta at (800) 223-7278. As far as blade info goes, manufacturers have brochures detailing blade types and uses, usually along with trouble-shooting charts. Unfortunately, every blade manufacturer has had, at one time or another, trouble with mis-aligned welds. These are annoying but so common that they hardly count as a defect. If you get a great blade, save it for special jobs.

You can sometimes true a bad weld by stoning the back of the

The Inca (above right) costs three times the price of the Wood-Mizer. Both machines sacrifice column rigidity for a wide throat area. The Inca, with flat rubber tires, tracks blades with their teeth overhanging the edge of the wheel (photo right). If you tension a wide blade much past 12,000 psi, it will ride off. The Wood-Mizer's rough-hewn block guides (far left) contrast with the Inca's three ball bearings, but both systems work.

Three-wheelers, two personalities
by John Kelsey

I like bandsaws. I've been shopping for a monstrous old cast-iron Crescent or equivalent, but I've also been curious about three-wheelers like the Wood-Mizer and the Inca. Thus, I was an eager volunteer when it came time to test those two machines. I used them to rip, to make veneers and to saw curvy little boxes. For a rigorous test, I asked each saw to make boards from half-rounds of apple wood, 8 in. from pith to bark, that had been drying since 1981. Apple is denser than cherry, but not as hard as sugar maple.

Wood-Mizer: If you were a pretty good basement tinkerer, and you welded your way through a whole lot of steel sheet, tube and channel iron, you could probably get pretty close to the Wood-Mizer. If I had made it myself, I'd be real proud.

I'd use it for everything, and I'd continue to fix, file and fit until eventually it grew into an absolute dream of a saw. It's a tempting purchase because it's cheap and American made. But if you do buy one, you'd best be prepared to fix and file as if you had built it yourself—there are rough edges and wobbly fits.

The saw has crowned wheels, which makes blade tracking easy. The steel-blade by hand. Another trick with stones is to pinch the blade lightly between the ends of two fine-grit whetstones and run the blade backwards through them by hand. This evens out the set of any errant teeth, and, with an older blade, sharpens the teeth, because it removes each tooth's rounded outside corner.

A final trick is worth noting. At any tension, bandsaw blades can develop a harmonic flutter, a sort of internal whiplash that can greatly reduce blade life through fatigue. This is visible as a series of waves in the blade as it runs. The waves at high tension can be as short as an inch or two, and are the most fatiguing. The trick is to tension and track the blade, then, with the saw running, look down the longest part of the blade you can see. Adjust the tension minutely until the waves disappear and the blade runs straight. Of course, any time you run a bandsaw with the wheel covers off, stand behind the saw and keep the area clear. □

Jim Cummins is an associate editor at Fine Woodworking *magazine. Some of the material in this article can also be found on the videotape* Small Shop Tips and Techniques *(The Taunton Press, Box 5506, Newtown, Conn. 06470).*

---

block guides adjust with six Allen screws, one of which is inaccessible. The throat is 26 in. wide, so you can saw to the middle of a piece of plywood. The table is too small and difficult to tilt accurately.

I couldn't resaw a flat board from the test apple, due to both bowing and wandering. However, all the blades Wood-Mizer supplied pulsed badly at the weld. Furthermore, there's a lot of vibration from the frame-mounted motor. If I owned the saw, I wouldn't give up. I'd remount the motor off the saw's frame, and shop for better blades.

Inca: The Inca is novel among bandsaws for having uncrowned wheels. There are two blade-tracking adjustments, one for tilt and one for tension, at the axle of the third wheel. Blades track with their teeth overhanging the wheels, and it takes some practice to learn how to track different widths of blades. You can't apply as much tension as I would like without throwing the blade. I had no luck with a ¾-in. blade; when it would track, it also bowed in the cut; with a little more tension, the blade ran off. On the other hand, a ½-in. blade and a slow feed produced flat apple lumber. I'd consider adding the 2-in. height extension.

For the money, you get some nice features. The blade guides are free-spinning bearings, very precise and responsive. You have to twist eight Allen screws to adjust the guides; if I owned the saw, I'd Krazy-glue eight Allen wrenches in place. A rack-and-pinion moves the top guide up and down, so it can't drop on the stock or your fingers. The stand-mounted motor doesn't contribute vibration. For the money you might also feel entitled to a legible manual with pictures matching the saw you bought (the photo-copied supplements are completely illegible).

This month of testing so whetted my appetite for a bandsaw, by the way, that I went out and bought a new 14-in. Delta with 6-in. height extension. I think it'll be pretty good, once I get the wheels trued round. □

John Kelsey sculpts and makes wooden boxes in Bethel, Conn.

The Rockwell/Delta 14-in. bandsaw (left) has served as the inspiration for Taiwanese copies, such as the AMT machine shown at right, which sells for less than half the price.

Delta, the imports, and Sears

I've owned a Rockwell 14-in. machine for more than five years; except for a few small differences, it's the same as the current Delta machine. Last spring, another editor here bought a bandsaw from American Machine and Tool (Fourth Ave. and Spring St., Royersford, Penn. 19468). The AMT bandsaw is a Taiwanese low-cost version of my Rockwell. It's made by the Yung Li Shing Electric Works Co Ltd, (whose trademark is an elephant cast into the plastic knobs) and sells for about $300. I've seen similar Elephant machines for as little as $189 (in a "buy from the truck" ad in a local newspaper). Elephant also makes bandsaws for such familiar names as Jet, Sunhill, Bridgewood, Bratton, Grizzly, Andreou, A.J. Tool, etc.

The wheels on the AMT machine were nicely round (my Rockwell's top wheel had a slight high spot in the tire). The top wheel on the Taiwanese machine was warped, or possibly bored crooked, as it was about ⅛ in. out of flatness. Curiously, this didn't affect the running of the blade. The wheels on both machines are aligned well, and tracking is no problem.

The AMT's table is a lighter casting than the Rockwell's, and flexes under heavy load. I doubt that the flexing would ever cause problems in normal use. The design of the trunnions (the table-tilt castings) is about the same on both machines, but the AMT's castings are lighter. I can't shift either table by pushing on it.

Here's the first problem with the AMT machine: I could not adjust the table so the miter gauge slot was parallel with the blade, although I disassembled the machine and shifted everything as far as I could. If you never intend to use the miter gauge, this should cause no problem, but

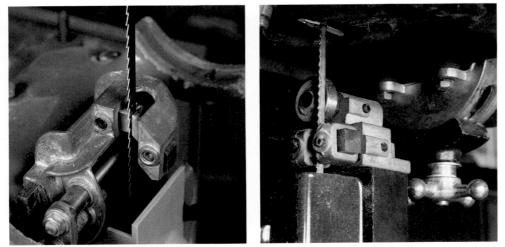

Delta's lower guides are designed with one side at a 45° angle, which allows them to be positioned close to the table for good support, while still allowing the table to tilt 45° to the right. In contrast, the Taiwanese saw's budget version uses the same guides top and bottom. To allow room for tilting, the guides must be positioned low, reducing support.

to get things right, you would have to re-drill some alignment-pin holes.

The second real difference between the machines is in the guides. Superficially, the systems seem equivalent, with the AMT, as usual, simply a stripped-down version of the Rockwell. In practice, however, the top and bottom guides on the AMT were poorly aligned, and, even after considerable fussing, still didn't end up quite right—they force the blade to twist a little. The bottom guides on the AMT, in addition, are the same as the top guides and have to be mounted some distance from the table to allow it to tilt (photo above). This reduces the support they give to the blade. The Rockwell has special 45° bottom guides, more expensive to manufacture. These two factors make the AMT less effective at resawing than the Rockwell.

Is the Rockwell, therefore, a very good machine, and the AMT a very bad one? Not quite. Let me knock the Rockwell a little: My machine vibrates more than I like. I balanced and trued the top wheel, but the bottom wheel may still be out of balance, and is too tight in its bearings to be checked. The accessory light fixture I bought with the saw will not extend far enough to throw light on the blade where it is cutting. The retractable caster wheels I bought couldn't be attached to the machine—the castings all cracked. Finally, I had to bend some of the sheet metal so the top wheel wouldn't rub.

On the plus side, the Rockwell—fitted with the blade described on p. 11—will cut anything I plan to feed it. It will hold its resale value indefinitely (maybe even go up). I will always be able to get parts. These considerations convince me I bought the right saw. That, in addition to better workmanship, is what you're buying for the price difference between Taiwan and Delta.

In spite of the fussing it took to get my saw running right, the problems were relatively minor compared with the worst that might come from Taiwan.

I talked to about a dozen importers of Taiwanese machines and everybody recited a litany of manufacturing shortcomings, most of which applied to an 18-in. model, but which also crop up on 14-in. Elephants. The squawks included guides machined crookedly, top wheels misaligned with bottom wheels, lumpy drive belts, pulleys machined off-center, cheap, unbalanced motors, ill-fitting fences, crooked or warped tables, and extension blocks that threw wheel alignment off. Some 220V motors were arriving with 110V plugs. The list could go on.

Many of the problems come about because Taiwan factories will make seemingly identical machines in a variety of grades, from almost-junk to pretty-competitive. Cost-cutting is a two-edged sword for importers—at some point you can end up with a machine that customers reject. Of course, every importer I talked with said the problems were with the other guy's machines, not his own.

These are things to watch out for if you're buying an import. But any of these problems should be immediately apparent and most can be fixed in one way or another, given patience and ingenuity.

Such things are not unheard of on domestic machines either. Take the Craftsman 12-in. saw, Sears "best," which is made by Emerson Electric in Paris, Tenn.

The older Sears machines enjoy an excellent reputation, and the new machine I bought *will* more or less cut wood. All in all, the machine is worth what it costs. I could live with it if I fixed the wheels, which are horrifically out of round—every revolution varies blade tension from 8,000 psi to 25,000 psi (to check for this, you turn the wheels by hand, pluck the blade, and listen for changes in musi-

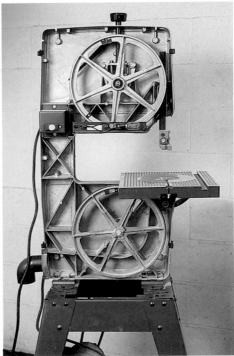

The Sears Craftsman bandsaw had very out-of-round wheels. In addition, the guide post needs shimming (top photo). It skews back almost ⅛ in. from top to bottom settings, leaving the blade unsupported by the backup bearing.

cal pitch). I'd shim the guide-post bracket, which, from top to bottom, skews about an eighth of an inch. The table could use bracing. Work hangs up on the table insert and the grooves, so I'd fill the table surface with auto-body putty and shim the insert level.

Just for a second, let me introduce a fourth machine here: the 12-in. Mini-Max, an Italian import built with welded steel construction. The point is that this is the smoothest running machine I encountered. It costs exactly double what the Sears does, and, in my opinion, it is at least twice the saw. Yet, right out of the box, the Sears saw will do most of the jobs the small shop asks. What the extra money buys is a bandsaw you won't have to re-manufacture yourself.

—J.C.

A bandsaw forum

EDITOR'S NOTE: Back in May, we asked readers to tell us about their bandsaws—bad points, good points, tips and tricks. We received more than a hundred letters, most of them several pages long. These hands-on impressions were invaluable in writing this article, and we'd like to express our grateful thanks to all who wrote. Here are excerpts from just a few. If there's a lesson here, it's that everyone has slightly different standards....

I have a Sears Craftsman 12-in. bandsaw that I purchased 6 or 8 years ago. Here are the details of the work I did on it:

The worklight is potentially dangerous, as it has no separate control and cannot be turned on without starting the motor. I replaced it with a Luxo-type lamp and added a separate switch to the front of the cabinet.

On the second day I had this saw, the centrifugal starter switch in the motor became fouled with sawdust and the motor would no longer start unless manually spun. Not realizing the cause of the problem, I replaced the motor under warranty, but of course the same thing happened again. A sheet-metal sawdust deflector has solved the problem.

I had to brace the stand with angle iron, also the table. I bored and reamed the table pivot for a bronze bushing.

Experiencing vibration, I rebored the upper wheel for bronze bushings. This did not cure the vibration, but solved an annoying blade-wander problem. I cured the vibration by replacing the motor-mounting plate. The blade thrust bearings wobbled; I replaced them with quality bearings. I replaced all cap screws and nuts with hardened ones.

I have extensively used a number of bandsaws, including this one, the Delta 14-in. saw, an older Jet saw and several large Yates-American saws. If I were to select, today, a saw to replace the Craftsman for the work I do, it would be the Delta. I do not feel, however, that my current level of use justifies the saw's replacement. This would hold true even if I had known exactly the work level required to repair my saw.
—*Steven S. Cushman, Sharon, Mass.*

My bandsaw experience goes back over 50 years, and includes an ancient 30-in. Tannewitz, a 30-in. Laidlaw, several other long-forgotten makes as well as both 20-in. and 14-in. Rockwells. Now in retirement, I have a 12-in. Craftsman. I haven't seen a bandsaw yet that couldn't use a tune-up.

Here's a tip: I find that holding a candle or some beeswax against the sides of the blade contributes to smooth running. Just one more thing. The miter slot on my machine is rarely used. On several occasions, I've had a piece of scrap fall into the slot and stick up just far enough to catch the work and throw me off line. So I made a press-fit insert to fill the slot level with the table. It can be removed instantly, should the need arise.
—*Kenneth A. Wolfe, Wausaukee, Wisc.*

I have a Grizzly 14-in. bandsaw. I season and use native woods such as dogwood, yew, madrone and apple, and find this machine, using a coarse ¾-in. blade, does an admirable job roughing pieces for turning squares, etc.
—*Donald M. Thomson, Vancouver, B.C.*

My 1980 Powermatic 14-in. bandsaw is a fine machine—no plastic parts and only two die-cast parts. My only real criticism is that the upper blade-guide rollers are not far enough apart—when using a ¼-in. blade, the back-up roller touches one of the side roller guides.
—*John W. Wood, Tyler, Tex.*

After having gained a limited amount of experience on a Shopsmith bandsaw, I feel that it represents fair value for the price. Just go slow and easy.

I'd wanted a three-wheel Inca for years and finally bought one for $2,000 plus (I bought every option available). I had initial problems, which would have been fewer if the dealer had been better qualified to set up and support the machine. In time, I took the machine apart, figured out how it should work, and realigned the wheels using a long straightedge. Since then, the unit has been a joy to use.

It is important to track the blade at the front of the wheels and to set the tension according to the manual. Too much or too little tension causes the blade to wander. Also, don't overtighten the drive belt. I use this saw almost daily, and slack off the tension overnight, so as not to create flat spots on the wheels. I've also found that the saw runs best at the slow speed, regardless of which blade I'm using.
—*James M. Watson, Beaverton, Ore.*

We have built a two-wheel, 18-in. Gilliom bandsaw at a cost, four years ago, of about $130 for the kit and another $30 for plywood. Built according to the plans, the machine is too flimsy for heavy work, and Gilliom doesn't pretend otherwise, but with a little reinforcing it can be made to resaw 12-in. oak with ease: We added a strip of plywood to enclose the H-shaped column, and poured it full of concrete, making it much more rigid and, of course, heavier. Three-inch angle iron set into the column and screwed to the wheel mounts top and bottom prior to pouring ensure that the wheels stay put

Interestingly, for three years we managed with a ⅓-HP washing-machine motor and never had any problems sawing stock up to 6-in.; the motor burned out recently and has been replaced with a ½-HP motor, which seems more than adequate, provided the blade is sharp.
—*Bon Dunstan, Wilson, Wyo.*

When I bought my Grizzly three-wheel bandsaw, I expected to use it for one job then unload it. Frankly, I bought this saw because it was cheap—I paid $120, delivered. Three years later, I still have the saw. While it doesn't compare with heavier, vastly more expensive machines, it cuts very cleanly and quickly through 4/4 and 8/4 stock—sufficient for my general needs.

Now for some negatives. The combined tilt-and-hold mechanism for the 15½-in.-square table is poor—adjustment is iffy, and even when snugged down, the table can be made to rock slightly when pressure is applied.

Although Grizzly has dropped the three-wheeler from its catalog, Shopcraft markets essentially the same saw. The one displayed at my local home center came with fewer attachments, but still included a miter gauge and the same ultra-basic rip fence as the Grizzly. On the day I stopped by, the saw was selling for about $160, but I've seen it for as low as $130.
—*Richard Cauman, Washington, D.C.*

I have had a 14-in. Rockwell/Delta for several years. Reverberations inside the enclosed steel stand made the saw very noisy; I built a heavy wood table with a fixed motor mount and the saw now runs very quietly. I replaced the flat blade-guide arm with the older V-shaped version. A wheel tire came off, but was successfully recemented.

There's still more vibration than I'd expect, but overall the saw operates very well and we are quite pleased with it.

Our second saw was an Inca 10-in. two-wheel model We really wanted this saw for exclusive use with ⅛-in. blades, but after extensive trial, including trips to the dealer for parts replacement and alignment, we had to return it (they gave a full refund). When the Inca was running, it was smooth as silk and cut beautifully, but we just couldn't stand the suspense of not knowing when the blade would jump forward off the wheels. The dealer said they had never seen a saw with this problem before.

Our next saw was a 12-in. Sears Craftsman, which, aside from a warped table that Sears replaced immediately, ran perfectly right out of the box.
—*H.E. Teagarden, Speedway, Ind.*

If you have the block-type blade guides, replace the metal blocks with lignum vitae. Press them lightly against the blade and tighten. After running the saw a couple of minutes, the wooden blocks wear-in and self-lubricate.
—*James J. Heusinger, Berea, Ohio.*

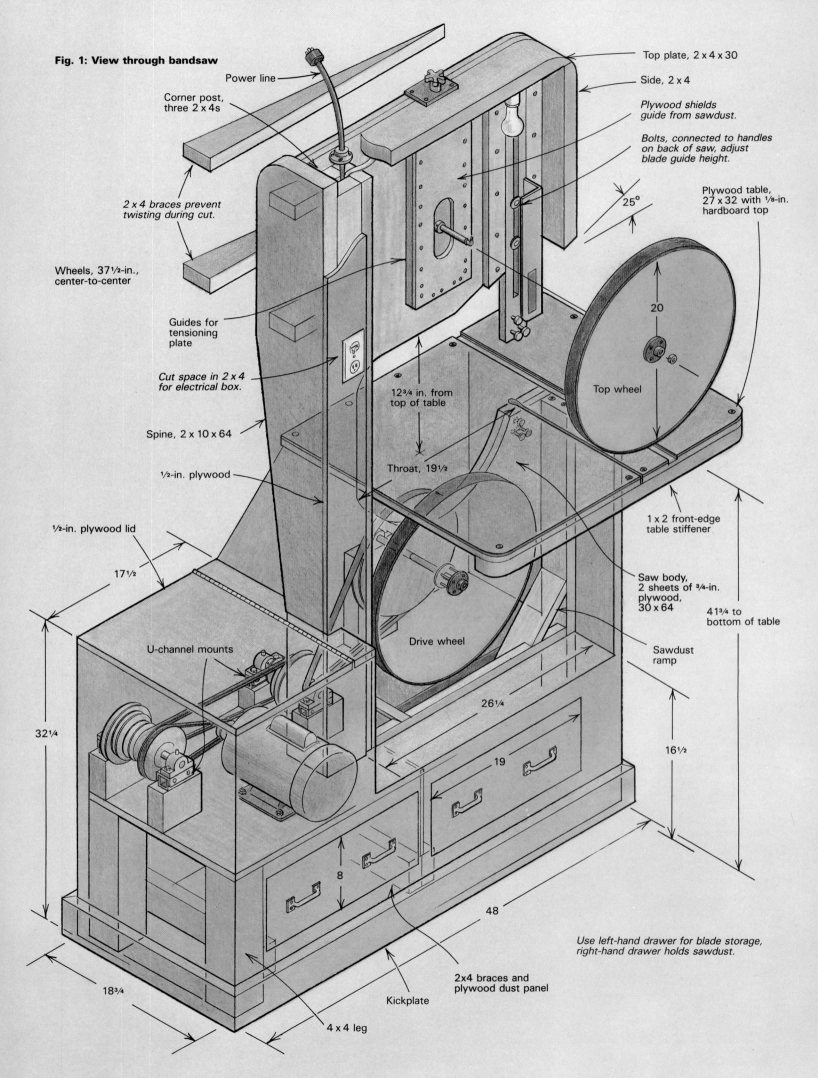

Fig. 1: View through bandsaw

Power line

Corner post, three 2 x 4s

2 x 4 braces prevent twisting during cut.

Wheels, 37½-in., center-to-center

Guides for tensioning plate

Cut space in 2 x 4 for electrical box.

Spine, 2 x 10 x 64

½-in. plywood

½-in. plywood lid

17½

U-channel mounts

32¼

18¾

4 x 4 leg

Kickplate

Top plate, 2 x 4 x 30

Side, 2 x 4

Plywood shields guide from sawdust.

Bolts, connected to handles on back of saw, adjust blade guide height.

25°

Plywood table, 27 x 32 with ⅛-in. hardboard top

20

Top wheel

12¾ in. from top of table

Throat, 19½

Drive wheel

1 x 2 front-edge table stiffener

Saw body, 2 sheets of ¾-in. plywood, 30 x 64

41¾ to bottom of table

Sawdust ramp

26¼

19

16½

8

48

Use left-hand drawer for blade storage, right-hand drawer holds sawdust.

2x4 braces and plywood dust panel

Shopmade Bandsaw

Plywood and basic tools build the saw

by William Corneil

Most woodworkers' thoughts turn to tablesaws and radial-arm saws when they're confronted with buying a large stationary saw. But I'm different in two regards. First, I chose a bandsaw, for reasons that I'll make clear in a moment. And, secondly, I opted to build the machine myself rather than buy it.

I chose a bandsaw because it can do many things a tablesaw can do, plus it can cut curves. As a project, it seemed less daunting than building a tablesaw or radial-arm saw, both of which would be great to own but are too expensive to buy on my budget.

My problem as an amateur woodworker is that I find it hard to justify (to myself and my spouse) the need to buy larger stationary equipment simply to "build better birdhouses." Granted, many cutting tasks are performed quicker on a tablesaw, but for the amateur, time doesn't mean money. Aside from cutting curves, I can resaw, rip and even cut lumber from logs on my saw. It also has five blade speeds: 120, 300, 600, 1,200 and 3,000 feet per minute (fpm). The slowest speed allows me to cut ¼-in. angle iron.

As machinery goes, the price was right. I built the 20-in. saw you see at left three years ago for under $100, Canadian (about $72 American today). I kept the cost down by using locally available materials and hardware. Most of the saw is built from ¾-in. interior-grade plywood and construction-grade lumber (which needs to be dried well first). I recently swapped the saw's ¼-HP motor for a used ½-HP model, but the smaller motor is more than adequate, unless you use the saw to cut lumber from logs, as I do.

It's ironic that my saw incorporates features that many store-bought saws don't, such as a worklight above the blade guard, one drawer for blade storage and another to catch sawdust, a built-in 110v AC power outlet and a conveniently located power cord.

Anybody who's built even a reasonably complex piece of furniture shouldn't find the saw hard to build. I built mine with the usual cast of characters: a saber saw, an electric hand drill and a borrowed belt sander. The only machine I used that many shops may lack is my homemade 12-in. disc sander.

I'll admit the project requires basic metalworking skills. If I were to build the saw again, however, I wouldn't use bushings for the wheels; I'd opt for roller or needle bearings instead. Although more expensive, bearings would eliminate much of the metalworking, and would also save time on building the machine.

Ball bearings would also have negated the need to run a network of copper-tubing lubrication lines throughout the saw to all the pillow blocks (for clarity, this network isn't shown in the drawing at left or those on p. 19). Similarly, two other jobs would also have been eliminated: drilling out the top wheel axle to fit it with a lubrication cup, and routing a groove in the saw body to run an oil line to the bushings in which the drive axle rides.

Even if you can't handle the more involved metalworking (such as building the wheel-tensioning assembly), a machine shop should be able to do it for a reasonable price—and you'll still accomplish the project for a lot less than what you'd pay for a good used machine of this capacity.

My bandsaw can be separated into three main components: the base, which supports the saw and table and contains the motor, drive components and two drawers; the saw body, which supports the wheels the blade rides on, along with the adjustment mechanisms and the door; and the mechanicals—the motor, pulleys, bearings, electrical wiring and adjustment mechanisms.

The logical place to start construction is with the base. This is no more than a ¾-in. plywood top, face, back and end pieces screwed to four 4x4 legs. A divider of ½-in. plywood separates the base into two drawer compartments and prevents sawdust from getting into the blade-storage drawer. The drawer runners are 2x4s with rippings glued to them.

After the base is built, begin work on the saw body by drawing its profile on two sheets of plywood that have been tack-nailed at the corners. Cut the profile and remove the scrap. The sole purpose for cutting an arcing, concave profile in the saw body's top is to conserve material for wheels, so handle the throat scrap carefully.

If you opt to use bushings instead of bearings, you'll have to run a lubrication line down to the bushings that the lower axle rides in. You'll also have to rout a groove large enough for the lubrication line (I used ¼-in.-dia. copper tubing for lube lines throughout) in one of the plywood sheets. The tube that feeds the lower bushings stops just above the axle and lubricates the bushings by dripping oil onto the axle.

Glue and screw the two plywood sheets that will form the saw body together. After the glue has dried, attach the 2x4 top plate, the 2x10 spine and the 2x4 braces on the back. Next, glue and screw the three 2x4s to the left of the front of the glued-up sheet so that they form a corner post. Be sure to leave a gap between the post and the sheet on the left-hand side—to provide room to run the switch and outlet wiring. Now, attach the top and bottom vertical 2x4s on the right-hand side of the saw body. Cut out and attach the ramps that spill the sawdust into the drawer.

Use the same pattern for the saw body to cut out the ½-in. plywood door. Then, rip the piece of plywood that's attached next to the door—the door swings from this piece by a piano hinge. Next, fasten another sawdust ramp at the bottom of the door, and cut out the oval slot in the door to allow the top axle to travel vertically.

Make up each wheel from the ¾-in. plywood throat cutouts. Rough out each piece, then glue a piece of ½-in. plywood on top of

Canadian woodworker Bill Corneil built this 20-in. bandsaw three years ago and has found it a reliable performer. Shown with its door and two drawers open, the saw is powered by a used ½-HP motor. It is built from construction-grade lumber and interior-grade plywood.

it, making each disc 1¼ in. thick. When the glue has dried, draw the 20-in.-dia. circles on each piece, and cut them out slightly oversize. I bored a ⅝-in. centerhole in each wheel, mounted the bushings to them and mounted the wheels, one at a time, on a jig on my disc sander. Then, I spun each one against the sanding disc to make it concentric with the axle and to make the edge perpendicular to the face. There's no need to put a crown on each disc to keep the blade on track; I'll explain more about this later.

Next, I bought an 18-in. bicycle inner tube, cut off the valve and split it into two large bands about 1 in. wide. I stretched these bands over each wheel—to prevent the blade's tooth set from wearing a groove in the wheel edge.

You can make your own bearings using bushings housed in floor flanges, which are threaded fixtures allowing plumbing pipe to be used as closet coatracks, machine stands and the like. You'll need four ½-in. floor flanges, two ⅜-in. floor flanges and four ¾-in.-long sintered bronze bushings with a ⅝-in.-dia. inside hole and ⅞-in. outside diameter. Drill out the centerhole in the ½-in. floor flanges to slightly under ⅞-in. dia., and press the bushings into the hole.

Pick one plywood disc as the top, free-running wheel and bolt a ½-in. floor flange to each side of the disc with flathead machine screws. I used a piece of ⅝-in. steel rod inserted through the

hole to keep both flanges aligned while bolting them to the wheel (and also to mount the wheel to my sanding jig).

Mount the top wheel-tracking assembly to the saw body. This assembly consists of a threaded rod with a knob mounted to it. Turning the knob clockwise threads the rod through a plate mounted to the saw body. The rod then pushes on the back of the plate to which the axle is welded, causing the wheel to tip back in relation to the front of the saw.

The wheel-axle plate hangs from the top of the saw and needs about ¼-in. clearance behind it. It's kept in side-to-side alignment by two pieces of 1-in.-thick wood—one on each side of the assembly—screwed to the saw body. A plywood shield is screwed to these pieces to serve as a cover.

Once again, if you decide to use bushings instead of bearings, you'll have to drill out the ⅝-in. steel-rod top axle. Bore a ⅛-in. oil channel down the center of the rod, then bore two ⅛-in. drip holes perpendicular to the oil channel—to lubricate the bushings the axle rides in. Use two collar stops to secure the top axle.

The other two ½-in. floor-flange bearings are attached to the saw body's laminated center—not to the lower wheel. The alignment of these lower bushings is critical. First, stand and plumb the saw body on its base and screw it down. Drop a plumb bob from the center of the top axle and mark the center of the bottom wheel with a vertical reference mark. Now, make a horizontal reference mark about 37½ in. down from the top axle. The bottom flange bearings are centered on these marks.

Drill out the two ⅜-in. flanges to ⅝ in. in diameter. Drill and tap three setscrew holes in each flange. Attach these two flanges to the bottom wheel in the same manner you attached the flanges to the top wheel. The setscrews—six in all—tighten the wheel to the axle. No collar stops are needed.

Cut a ⅝-in. steel rod to 12 in. long and push it through both the drive wheel and the bearings attached to the laminated body. The rod should almost touch the back of the base.

Install a piece of 2x6 to support the pillow block that the drive axle will rest on, then mount the pillow block itself (see figure 2). Next, install the V-belt and the 12-in.-dia. V-belt pulley on the lower axle. Finally, mount the axle to the pillow block.

The key to blade-tracking success is shimming the pillow block that the drive axle rests in. This will make the axle run downhill, tipping the lower wheel slightly. The lower inside face of the wheel is closer to the saw body than the top by about ⅛ in. (or a little less). You might have to experiment with shimming the axle to get the blade to track correctly, but, once done, the blade tracks extraordinarily well. Mine hasn't come off the track in more than three years of heavy use, even after ripping more than 200 logs into lumber.

Next, mount the two sets of intermediate five-step pulleys to their axles which, in turn, ride in pillow blocks bolted to 3-in. U-channel mounts (see figure 1). Slotted holes for bolts allow the pillow blocks to adjust horizontally, and the U-channels to adjust vertically, for fine-tuning alignment.

Build the sliding blade guard as shown in the photos, facing page. The blade guard slides between two pieces of wood screwed to the saw body. The bearings are positioned by nuts (threaded to either a rod or a bolt) after a blade has been installed. Two of the bearings in each trio should be located to ride along both faces of the blade, while the third backs up the blade from behind.

Bolt the motor in its compartment using the inside face of the base as the reference point. Use a straightedge or a steel square to align the pulleys before tightening down their setscrews. Run the power cord in through the top of the saw, and fish the wiring

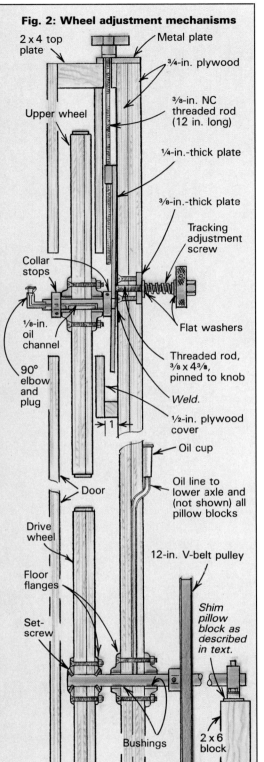

Fig. 2: Wheel adjustment mechanisms

- 2 x 4 top plate
- Metal plate
- ¾-in. plywood
- ⅜-in. NC threaded rod (12 in. long)
- Upper wheel
- ¼-in.-thick plate
- ⅜-in.-thick plate
- Tracking adjustment screw
- Collar stops
- ⅛-in. oil channel
- Flat washers
- Threaded rod, ⅜ x 4⅜, pinned to knob
- 90° elbow and plug
- Weld.
- ½-in. plywood cover
- 1
- Oil cup
- Door
- Oil line to lower axle and (not shown) all pillow blocks
- Drive wheel
- 12-in. V-belt pulley
- Floor flanges
- Shim pillow block as described in text.
- Set-screw
- Bushings
- 2 x 6 block

With its guard and the top wheel removed, the saw's blade-tensioning assembly (above, left) is exposed. The assembly is raised higher than normal to show the tracking assembly behind it. The blade guard slides in tracks screwed to the saw body. Blade guide bearings (top right) are made of ball bearings on threaded rods or bolts. The top backup bearing in the upper trio is smaller that the bottom backup bearing because it's a temporary replacement. The author burned out the original bearing after three years of use, milling logs into lumber.

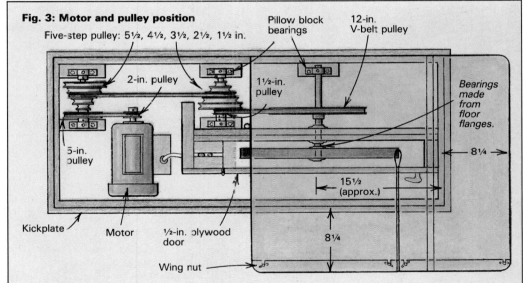

Fig. 3: Motor and pulley position

- Five-step pulley: 5½, 4½, 3½, 2½, 1½ in.
- Pillow block bearings
- 12-in. V-belt pulley
- 2-in. pulley
- 1½-in. pulley
- Bearings made from floor flanges.
- 5-in. pulley
- 8¼
- 15½ (approx.)
- Kickplate
- Motor
- ½-in. plywood door
- 8¼
- Wing nut

down through the support post to the switch/receptacle. Wire the motor between the switch/power outlet and the light. When wired correctly, the bulb should light when the saw is turned on, and the receptacle should have power at all times. By having the power cord exit the top of the saw, you can plug it into a ceiling receptacle, keeping the cord high and out of the way.

The remaining work is simple. Attach the hinged cover for the motor compartment, build the drawers and the saw table, attach hardware, cover blemishes with filler, then sand and paint.

While the saw accepts blades from 138 in. to 146 in. long, I use a ¾-in. by 144-in.-long blade most of the time. Take the blade on a test run by slipping it over both wheels. You should also snug up the blade tension; the blade should be snug enough to ring when you strum it like a guitar (see hints under "Tension gauges" on p. 10). With the saw unplugged, turn the top wheel over by hand and adjust its tracking.

Now comes the moment of glory. Quickly flip the switch on and off a couple of times to test how the blade tracks. All that's left is to take it for a test drive down a long and winding cut. □

Bill Corneil lives in Thorndale, Ontario. Eight detailed sketches of his shopmade bandsaw are available by sending a self-addressed #10 envelope and 45¢ in stamps to Corneil Bandsaw, The Taunton Press, Box 5506, Newtown, Conn. 06470. Photos by author.

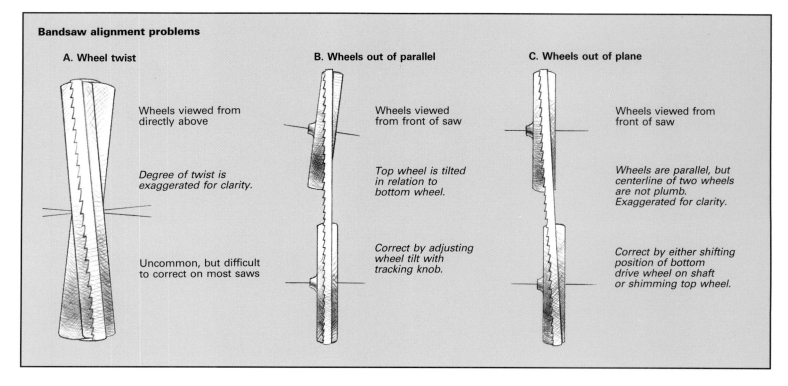

Bandsaw alignment problems

A. Wheel twist

Wheels viewed from directly above

Degree of twist is exaggerated for clarity.

Uncommon, but difficult to correct on most saws

B. Wheels out of parallel

Wheels viewed from front of saw

Top wheel is tilted in relation to bottom wheel.

Correct by adjusting wheel tilt with tracking knob.

C. Wheels out of plane

Wheels viewed from front of saw

Wheels are parallel, but centerline of two wheels are not plumb. Exaggerated for clarity.

Correct by either shifting position of bottom drive wheel on shaft or shimming top wheel.

Adjusting Bandsaw Wheels
Small alignment changes improve performance

by Mark Duginske

The bandsaw can be one of the most useful tools in the shop: It can resaw thick stock or slice off thin veneer and cut curves, circles, tenons, dovetails and more. But don't expect it to do all these jobs well straight from the factory. For top performance, you must fine-tune the saw, paying special attention to wheel alignment. This takes no special tools, gadgets or miracle blades, just a little time and attention, and a shim or two.

In the course of my travels in the past 10 years, teaching classes and giving seminars on woodworking tools and techniques, I've adjusted at least 100 different bandsaws. Most of these were poorly tuned, and many were miserably out of adjustment. Unfortunately, when a bandsaw doesn't work correctly, people tend to blame the machine, the blade or themselves rather than alignment or any other adjustment. Some workers seem almost afraid to mess with the machine, but the method I'll describe here is simple and virtually foolproof, if you follow the steps properly. But before getting into the "how to," I'll explain a bit about the dynamics of a bandsaw and why misalignment can be such a complex problem.

Good alignment—For any blade to cut accurately, the wheels of the bandsaw must drive it smoothly and continuously. Proper wheel alignment is essential for this to happen, just as correct wheel alignment is necessary for a car to travel in a straight line without

excessive vibration. For top performance, the wheels must line up with each other in three ways, as shown in the drawing above. The wheels must align in the vertical axis, be in the same plane and be parallel to each other. When the wheels are aligned all three ways, I refer to them as being "coplanar." With poor wheel alignment, the blade can hop around on the wheel, yielding an erratic cut. These undesireable movements will shorten the life of the blade and the thrust bearing, as well as wear the guides unevenly.

Because bandsaw wheels have no rims, the only thing that holds the blade on the tire covering the wheel is proper tracking. To adjust the tracking, you must alter the angle of the bandsaw's nondriven wheel while the blade is running. On most saws, this adjustment is made by screwing a knob in or out. This tilts the arbor supporting the top wheel, which in turn causes the blade to run or track on a different section of the tire. The goal is to keep the blade riding evenly on the wheel: A properly tracked blade will run without rubbing hard against the thrust bearing or coming off the wheel.

Blade tracking is also enhanced by the crowned wheels found on most small American and Taiwanese bandsaws, like the Delta, Sears and Grizzly. The wheels' convex profiles tend to automatically center the blade in the middle of the wheels, just as the crowned front roller on a belt sander tends to center the belt. This natural centering occurs because the blade wants to equalize the tension

From *Fine Woodworking* magazine (March 1989) 75:75-77

With the table tilted out of the way, the author uses a strip of plywood with a straightedge jointed on it to check the wheels of a Delta 15-in. bandsaw for plane and parallel alignment.

on its inner and outer edges. Crowned wheels also buffer many wheel-alignment problems and even compensate for irregularities in the blade's thickness and width.

Variables of poor tracking—Despite the crowned wheels and tracking adjustment, there are several variables that constantly work against good tracking and often make even a high-quality bandsaw perform poorly. First, bandsaw blades are rarely perfect. Each blade has its own performance characteristics or "personality." If the weld joining the ends of the blade is uneven, the front and back edges of the blade won't be the same length, and the blade may track poorly and tend to hop around on the wheels. Blade straightness is also affected by the manufacturing process: When the front of the blade is heat-treated to harden the teeth, it often contracts, making the back of the blade longer than the front.

Other variables include wheels that are out of round, causing the blade to loosen and tighten on every revolution, or tires that are worn unevenly. Even the self-centering quality of crowned wheels can be a disadvantage with misaligned wheels: The two crowns compete for control of the blade, rocking the blade back and forth, producing a crooked cut. This is similar to what happens when you drive down a rutted dirt road: The car will jerk from side to side as the wheels slip into one rut, then the other.

Tension and tracking—Even though we can't always change the variables described above, we can cure the biggest cause of tracking problems: misalignment of the bandsaw wheels. If poor alignment isn't remedied, an excessive amount of wheel tilt, via the tracking adjustment, may be needed to keep the blade tracking properly. In extreme cases, it's nearly impossible to keep the blade on the wheel or to keep it from riding so hard against the thrust bearing

that it prematurely wears the bearing and the blade.

If wheel alignment is so critical, why don't manufacturers take care of it? In fact, the wheels *are* aligned at the factory, but before a blade is installed. This presents yet another variable: blade tension. Wheels that are coplanar under no tension can be forced out of alignment when the blade is mounted and brought up to proper running tension. Also, a saw that is coplanar at normal tension can become misaligned under excessive tension. When a wide blade that runs at a higher tension than a narrow one is installed, the misalignment may become even greater. That is why a saw that runs fairly well with narrow blades can perform poorly with wide blades. For this reason, bandsaw wheels should be aligned while a wide blade is fully tensioned on the saw. This will ensure that the wheels are coplanar when the relationship is the most critical.

Some authors claim that many bandsaw problems can be cured by drastically increasing blade tension beyond the manufacturer's specifications (see article on pp. 8-15). This is something I am strongly against, because I think it reduces the quality of cut and can eventually damage the saw. Bandsaws, as well as bandsaw blades, are designed to work at specific tension settings; higher blade tensions unduly stress the saw and make the blade much more susceptible to harmonic flutter, a rhythmic vibration that results in poor cuts. In contrast, blades will run truer and last longer on a bandsaw with coplanar wheels, because there is no binding or twisting of the blade. You will notice more accuracy and power, with less vibration and less blade wander.

Checking wheel alignment—This simple procedure only takes about half an hour. As already mentioned, the alignment should be checked with a blade in place. Tension the widest blade you use on your saw according to the gauge on the saw. In my opinion, a ½-in. blade is the largest practical size for a consumer bandsaw. If your saw is old, or if you do not habitually release the tension after using the saw, the spring may be compressed and not give you a true tension reading. You can check this by raising the upper guide assembly for a 6-in. cut and pushing sideways on a ½-in. blade: The blade should only deflect about ¼ in. If it's a lot more, you should increase the tension until the deflection is right. If you're using a wide blade, you may need to increase the tension slightly past the highest mark, but not to the point where you're at the end of the adjustment screw. When the spring is compressed completely (you can see if it's squashed all the way down), it loses its ability to function as a shock absorber, which is its secondary purpose.

Use a straightedge, a board or a piece of plywood with a true edge on it to check if the wheels are parallel and in plane with each other. Hold the straightedge vertically and lay it across the middle of the wheels, as shown in the photo on this page, but avoid the hubs if they protrude. If the straightedge touches on the top and bottom rims of both wheels, the wheels are parallel and in the same plane. If this is the case, rest easy: The wheels are aligned and you're ready to check for twist, as described at the top of the next page.

If the wheels are out of alignment, the straightedge will touch at two or three points. In most cases, only the top wheel or only the bottom wheel will touch the straightedge. In either case, one of the wheels will have to be moved to make both wheels coplanar.

It is important to know exactly how far to shift the wheels. This eliminates a lot of trial and error in adding and subtracting washers from behind the wheel. The measurement is made at two points: at the top and bottom edge of the wheel not touching the straightedge. The distances between the straightedge and the two points should be exactly the same; if they're not, tilt the top wheel with the tracking adjuster until they are. This will make the top wheel parallel to the bottom wheel. The distance from the straightedge to the wheel is the amount the wheel must be shifted to be in the same plane.

Finally, you need to check the wheels for twist by laying the straightedge diagonally across the wheels, as shown in the lower photo at right. Check both diagonals. You may have to tilt or remove the saw table to accomplish this. The straightedge should contact each wheel on both rims; if it doesn't, the wheels are twisted. Don't worry if your saw doesn't have an adjustment for wheel twist; it is very uncommon and doesn't affect the saw's performance nearly as much as the other misalignments. Some old bandsaws and European saws have top wheels that tilt from side to side, allowing the blade to find its alignment in this vertical plane (twist).

All the above procedures can be done on a three-wheel bandsaw as well: Just check the relationship of the drive wheel to one nondriven wheel, then the other. Finally, check the two nondriven wheels to each other. One or two wheels may need to be shifted to get them into plane with each other.

Shifting the wheels—Each bandsaw will require a slightly different method for shifting the wheels to get them coplanar. Some manufacturers, such as Sears and Inca, allow for an adjustment with a movable bottom wheel. This is the easiest kind of saw to adjust. The bottom wheel is mounted on a shaft with a keyway and locked in place with a setscrew. To adjust the wheel, loosen the screw and slide the wheel the desired amount, then tighten the screw.

Delta and some Taiwanese saws must be adjusted by shifting the top wheel, which is mounted on a threaded shaft and held secure with a nut. Unscrew the large nut and remove the wheel, as shown in the top photo at right. The wheel is shifted by either adding or subtracting the shims or washers on the axle behind the wheel. Some saws won't have any shims to remove, but it's almost always necessary to add shims, so this isn't a problem. The Delta bandsaw has a ⅝-in. axle that standard hardware-store washers will fit. If a smaller adjustment is necessary, you can make shims from sections of an aluminum can. Replace the wheel and tighten the nut snugly.

After you make adjustments, rotate the wheels several times to make sure the blade is tracking properly. On machines with crowned wheels, the blade will often find a new equilibrium that's not in the middle, so don't worry. Recheck the plane and parallel alignment one more time. It is a good idea to mark the original wheel positions relative to the straightedge so the reading won't be thrown off by an uneven section of the wheel's rim. Use a pencil or magic marker to mark the wheels.

Don't be afraid to realign your saw often—think of it as part of your regular maintenance. If you plan on doing much work with one blade, it's not a bad idea to align the saw for that blade. It is important to continually monitor the performance of your saw. New blades often stretch, and any blade will expand as it gets warm from sawing, and this may affect blade tracking. Remember, wheel alignment is the best adjustment. You can still use the top-wheel angle to fine-tune the running blade, but don't depend on it too much. After you align your saw a couple of times, it will become very quick and easy to do. The minute it takes to align the wheels is a small price to pay for good performance.

Final tricks—There are two more things you can do to make your bandsaw a pleasure to use. With the blade running, gently round the blade's back corners. This simple modification makes an enormous difference. I use a diamond hone, but you can use a fine sharpening stone or even 100-grit sandpaper on a block. A blade with rounded corners catches less at the back of the cut, especially in tight turns, and tends not to dig into the thrust bearing during curved cuts, preventing excess heat and wear. The second trick is to exchange your saw's stock guide blocks for a new type of block made from

Slipping a regular ⅝-in. hardware-store washer on the axle of the Delta bandsaw's top wheel shifts its position sideways to put it in plane with the lower wheel.

Laying a straightedge diagonally across the bandsaw's wheels allows the author to check the wheels for twist. This often requires the bandsaw table to be tilted out of the way.

graphite-impregnated phenolic. The replacements, called "Cool Blocks," can be set tight to the blade, for more cutting control and accuracy, without heating up the blade or wearing down excessively fast. They're made to fit most popular bandsaws and are available from Garrett Wade Co., Inc., 161 Ave. of the Americas, New York, N.Y. 10013; (800) 221-2942 or (212) 807-1155 in New York. Custom block sets can also be ordered to fit practically any saw. □

Mark Duginske is a woodworker and author. He also teaches woodworking at his shop in Wausau, Wis. He has written a book on the bandsaw that's due to be out in the fall of this year (Sterling Publishing Co., Inc., 2 Park Ave., New York, N.Y. 10016).

Shopmade Scroll Saw
Eccentric drive simplifies construction

by Mark White

I was a high-school student in the mid-1950s when I attended my first industrial-arts conference in Oswego, N.Y. One of the displays there featured a cheap kit for a motorized version of the wooden scroll saw my great uncles had used to cut fretwork for fancy houses they built at the turn of the century. The saw was made almost entirely of unfinished, ¾-in. ash. It was simple and homely, but boy could it cut. For years, I've tried to lay my hands on one, but the manufacturer has disappeared without a trace.

Since I had already built a large, inexpensive and versatile walking-beam saw (sort of a "poor man's band saw"), I finally decided to design my own scroll saw. I ended up with a saw that performs as well as any of the factory-made machines I've tried and will saw very tight curves in wood up to 2 in. thick, leaving a smooth surface that requires no sanding. For inside cuts on fretwork, the blade can be removed, threaded through a hole in the wood and reinstalled in less than 30 seconds.

Inspired by the homely kit I'd seen years earlier, I made my saw as simple as possible. Basically, it consists of two parallel wooden arms mounted on a rigid wooden frame and kept in tension by the blade at one end and a stout nylon cord at the other end. The blade is driven by the reciprocating motion generated by a pair of eccentric, rotating weights attached to the lower arm with a shaft and pillow block. An old clothes-dryer motor drives a section of rubber hose that acts as a flexible shaft to spin the weights. Because the weights are eccentrically mounted, they actually unbalance the pillow-block shaft, causing it to oscillate one cycle for every revolution of the motor. Although the stroke can be varied by changing the length of the weights, I've found that weights made from 2-in. bar stock, 3½ in. long, work best with the 6-in. coping sawblades I use in the saw. These longer blades produce a more aggressive cut than the 4-in. blades most scroll

saws use. As shown here, the saw has a 24-in. throat, but if you need a smaller or larger throat, you can scale the dimensions up or down without affecting performance.

Building the frame and arms—When choosing wood for the frame, pick a stable and warp-resistant material. For this saw, I used two Sitka-spruce 2x12s about 32 in. long, because that's what I had. White pine or fir would work as well, or if you want a nicer-looking saw, use walnut, beech or maple. To ensure precise alignment of the arm pivot holes, screw the boards for the frame together and machine both parts at once. The pivot holes—½ in. dia. for the top arm and ¾ in. dia. for the bottom arm—should be bored on a drill press. Bore the large access holes for the rotating weights with a Forstner bit or a hole saw, or saw them out with a jigsaw and much patience. After bandsawing the frames to shape, I separate the two sections and rout a radius on all the edges except those that mate to the base and the saw table.

I also used spruce for the arms, but ash, cherry and pine are good choices, too. Whatever wood you pick, keep the weight of the arms as low as possible near the blade end. If the arms are too heavy, excess vibration and poor reciprocating action will result. One advantage of spruce is that it has sound knots hard enough to serve as bearings for the bolts or rods on which each arm pivots. On one of the saws I've built, a 1¼-in. knot drilled for the pivot shaft and regularly lubricated with gear oil has lasted four years as a bearing. The lower pivot on the saw shown here is a ¾-in.-dia. steel rod in an Oilite bearing of the equivalent inside diameter. Oilite bearings—self-lubricating, sintered bronze sleeves—are available in a range of sizes. Refer to the supplies box for a source.

As the drawing shows, the distance from the pivot point to the blade mount is ¼ in. longer on the top arm than it is on the bottom arm. This causes the blade to back out of the cut on the upstroke and advance into the material on the downstroke, increasing blade life and improving performance. Reducing the blade rake (angle) to ⅛ in. will make the blade less aggressive and the cut more precise.

The eccentric drive—For the drive, you'll need some ¼-in. by 2-in. mild steel bar stock, a 3½-in. to 3¾-in. bolt to serve as a shaft and a ¾-in. ID pillow block. As shown in detail C, the weights are fashioned from the bar stock, then mounted on either side of the pillow-block bearing by the shaft. The threads on the bolt's excess length are filed or ground off to give the rubber-hose coupler good purchase. To make the weights, I first bored the bar stock, then cut them to final size. It's tough boring large holes in heavy steel, so I started by boring a ¼-in. hole, which I then enlarged to ¾ in. Do this boring on a drill press and be sure to clamp the steel firmly and keep your hands well clear of the work.

I assembled the drive mechanism by holding the bolt head tightly in a vise while the nut was drawn up very lightly. Washers, or a ⅞-in. nut, can be used as spacers to keep the weights from striking the arm as they rotate. As you tighten the nut, make sure the weights are aligned so they'll rotate in unison, otherwise the reciprocating action will be uneven. Once it's assembled, position the pillow block on the lower arm, as shown in the drawing. Before bolting the pillow block down, make sure the weights rotate through their full arc without striking the arm. If they strike the arm, add a thicker spacer. By the way, the drive can be positioned so the motor is on either side of the saw.

Assembling the saw—Begin assembly by inserting the arm pivot bolts in their holes and positioning the upper and lower arms on the frame. Rotate the eccentric weights by hand, and on the inside of the frame, mark the path they describe. With a large Forstner bit and/or a chisel, chop clearance cavities in both frame pieces to accommodate the rotating weights. Remember, the arm's travel is at least 1 in. in both directions, so be sure you've provided enough clearance. Although the spinning weights are well protected by the saw's frames, it's probably not a bad idea to fashion some sort of a removable guard for the back of the saw as an added safety feature. Before proceeding with final assembly, the blade holders and tensioner must be made.

I made the blade holders from ⅜-in. key stock, as shown in the drawing. Each blade holder fits into a slot cut into the end of the arm and is held in place by a ³⁄₁₆-in. steel pin. If you can find them, pins that are hardened and ground will work best with the softer key stock, but in a pinch, a small bolt could also suffice. The blade itself is inserted through the holder's slot and held in place by pins on the ends of the blade.

To cut well, the blade must be under considerable tension; and on commercial saws, this is usually done with a threaded rod. But in keeping with my saw's low-tech design, my tensioner is simply a loop of nylon cord that passes around a ¼-in. pin in the lower arm and through a hole in the upper arm, where it wraps around a dowel. Twisting the loop tensions the blade, as with a bowsaw. This setup may sound crude, but it's effective, and because it's flexible, the saw won't shake itself apart when a blade breaks. Sometimes, vibration will tend to unwind the tensioner, a problem that can be remedied by carving a detent notch for the dowel where it seats against its mounting knob.

To minimize warping, I finish both sides of the frames with varnish or shellac before assembling the saw. Once the finish is dry, I test assemble the parts, tightening the fasteners fingertight.

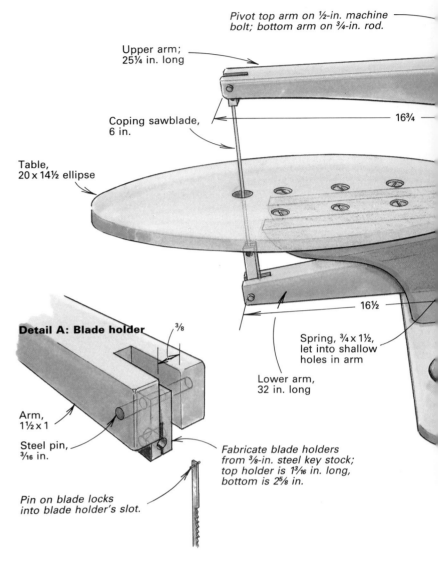

Fig. 1: Scroll saw plan

Pivot top arm on ½-in. machine bolt; bottom arm on ¾-in. rod.

Upper arm; 25¼ in. long

Coping sawblade, 6 in.

16¾

Table, 20 x 14½ ellipse

16½

Detail A: Blade holder ⅜

Spring, ¾ x 1½, let into shallow holes in arm

Lower arm, 32 in. long

Arm, 1½ x 1

Steel pin, ³⁄₁₆ in.

Pin on blade locks into blade holder's slot.

Fabricate blade holders from ⅜-in. steel key stock; top holder is 1³⁄₁₆ in. long, bottom is 2⅝ in.

With a blade installed and lightly tensioned, I move the arms by hand. They should slide lightly against the sides of the frame. If there's binding, trim as needed with a handplane. To keep the lower arm roughly centered in its swing and to give the rotating weights some resistance to work against, I mounted three coil springs between the lower arm and the saw's base. The springs—straight from the hardware store—are 1½ in. long, ¾ in. in diameter. To hold each spring fast against vibration, I bent one end of the coil down and threaded it into a small hole bored in the base. Long finishing nails will temporarily hold the coil springs in place while the saw is attached to its plywood base.

Trial run—To test the saw, I chuck a bolt into a variable-speed drill and connect this through a section of rubber hose to the eccentric drive shaft. I run the machine for a few minutes at slow speed to check everything out. Both arms should reciprocate freely with minimal vibration. If the front or back of the bottom arm strikes the base, adjust the position of the springs or install stiffer ones. Once this test is done, I connect a permanent motor and switch. The saw doesn't require much power—⅓ HP to ¼ HP should be plenty at 1,720 RPM. Do not, under any circumstances, use a 3,450-RPM motor. Unless you reduce its speed through pulleys, a motor this fast will cause dangerous vibration.

To finish up the saw, I make a 20-in.-dia. elliptical saw table out of ¾-in. plywood and screw it to the frames with drywall

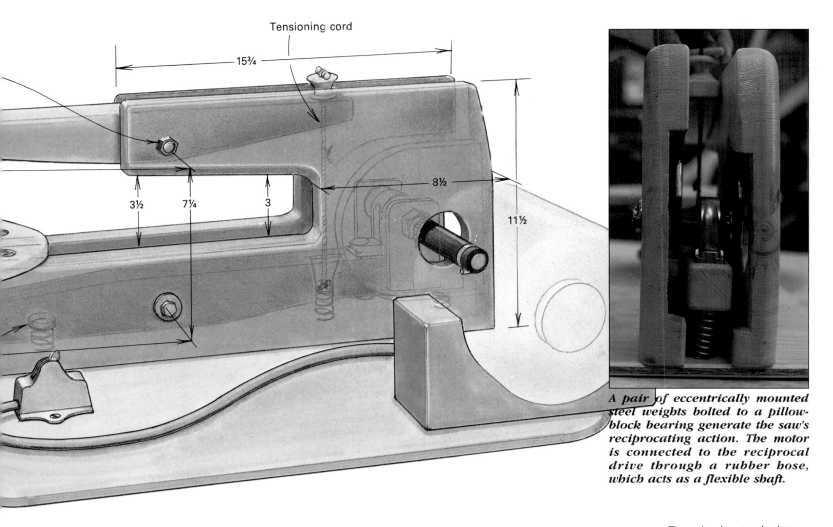

Tensioning cord

15¾

3½   7¼   3

8½

11½

A pair of eccentrically mounted steel weights bolted to a pillow-block bearing generate the saw's reciprocating action. The motor is connected to the reciprocal drive through a rubber hose, which acts as a flexible shaft.

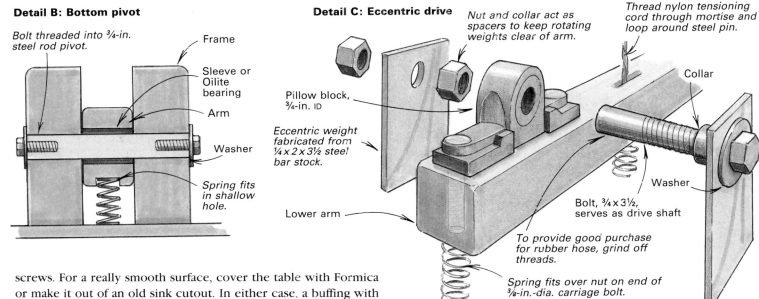

Detail B: Bottom pivot

Bolt threaded into ¾-in. steel rod pivot.

Frame

Sleeve or Oilite bearing

Arm

Washer

Spring fits in shallow hole.

Detail C: Eccentric drive

Nut and collar act as spacers to keep rotating weights clear of arm.

Thread nylon tensioning cord through mortise and loop around steel pin.

Pillow block, ¾-in. ID

Eccentric weight fabricated from ¼ x 2 x 3½ steel bar stock.

Lower arm

Collar

Washer

Bolt, ¾ x 3½, serves as drive shaft

To provide good purchase for rubber hose, grind off threads.

Spring fits over nut on end of ⅜-in.-dia. carriage bolt.

screws. For a really smooth surface, cover the table with Formica or make it out of an old sink cutout. In either case, a buffing with paste wax will make maneuvering the workpiece easier for small-radius scroll work. I've come up with solutions for the two aspects of using a scroll saw that I find most unpleasant: vibration and dust. A 3-in.-thick foam-rubber pad placed under the saw's base dampens noise and vibration considerably and keeps the saw from walking across the table. On a few of the machines I've built, I tapped into the airstream coming off the motor's cooling fan and diverted it through a ½-in. copper tube to a point just in front of the blade. If you do this, make sure to orient the tube so it blows dust toward the back of the saw and not toward the operator. □

Mark White teaches woodworking, welding and house construction at the University of Alaska outpost on Kodiak Island.

Sources of supply

Pillow blocks and motors are available locally from Grainger's. For a catalog and list of distributors, write W.W. Grainger, Inc., 5959 W. Howard St., Niles, IL 60648; (312) 647-8900.

Bar stock, Oilite bearings and hardware are available from Small Parts, 6901 N.E. Third Ave., Miami, FL 33238; (305) 751-0856.

Key and bar stock is available from Metal by Mail, 18170 W. Davidson Road, Brookfield, WI 53005; (414) 786-4276.

Modern scroll saws are more than just hobby machines. They can do a wide variety of sawing jobs, from cutting delicate marquetry patterns in thin veneers to sawing fretwork in thick hardwood.

The saws, from left to right, are the Hegner Multimax 2, Lancaster Machine Co.'s Pro-Cut 20 in., RBI's Hawk 220 and Delta's 18-in. Electronic. The stand is optional with the Pro-Cut.

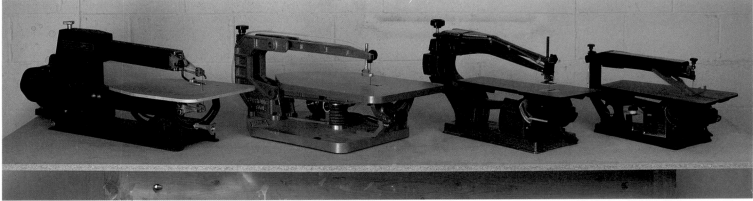

The scroll saws from left to right include Excalibur's Excalibur II, Strong Tool's 2015, American Machinery Sales' Superscroll 18 and

Penn State Industries' Super 15. The Strong 2015 is shown without its bolt-together stand, which does come with the saw.

Testing Scroll Saws

Smooth and precise cuts, even in thick stock

by Greg Bover

From *Fine Woodworking* magazine (January 1989) 74:50-54

I had always been a little skeptical of scroll saws: They seemed to be designed more for hobbyists cutting out whirligigs and knickknacks rather than for the needs of a professional shop. Although our pipe-organ building company, C.B. Fisk Inc., had used a 1940's Boice Crane scroll saw to cut curves smaller than our bandsaws could handle, the saw never cut thick hardwood well. Consequently, it mostly sat and gathered dust.

But when I saw a guy at a woodworking trade show last year cut names out of 8/4 oak, I began to think that modern scroll saws were more than just toys. They seemed capable of doing difficult, precise work, cutting tight-radius scroll work in thick hardwoods smoothly enough that the sawn surfaces were ready to finish with only light sanding. While pricing a few scroll saws, I discovered that there are vastly differing prices between various makes and models with seemingly similar capacities and features. To determine how the scroll saws differ and how a modern scroll saw would work in our shop, we picked eight scroll saws, ranging in price from $129 to slightly more than $1,000, and tested them over a period of several months. Our observations and opinions are stated below, and a chart of specifications for the eight models is located on p. 29. But first, let's look at how modern scroll saws work.

Saw anatomy—The tool itself is pretty simple. Basically, it's nothing more than a stationary table with a thin blade coming up through the center, secured by arms at top and bottom. To make the blade cut, the arms move up and down in a reciprocating motion, or stroke. The arms are driven by an eccentric shaft (or gear drive on some saws) powered by an electric motor. On all modern scroll saws, the blade is attached to both arms and kept in constant tension. On older, rigid arm designs, like our Boice Crane, the top of the blade is attached to a spring, which doesn't provide the same constant blade tension throughout the stroke. The constant-tension design allows the perpetually taut blade to cut tight-radius curves in thick wood without excessive flexing, which would cause a low-tension blade to break or bow in the cut.

Because the blades are under constant tension and don't flex very much, scroll saws can use very thin blades, like jewelry-saw blades, as small as .010 in. thick and .022 in. wide. These small blades allow delicate cuts for fretwork patterns; the thin-blade kerf makes the scroll saw perfect for cutting marquetry patterns in veneer or for sawing out jigsaw puzzle pieces that fit tightly together. Because the blades can be quickly removed from the clamps on the ends of the arms, it's easy to replace a blade or insert it through a small hole drilled in the middle of a piece, for doing fretwork or cutting out a marquetry background (see top photo this page). Compared to most other woodworking machinery, the scroll saw is quite safe to use: The teeth on the blade are fine and don't cut very aggressively.

Although the saws look similar, the eight models we tested can be divided into two basic types based on the design of their arms. Most saws employ the parallel-arm design: The two arms pivot independently, and only the lower one is powered. The blade is secured to both top and bottom arms via blade clamps, and a knob on a threaded rod connecting the back ends of the arms is tightened to tension the blade (see bottom photo this page). The main advantage with the parallel-arm design is that by pivoting both arms, the blade stays almost perpendicular to the saw table throughout its stroke, for a square cut in tight curves with little blade flexing. If the blade breaks, the upper, nonpowered arm stops running (the exception is the Excalibur, see below), and the broken end of the blade won't stab the top of the workpiece, or your finger—another advantage.

On the other hand, C-frame saws, like the Delta and Superscroll 18, hold the blade between the points of a deep, C-shape casting

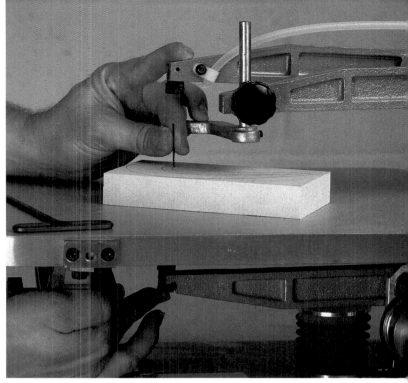

By drilling a hole in the workpiece and threading the blade through before tightening the blade clamps, the scroll saw can cut out patterns in the middle of a panel, handy for fretwork or marquetry. As shown above, the removable bottom blade clamp on the Strong 2015 is held with a finger while the upper arm is brought into position; the blade is then aligned in the clamp and tightened.

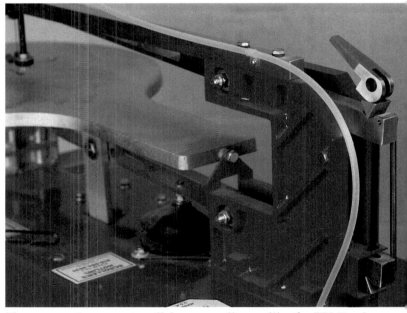

The rear casting on a parallel-arm scroll saw, like the RBI Hawk 220 shown here, houses the pivot bearings for the two arms and supports the saw's hold-down arm. The threaded rod and hand knob at the back of the arms tensions the blade during the cut and must be released before blades are changed.

that rotates up and down in a short arc. Because both arms are part of the same casting and are not independently pivoting, as on the parallel-arm scroll saws, the blade is tensioned with an eccentric cam or hand screw that pulls up on the upper blade holder. The disadvantage of this design is that the blade moves through an arc rather than straight up and down, which can strain the blade when cutting tight corners in thick stock. Also, because both arms are driven during the stroke, a broken blade will continue to stab the workpiece until the saw is turned off.

Testing eight models—Most of the saws arrived at our shop in time to help us rough out a lot of Gothic tracery for our Opus 92—

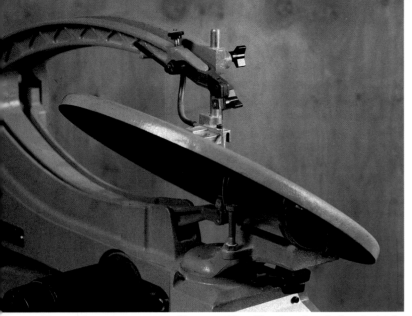

The tables on most scroll saws tilt, allowing beveled cuts to be made. Here, the table on the Delta is tilted to 45°, revealing the two trunnions that suppport the table, as well as the stop bolt that accurately references the table when it's returned to square.

a large pipe organ we built for The Church of the Transfiguration in Manhattan, N.Y. The tracery, which provides the grillwork around the tops of the organ's fascade, had to be cut out of 4/4 and 6/4 white oak. We broke blades left and right until we got used to the machines. Of course, we learned a lot about changing blades, and as we got the hang of running the saws, we began to understand their individual merits and shortcomings. Before getting into specifics, here are some general observations from our work with the saws:

All eight saws worked reasonably well, cutting tracery in thick oak or fretwork in thin stock, regardless of whether the saws were of aluminum or cast-iron construction. However, we found that the heavier machines with cast-iron frames and tables, like the Delta and Superscroll 18, vibrated less and thus felt more solid and were more pleasant to use. This is important, because the vibration caused by the saw's reciprocating action can be distracting, especially when turning a thin piece constantly to cut a delicate pattern. Heavy, well-braced stands increase a saw's stability, and three-legged stands, like the Delta's and Hegner's, don't rock even on an uneven floor. For lighter machines or ones without stands, good performance can be had by bolting the saw to a heavy workbench. Although most scroll-saw tables are flat, they tend to be fairly rough; therefore, they must be smoothed with a block and 320-grit or 400-grit silicone carbide paper, then waxed before workpieces can be turned freely. The tables also tilt for beveled cuts, as shown in the photo above, but few of the saws tilt 45° to both the left and the right, which is necessary for cutting dovetail pins.

Despite the the manufacturers' advertisements, power isn't much of an issue with a scroll saw, because the blade always breaks before the motor strains. Because of this, saws with even the smallest motors aren't underpowered. Further, we found speed-change pulleys and control devices unnecessary for most woodworking: It's best to run the machines at full speed, except when cutting thin veneers or metal. High speeds generally produce smoother cuts, except when cutting tight curves, which may cause the blade to burn. All the saws feature built-in blower systems designed to clear sawdust from the workpiece, and most of them blew away enough dust to let us see where we were cutting.

Although we assumed the blade on a parallel-arm saw is supposed to move straight up and down during cutting, we found that the blades on most of these saws move slightly forward and backward, as well as up and down. Saws with blades that move forward on the downstroke, like the Hegner and the Hawk, proved best,

because they cut more aggressively and saved the blade from wear by moving slightly backward and clearing the cut on the upstroke. The blades on the Excalibur and Strong 2015 scroll saws actually move slightly backward on the downstroke and forward on the upstroke—the opposite of the optimum blade movement.

Most saws have blade clamps that will accept any 5-in.-long blade, from #2/0 to #12, and some can even clamp a cardboard emery board for sanding. The blades that came with the saws all performed about the same, but we found that #9 12-t.p.i. blades are best for all-around woodcutting. Any blade is subject to deflection from the pressure of cutting, especially in thick hardwoods. Therefore, a blade clamp that allows the blade to flex freely over its entire length rather than at just the clamp points is better for smooth cuts and longer blade life. The machines with pivoting clamps, like the Hegner, Delta and Superscroll 18, had the least blade breakage.

Generally, we felt all the machines were safe to operate. The hold-down arms featured on all the saws tested offer some protection from the blade and are useful for keeping tiny workpieces from jumping around during a cut. For most cuts, the work can be controlled by pushing down and in at about 45°. It's also worth noting that the thickness-cutting capacity of most saws with their hold-downs in place is less than what manufacturers state in their literature.

Delta Electronic—The Delta saw, manufactured by Delta International Machinery Corp. (call 800-438-2486, or 2487 in Pennsylvania, for a local distributor), is built like a battleship, with its heavy cast-iron frame. We set the saw up in about 45 minutes, and once assembled, the Delta was clearly the most ruggedly built saw in our review. Its round cast-iron table is supported by two trunnions, and a built-in 90° stop makes squaring the table to the blade quick and positive. The saw vibrated very little, even when we cut 8/4 material.

The blade tension lock/release and adjustment knob are on top of the upper arm instead of at the back of the arm, as on the parallel-arm saws, so it's very convenient to reach. Blade change on the Delta is a bit slow, because a pin must be inserted to lock the pivoting blade clamps before their Allen screws can be loosened or tightened. An optional hand screw replaces the Allen screw, making blade changes quicker, but the hand screw gets in the way when the hold-down is raised for deep cuts. The hold-down on the Delta, as well as on the Excalibur and Superscroll 18, is adjustable for bevel cutting. On most other saws, the hold-down must be removed for tilt table work.

The Delta features an electronic speed-control knob and a digital readout, which shows the number of blade strokes per minute (SPM). The knob allows instant speed changes, but the tool's range of 40 SPM to 2,000 SPM was excessive for any work we tried. Because fancy electronic devices are often prone to breakdown, we feel the device is more a gimmick than a bonus for an otherwise fine machine.

Excalibur II—The Excalibur, manufactured by Excalibur Machine & Tool Co. (210 8th St. S., Lewiston, N.Y. 10492), features alloy castings, extruded steel arms and a smoothly surfaced aluminum table. The saw comes without a stand, so it must be bolted to a table or bench. This saw was the hardest to set up: Instructions were sketchy, some hardware was missing and the process took more than three hours. The saw comes motorless, which can save money if there's an old 1,725-RPM motor around with a ⅝-in. shaft to fit the supplied three-step pulley. The motor mount is designed to hang the motor off the back of the saw, and a nice lever arm releases belt tension for speed changes. The cord and switch are supplied, but the switch is on the cord rather than up front on the machine, which can be a problem if the saw needs to be turned off in a hurry.

The Excalibur drives the blade with a "double parallel-link" sys-

Company and model	List price	Throat depth	Cut † thickness	Motor speed SPM	Stroke length	Arm design	Drive method	Table size	Table tilt left/right	Stand
American Machinery Sales Inc. Superscroll 18	$387	18 in.	1¾ in.	1,650	¾ in.	C	Direct	8¾ x 17½	45°/0°	No
Delta International Delta Electronic	$699 $1,014**	18 in.	1¾ in.	Variable 40 to 2,000	⅞ in.	C	Gear	16 in. dia.	30°/45°	3 leg, bolted
Excalibur Machine & Tool Co. Excalibur II	$579*	19 in.	1¼ in.	400/800/1,400	¾ in.	P††	Belt	12 x 17	45°/45°	No
AMI Ltd./Hegner Hegner Multimax 2	$995**	14½ in.	1¾ in.	1,660	15/16 in.	P	Direct	9 x 17	45°/0°	3 leg, welded
Lancaster Machinery Co. Pro-Cut 20 in.	$799	20 in.	2½ in.	800/925/ 1,000/1,150	1 in.	P	Belt & gear	16 in. dia.	45°/45°	Opt. 4 leg, bolted
Penn State Industries Super 15 in.	$129	15 in.	1¾ in.	1,650	¾ in.	P	Direct	7¾ x 17	45°/0°	No
RBI Industries Hawk 220	$799**	20 in.	1¾ in.	700/1,300	1⅛ in.	P	Belt & gear	13¾ x 22½	45°/45°	4 leg, bolted
Strong Tool Design Strong 2015 Two Speed	$999**	20 in.	2 in.	728/1,028	1 in.	P	Belt	13¾ x 22	45°/12°	4 leg, bolted

*, without motor   **, stand included   †, with hold-down in place   ††, both arms powered
SPM = strokes per minute   C = C-frame   P = parallel arms

tem, powering both the upper and lower arms. Unfortunately, this design makes the Excalibur subject to blade stabbing. Despite this shortcoming, the Excalibur performed well and consistently gave us clean cuts, though its short ¾-in. blade stroke didn't cut fast in thick stock. With the saw mounted to a bench, it was the quietest of all the machines tested. Although the blade clamps don't pivot, the saw wasn't particularly prone to breaking blades, and we judged it the easiest saw to change blades on.

Hegner Multimax 2—The Hegner, imported by AMI Ltd. (2 McCullough Drive, Southgate Industrial Park, Box 312, New Castle, Del. 19720), has a cast-alloy frame and arms, and it was a breeze to put together—a set-up time of only 15 minutes. The saw has an extremely smooth finished alloy table, which we judged the best in the test. Although the table only tilts one way, the trunnions were well machined, and the table locked where it was put without excessive finger pressure on the lock knob. The Hegner runs at 1,660 SPM, the highest speed next to the Delta in the test, and is powered by a direct-drive 1.9-amp AEG motor, with no speed controls. (Hegner has a new line of variable-speed saws that should be on the market by the time this article is in print.) With a #9 blade, the Hegner cut 1½-in.-thick maple well. Its welded tubular-steel stand is heavily braced and stable.

Besides being an all-around well-built saw, the blade clamps on the Hegner had the best design and construction: They allow the blade to pivot freely and make blade changes easy. The Hegner's blade clamps have 3/16-in.-sq. head machine screws that tighten with a large clock-winding type key, an improvement over the small easy-to-strip Allen screws used on the other saws. To make the blade changes even easier, the Hegner has a blade-clamp holder on its table edge that holds and aligns the blade and clamp while they're tightened (see the photo on the next page). An accessory called the "Pierce Pal" allows the blade to be aligned and clamped in the blade holder after it has passed through a hole in the workpiece, for cutting out a pattern in the middle of a panel. Also, because the blade clamps aren't fixed on the arms, one can

buy several extra pairs. If a blade breaks, just install a new blade already fixed in its clamps. Overall, the Hegner machines (including the larger Polymax 3, which we also tried) are beautifully built and highly favored by our woodworkers.

Pro-Cut 20 in.—This machine, sold by Lancaster Machinery Co. (715 Fountain Ave., Lancaster, Penn. 17601), has cast-alloy arms, frame and table and an optional four-leg stand with braced legs. The saw has a nicely surfaced table that's stabilized by dual trunnions—a sturdy arrangement. The belt-driven machine has a two-step pulley, and changing speeds was very easy, despite the tiny, hard-to-grip thumbscrew on the belt guard. Even with four speeds though, the Pro-Cut's maximum speed of 1,160 SPM seemed slow; we felt the saw would have cut better at a higher speed. The Pro-Cut, as well as the Hawk and the Strong 2015, has a large 20-in. throat capacity, which is useful for cutting out fretwork patterns in large panels.

Blade change is a real ordeal on the Pro-Cut, because the top blade clamp is hidden under a shroud on the upper arm, and a special tool and Allen wrench are needed to set the lower blade clamp. The Pro-Cut comes with a foot pedal on/off switch that plugs into the cord. This feature came in handy a couple of times, but we didn't need to start and stop the saw too often.

Hawk 220—The Hawk, made by RBIndustries Inc. (1801 Vine St., Box 369, Harrisonville, Mo. 64701), has a cast-alloy frame and table supported by a sheet-metal stand with four unbraced legs. It is light and wobbly but the solid bar stock arms are sturdy. Its rubber glides might lessen the bad vibration we experienced. The table tilts 45° both ways, but the trunnions are sloppy, and the table was difficult to lock in place. Despite its pivoting blade clamps, the saw broke more than its share of blades and was prone to burning in the kerf when we cut 1¾-in.-thick oak.

The Hawk has two speeds and a motor that's mounted under the saw, out of the way. Unfortunately, making speed changes becomes difficult, because the motor pulleys are located under the

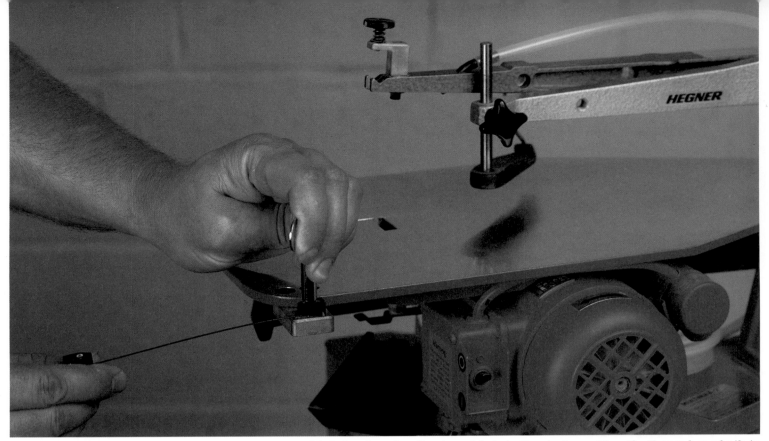

Besides providing a pivoting blade clamp that prevents blade breakage by allowing a blade to flex during cutting, the Hegner has a built-in holder that supports and aligns a blade in the clamp while it's tightened in place.

saw. Two different length V-belts are required, one for each saw speed pulley. Blade change requires a special rod and an Allen wrench to secure the pivoting top blade clamp. The blade tensioning/release adjustment features a convenient cam lock that takes only a flick to engage or loosen for blade changes.

Strong 2015 Two Speed—This saw, made by Strong Tool Design (20425 Beatrice, Livonia, Mich. 48152), has a cast-alloy frame, arms and large 13¾-in. by 22-in. table. The stand has four legs that are splayed in lieu of bracing to give the saw stability, but we found the legs to be always in the way. The table surface was adequately smooth, but the single trunnion didn't lock well enough to keep the table steady when cutting heavy work. The hold-down can be bolted on either side of the frame, making it easier for left-handers.

Cuts with the 2015 were generally smooth, but the light saw vibrated considerably. A few times after tightening the blade-tensioning adjustment, the pivot on the end of the bolt didn't engage correctly and tension would suddenly release in the middle of the cut. The blade clamps are designed to pivot with the blade, but unfortunately, arm design makes the blade move back on the downstroke. Blade changes were relatively easy with the provided Allen wrench. One problem, however, is that the lower blade clamp barely fits through the table, so the blade needs to be bent and worked through the opening. Since our test, the 2015 has been superceded by a new model, the Strong Prospector, also with a 20-in. throat.

Super 15 in.—This saw is the least-expensive saw in the sample: a fraction of the price of the $1,014 Delta, the most expensive saw we tested. Manufactured in Taiwan and imported by Penn State Industries (2850 Comly Road, Philadelphia, Penn. 19154), the Super 15 looks like the Hegner and is remarkably similar to Taiwanese saws sold by Grizzly and Delta. Although Penn State's ads claim the saw has professional quality and precision, it simply doesn't. The overall quality of the castings and the saw's fit and finish is poor. For instance, the Super 15 has a cheap plastic hold-down and miniscule pump bellows that are absolutely useless. Also, the blade clamps

are badly machined and don't grip the blade well.

Like the Pro-Cut 20 in., the Super 15 features a covered top arm for safety. But on the unit we received for testing, the cover had been bent, and the arm hit it on every stroke, making a terrible sound until we bent it back to shape. On the positive side, the saw can cut cleanly enough (albeit with a lot of vibration), no doubt thanks to its high 1,650 SPM. Also, the Super 15, like the Superscroll 18, has a power-switch lock so it can be child-proofed.

Superscroll 18—Imported by American Machinery Sales Inc. (Box 5285, Marshallton, Del. 19809), this Taiwan-made saw is heftily built and doesn't offer many frills. Although the table surfacing and machining are still pretty rough, this saw is a step up from the Super 15, both in capacity and performance. The Superscroll's 18-in.-deep throat is enough for fairly large work, and with its hold-down in place, the saw has the same depth-cutting capacity of most other, more expensive scroll saws. The saw is a hybrid design: It features direct drive, like many parallel-arm saws, but is a C-frame saw, like the Delta.

The Superscroll 18 has pivoting blade clamps that allow for a fair amount of blade flex. Plastic hinged covers flip over the blade clamps (I can't see why), and a removable table insert makes accessing the lower arm for blade changes easier. The Superscroll 18 produced a moderate amount of vibration during cutting, which decreased when we bolted the saw to a heavy workbench. Cutting action was solid and yielded smooth cuts in all but thick hardwoods. Overall, the Superscroll 18 is a lot of saw for the money.

Other models—As interest in scroll saws grows, manufacturers continue to offer additional models, which we were unable to include in this test. Companies offering other scroll saws include AMT, Grizzly, Sunhill, Sakura U.S.A. and Transpower. □

Greg Bover is the woodshop foreman of C.B. Fisk Inc., pipe-organ makers in Gloucester, Mass. Shop members Rob Hazard and John Schreiner helped with the testing for this article.

Tight Quarters

Here's a sample of some ways readers cope with what seems to be a universal problem—not enough room. Robert Henderson, a woodworking teacher in the Detroit public schools for 21 years, tells how he rolls tools out of the way in his garage shop; Mike Drummond, a woodworker and writer from Grass Valley, Calif., tells how a nearby craftsman adapted to the cramped space in a tractor trailer; Vic Mumford, a retired executive who turned his garage into The Whittle Shop in Ventura, Calif., has come up with the fastest tablesaw/router-table conversion yet; and Michael K. Brouillette, a database designer in Fairfax Station, Va., writes about an ingenious workbench/lathe combination. What they all have in common could be summed up by the old magician: Now you see it...Now you don't....

Wheel away your troubles

by Robert Henderson

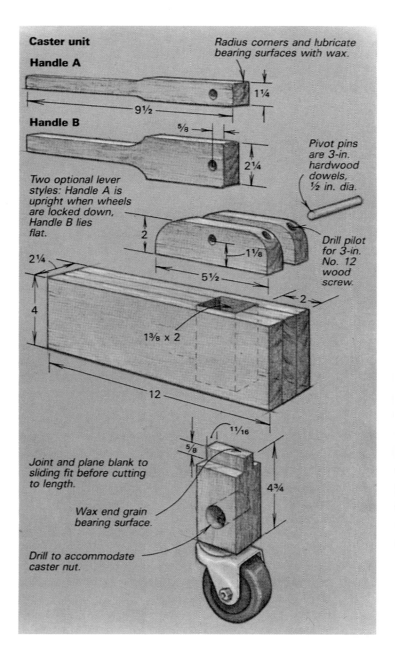

I've moved three times in the past 20 years, and each time my workshop got a little bigger and better planned. With every move, I anticipated that the new shop would be big enough to spell an end to my space problems. Not so—I've come to believe that a big-enough workshop truly is the "impossible dream."

A few years back I installed a commercially made caster set on the base cabinet of my radial-arm saw in hopes that it would help. But I found the adjustable casters cumbersome to use, and the wheels were too small to work well. What I needed was big wheels that lowered and retracted without a lot of fuss.

The system I finally came up with has solved most of my problems. The hardwood base adapts to various machines with a little ingenuity, and the casters can be selected to bear whatever weight is required. As equipped here, with medium-duty casters from the hardware store, the setup will carry a 500-lb. machine very well and when the wheels are retracted the machine sits firmly on its own weight.

The levers shown in the drawing provide ½ in. of lift, which should be enough to traverse the most uneven floor. If necessary, the amount of lift can be easily changed by slightly altering the design. In addition, I've shown two lever styles: one positions the handle up when the wheels are extended, as shown in the photo; in the other style, the levers lie flat.

So far I have fitted casters on three of my heavier machines with excellent results. In fact, they work so well that at least three more of their relatives will soon have wheels of their own.

Author

One version of Henderson's retractable casters bolts directly to the sides of his tablesaw; another version, not shown, has a four-sided wooden frame that supports his Hitachi planer.

From *Fine Woodworking* magazine (September 1985) 54:68-70

For additional space and light, Clay cut and hinged two sections of the trailer's sides so they would fold out as decks supported by adjustable metal legs. In bad weather they can be shielded with corrugated fiberglass and plywood panels.

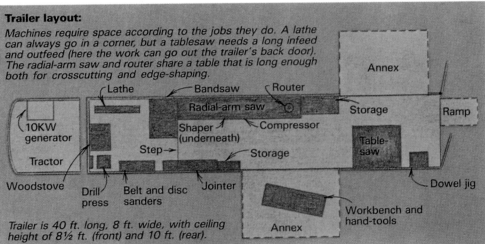

Trailer layout:
Machines require space according to the jobs they do. A lathe can always go in a corner, but a tablesaw needs a long infeed and outfeed (here the work can go out the trailer's back door). The radial-arm saw and router share a table that is long enough both for crosscutting and edge-shaping.

Lathe — Bandsaw — Router
Radial-arm saw
Annex
10KW generator
Shaper (underneath) — Compressor
Storage
Ramp
Step
Storage
Table-saw
Tractor
Woodstove — Drill press — Belt and disc sanders — Jointer
Dowel jig
Annex
Workbench and hand-tools

Trailer is 40 ft. long, 8 ft. wide, with ceiling height of 8½ ft. (front) and 10 ft. (rear).

Mobile Wood Works

by Mike Drummond

Gary Clay took delivery of a 40-ft. truck trailer a year ago intending to use it as storage. But he soon saw it in a different light, as a complete wood shop on wheels.

The wheeled workshop is only 8 ft. wide, which would have made a discouragingly narrow and dark work space, so Clay modified the trailer as shown in the floor plan and photos above. The trailer can tap into a power source on the job site, or run off its own 10KW generator, which Clay mounted in place of one of the truck's 80-gal. fuel tanks.

The machines are situated according to the jobs they have to do, and the heights of the tables are also taken into account—the

tablesaw feeds under the dowel jig; the bandsaw feeds over the radial-arm saw and the lathe. The jointer is angled just enough that long work can bypass the sanders. In places where much vertical clearance won't be needed, such as above the radial-arm saw and the jointer, 10-in.-deep shelves provide storage, and pegboard above the router table keeps much-used handtools central and handy.

Clay is after jobs where he can set up on site for several days or weeks at a time. He is an all-around woodworker: In the past he has done circular windows, arches, custom bars, cabinetry, stairways and office furniture. One early job was building a 7½-ton sailboat; a recent one was customizing a recording studio for a member of the rock group SuperTramp.

Clay, who recently drove his shop from Nevada City, Calif., to a new home in Telluride, Colo., has been partial to Sears Craftsman machines for many years, and now appreciates a feature he never thought much about before—the tools have excellent warranties, parts and service—nationwide.

Drop-in router table

by Vic Mumford

In my 400-sq.-ft. shop there wasn't room for a regular router table, so I decided to mount my Makita 3600B in one of the plywood extension wings on my tablesaw. Past experience with space-saving ideas taught me that unless a conversion is foolproof and dead easy, the changeover simply isn't used very much. So I wanted a mounting system that required no screws, no clamps and no fasteners, one that would allow instant setup and takedown, with no-hassle bit changes. The photos at right show the simple drop-in design I came up with. The router is inserted down through an access hole that is large enough to admit the handles, then it slides into a tight-fitting mounting bracket and is locked in place by the access hole's cover plate.

I cut the holes with the router, a straightedge and some hand-tools, then glued and screwed wooden strips beneath to form rabbets that support the router and the cover plates. Where the wooden strips met, I left spaces at the corners to make sawdust removal easier. You could mount a round-base router in a similar way, by cutting half the mounting hole in the table surface, and the other half in the access hole's cover plate.

Mumford's Makita router plugs into a switched outlet, then is inserted through a hole large enough to admit the handles. Gravity and the access-hole cover plate hold it in place.

Workbench top swings up on hinges, as shown in center photo. Lathe is then raised into position. A length of angle iron on a hinged wooden strip at the front of the bench holds the lathe base up, as shown in the photo at right.

Lathe/workbench duo

by Michael K. Brouillette

Despite my workshop's size—a double garage measuring 20 ft. by 22 ft.—I never seem to have enough room. To make matters worse, I recently decided I needed a second workbench, so I could work on more than one project at the same time. My quandary was that regardless of where I placed it, the bench would occupy 18 sq. ft. of precious floor space.

I spent weeks puzzling out the situation until my wife, Jane, gave me the solution. Why not remount the lathe on a hinged board under the workbench top, like a sewing machine?

The photos above show the general idea. The important de-sign considerations are the length of the lathe and the height of the headstock, for which you have to allow clearance. I made my base from heavy construction lumber, and mounted the lathe on butcher-block. The workbench top is an old solid-core door.

I counterweighted the lathe with a spring-and-cable setup at both ends, running over pulleys mounted inside the base frame. My local hardware store carried the necessary hinges and the other hardware 2-in. pulleys, heavy-duty springs about 1 ft. long, ¼-in. vinyl-coated steel cable and 2½-in. eye screws. Depending on the weight of your lathe, you might want heavier or lighter springs (or maybe none at all), but considerable leeway is possible by adjusting the mounting positions.

The workbench is mounted on casters, like most of my other heavy machines, and it does its double-duty with aplomb. I may not have any more room than I had before, but at least for the time being, I don't have any less. Now where, if I had the chance, would I put a nice little planer...? □

Radial-Arm Saws

Sizing up six popular models

by Sandor Nagyszalanczy

Fig. 1: Radial-arm saw anatomy

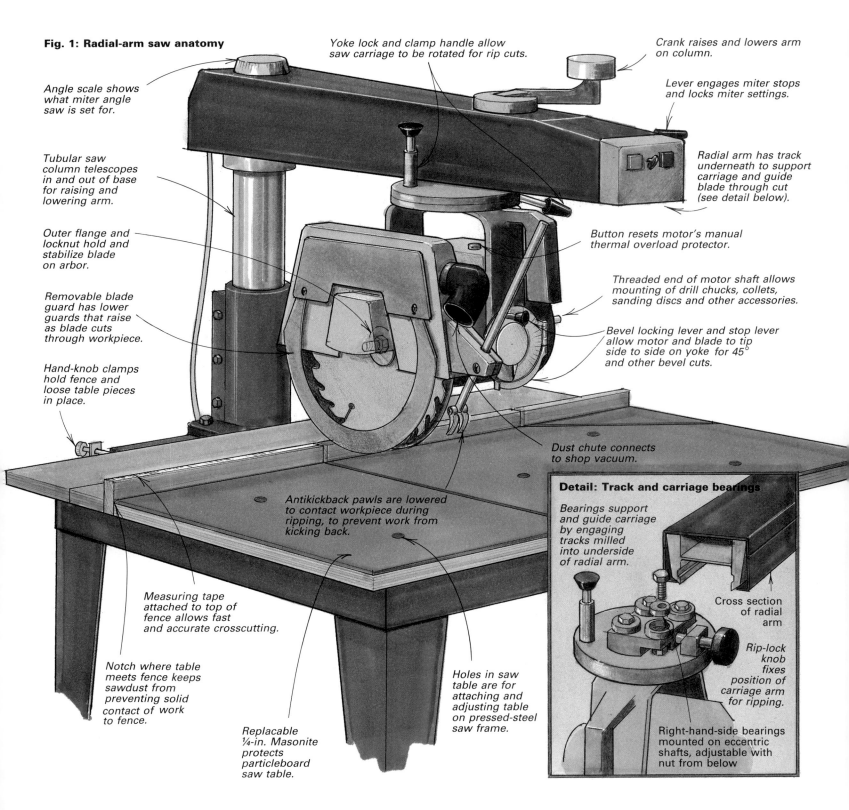

Yoke lock and clamp handle allow saw carriage to be rotated for rip cuts.

Crank raises and lowers arm on column.

Angle scale shows what miter angle saw is set for.

Lever engages miter stops and locks miter settings.

Tubular saw column telescopes in and out of base for raising and lowering arm.

Radial arm has track underneath to support carriage and guide blade through cut (see detail below).

Outer flange and locknut hold and stabilize blade on arbor.

Button resets motor's manual thermal overload protector.

Threaded end of motor shaft allows mounting of drill chucks, collets, sanding discs and other accessories.

Removable blade guard has lower guards that raise as blade cuts through workpiece.

Bevel locking lever and stop lever allow motor and blade to tip side to side on yoke for 45° and other bevel cuts.

Hand-knob clamps hold fence and loose table pieces in place.

Dust chute connects to shop vacuum.

Antikickback pawls are lowered to contact workpiece during ripping, to prevent work from kicking back.

Detail: Track and carriage bearings

Bearings support and guide carriage by engaging tracks milled into underside of radial arm.

Cross section of radial arm

Measuring tape attached to top of fence allows fast and accurate crosscutting.

Rip-lock knob fixes position of carriage arm for ripping.

Notch where table meets fence keeps sawdust from preventing solid contact of work to fence.

Holes in saw table are for attaching and adjusting table on pressed-steel saw frame.

Right-hand-side bearings mounted on eccentric shafts, adjustable with nut from below

Replacable ¼-in. Masonite protects particleboard saw table.

Drawings: Kathleen Creston

The radial-arm saw has a split personality. Manufacturers have hyped it for years as the "all-in-one" shop tool, because it can single-handedly rip and crosscut, cut joinery, and with attachments, shape, drill, sand and even plane wood. On the other hand, many serious woodworkers have shied away from the radial-arm saw because of it's notorious reputation for inaccuracy. In fact, getting even a simple square crosscut with a poorly adjusted saw can be an exercise in frustration.

When I was making furniture full-time, I avoided the radial's personality dilemma by relying on an old cast-iron monster with an arm beefy enough to be used as a crane and a giant blade that could tear through tree trunks, with power to spare. Unfortunately, small shops usually don't have the room or the budget for an industrial-size radial and are left to buy a saw from the ranks of smaller, lighter-duty machines. But do all new small radial saws deserve the bad reputation alluded to above, or can small design variances and manufacturing quality make all the difference between a junker and a dream saw? To find out, I tested radial-arm saws made by six manufacturers, one model from each: Black & Decker 1712, Delta Model 10, DeWalt 7770-10, Inca 810, Ryobi RA200 and Sears 19825. I've summed up my observations and experiences with these saws and added a chart of their vital statistics on p. 36. As I discovered, design and construction aren't the only culprits for giving radial saws a bad name. In fact, these differences aren't as important to good performance as proper adjustment and good-use habits. Therefore, accompanying this article are two sidebars on adjusting and using a radial, which contain some hints to help you turn your recalcitrant machine into a sweet-cutting saw.

The radial-arm saw is an intimidatingly complex piece of machinery, as you can see from the drawing on the facing page. It's design, however, is based on a simple cutting principle that distinguishes it from most saws: For all crosscutting jobs, the workpiece remains stationary and the blade moves to make the cut (a powered miter box does this, but it doesn't have the crosscut capacity of the radial). This feature makes the radial great for crosscutting long or heavy boards, which would be difficult to push accurately across a tablesaw.

The radial-arm saw is basically a motor-driven circular sawblade mounted on a carriage that rolls the length of an arm suspended over a saw table. The workpiece is supported by the saw table and aligned by the saw fence during cutting. In addition, the saw's arm pivots, raises and lowers, the carriage tilts and the yoke rotates. All these settings change the orientation of the blade relative to the workpiece for different kinds of cuts. This is what gives the radial-arm saw such tremendous woodworking versatility: By pivoting the radial-arm saw from side to side, you can make miter cuts up to 45° or more. Tilting the carriage so the blade is angled relative to the saw table allows for bevel cuts. By setting the saw to both bevel and miter at the same time, you can cut compound angles. The carriage can be rotated so the blade is parallel to the fence in order to rip boards to width between the fence and blade. Once set, the angles of the arm, carriage and yoke are locked in place either with screw knobs or lever locks. Often-used angles, such as 90° and 45°, have positive stops, such as tapered pins or bolts that lock into holes or slots and quickly and accurately set the saw to those angles. The radial arm can be raised and lowered to set the blade's height relative to the saw table.

The price you pay for all of the radial-arm saw's versatility is that you must carefully keep all the saw's moving components adjusted and aligned in order to get consistent, accurate cuts. Practically everything on a radial is subject to adjustment, including the table, arm, yoke, carriage bearings and column. Some of these adjustments allow you to fine-tune the accuracy of the stops used

in setting the saw to often-used bevel and miter angles (like for regular square cuts or 45° miters). In addition to the adjustment of the stops, adjustment of the saw blade's horizontal and vertical alignment relative to its travel along the arm is necessary for a true, clean cut. For an explanation of alignment and to get an idea of how to go about adjusting a radial-arm saw, see the sidebar on p. 40.

Saw construction – To handle the weight of the motor carriage and the tremendous stress that cutting exerts on the radial arm and column, a radial-arm saw has to be built sturdy. Ideally, the arm should be cast iron (cast alloy is used on cheaper saws) and reinforced with ribs to help resist deflection. The track for the carriage needs to be ground straight and true for the saw to achieve straight cuts. Since these tracks are subject to wear, the most durable tracks are either machined cast iron or made up of two replaceable steel rods. The tracks should also be designed to shed sawdust, which can foul the smooth motion of the carriage and ruin the cut. Depending on the saw's design, three or four replaceable ball-bearing rollers ride in the track to support and guide the carriage. The roller assembly adjusts to set the tracking pressure so the carriage can roll smoothly but without play.

The yoke connecting the motor and the blade assembly to the carriage should mount at both front and rear to stabilize the blade during cutting. The motor should have built-in thermal protection and an arbor long enough to hold a dado set. The saw's blade guard should be easy to remove for blade changes, and it should have antikickback pawls and a splitter for ripping. To be useful to the cabinetmaker, a radial should have the power and capacity to cut through at least 8/4 hardwood in one pass.

A tubular steel column supports the arm and is housed in a cast base bolted to a sheet-metal saw frame. The column supports the arm and allows the arm to pivot for miter cuts. The column telescopes in and out of the base via a crank-driven screw to set blade height. The saw table is typically a piece of ¾-in. particleboard fastened with brackets to the saw frame. The brackets allow the table to be adjusted parallel and square with the arm. Screw knobs at the back of the saw table clamp two or three loose table inserts and the fence in place. The clamps allow these pieces to be reassembled in any order. This is because, on miter cuts, the fence must be moved closer to the column to get the maximum width cut. Even so, most radials give 3 in. to 4 in. less capacity mitering to the left than to the right.

Testing the saws – I made numerous crosscuts, miters and bevels in both hard and soft woods to see how smoothly and accurately each saw performed. For consistency, I used a 10-in. DML (1350 S. 15 St., Louisville, Ky. 40210-1861) "Radi-All" blade on the four 10-in. saws and comparable carbide-tooth crosscut blades on the other two radials. Because I could only try each saw for a limited time, I spoke with saw owners and manufacturers to get an idea of each saw's reliability and possible problems.

I found all the saws capable of delivering fairly smooth, accurate cuts, but this is greatly dependent on how well the saw is adjusted, and some saws are much more apt to come out of adjustment than others. In some cases, just bumping into the arm or hitting a knot with the blade throws the saw out. Generally, the more expensive the saw, the more it seems suited for heavy- or continuous-duty work.

Black & Decker 1712 – Made in Italy, this 10-in. radial is Black & Decker's portable model, with the power and capacity of a stationary machine. The 1712's column attaches to the frame with a cast-alloy pivot that allows the entire arm, head and column to

Radial-arm saws

Manufacturer model number	List price	Blade diameter	Motor HP/ Amps at 110v	Maximum depth of cut	Maximum crosscut at 90°	Maximum crosscut at 45° (3/4 in. deep)		Maximum rip capacity	Table size
						Left	Right		
Black & Decker, 1712	$400	10	2/11†	2¾	13½	6	9½	19⅜	21×34
Delta, Model 10	$694	10	1½/11.5** (5.75 amps) (at 220v)	3	14¾	9	10½	24	24¾×42
DeWalt, 7770-10	$990*	10	3½/17** (8.5 amps) (at 220v)	2¹³⁄₁₆	15½	8½	11	25¼	26⅜×36
Inca, 810	$599	9	NA/9	2⅛	16½ 27½††	12¼ 20††	12¼ 20††	25	23½×5⁵⁄₁₆
Ryobi, RA200	$515	8¼	2/11	2¼	12	22½° only	7½	17¾	21½×27½
Sears, 19825	$399*	10	1½/11**	3	13	6	8⅝	26	27×40

All dimensions above are in inches. * includes stand, ** automatic brake, † manual brake, †† with optional extension arm

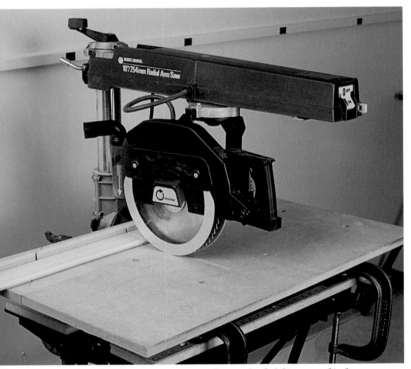

The Black & Decker 1712 is the only folding radial-arm saw with a 10-in. blade. The saw shown above is clamped to a Black & Decker Workmate to give it stability during cutting. Once the saw is positioned correctly and the loose table inserts are removed, the 1712 folds flat, below, for compact transport.

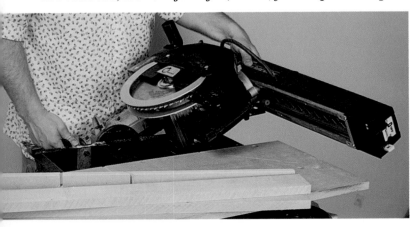

fold down and be carried to the job site or stored flat (see the bottom photo on this page).

The Black & Decker's 11-amp induction motor has an aluminum housing that has fins to dissipate motor heat. The motor has no accessory shaft: Accessories mount directly on the saw's arbor shaft, which is, unfortunately, too short to hold a full ¹³⁄₁₆-in.-wide dado set. A manual brake button is mounted on top of the motor housing. A metal blade guard provides upper and lower blade protection, but I found it apt to bind against the workpiece, especially on miter cuts, and a real pain to take off for blade changes, requiring the removal of three wing nuts.

The motor attaches to a cast-alloy yoke assembly that supports it at both front and rear, but there's no way to set the horizontal alignment. The yoke head has three steel bearings that ride in tracks cast into the underside of the saw's generously ribbed cast-alloy arm. These bearings are arranged so that two oppose one, therefore only one needs adjustment to set the tracking. Because the steel bearings ride in a nonreplaceable cast-alloy track in the arm, I would question how well this track would wear over time.

Although I found setting the 1712 to be straightforward, the elevation crank atop the column and the miter locking lever next to it were a bit hard to reach from the front of the saw. Both the bevel-lock and rip-lock levers are spring loaded and pull out so you can adjust the locking pressure without a wrench. Bevel and miter stops are set using a plunger lever, which provides a positive reference, but the stops stuck easily and were occasionally hard to disengage.

The Black & Decker performed smoothly and consistently gave me straight, true cuts while crosscutting and ripping. While the motor was adequately powerful for maximum depth cuts through maple, it seemed to take the blade an inordinate amount of time to get up to speed. The manual brake required brute force to press and even then was mostly ineffective. I found the saw arm easy to deflect accidentally by pulling the handle slightly to one side while advancing through a crosscut. The saw folds easily for transport, but you must first carefully set the elevation and rip-lock positions and remove part of the table. At 65 lbs., the saw is light enough to carry single-handed, but the handle of the folded saw is close to the table and makes for a cramped grip.

Delta Model 10—This Delta radial is a heavy stationary machine with a ribbed cast-iron arm. The Delta's 11.5-amp motor assembly, however, is housed in plastic and supported in the front and rear by a cast-alloy yoke. The motor, featuring built-in thermal protection and an automatic blade brake, can be wired for either 110v or 220v. The on/off switch is located right next to the handle and is operable with the right-hand thumb—a refreshing convenience compared to the end-of-arm mounted switches on other saws. The upper/lower blade guard is designed so that the blade must be removed before the guard comes off—a definite inconvenience. Like the Black & Decker and the Inca, the Delta guard has the dust chute at the rear. Other saws have them at the front, and I found a front-mounted hose much more likely to get in the way. The head carriage is supported by four ball bearings, and one pair is adjusted to set tracking. Unlike other radials though, bearings can be conveniently adjusted from the top of the saw.

The Delta Model 10 is designed to be set from the front. The elevation crank is just below the table, and the miter stop and locking screws are big wing nuts on the front of the arm. The bevel, yoke and rip-lock knobs and levers are large, easy to grip and generally positive to set and lock. The bevel stop locked easily and securely; however, the lever-action yoke stop didn't engage very positively and needed some fooling with for a true 90° or 45° cut.

When I tried the Delta, the carriage rolled with little effort, and all the cuts were straight and true. The saw ripped well thanks to the adjustable-kerf splitter/antikickback pawls, and I like its large 24¾-in. by 42-in. particleboard table, with lots of room for miter cuts to the left of the column. To get its arbor to hold more than ½ in. of dado cutters (up to ¹³⁄₁₆ in.), use the thin arbor flange on the inside and the arbor nut on the outside without an arbor flange.

DeWalt 7770-10—This is a heavy stationary radial built in traditional DeWalt fashion, with lots of machined cast-iron parts. The model 7770-10 is DeWalt's top-of-the-line 10-in. saw and is now distributed by Black & Decker. It is also the most expensive radial-arm saw in the survey. For the extra money, you definitely get a lot more saw: Its 17-amp motor (8.5 amps when wired for 220v) and cutting capacities equal many 12-in. radials, although at 2¹³⁄₁₆ in., the depth of cut is just shy of the 3-in. cut possible on the Delta and Sears saws.

The DeWalt's thermally protected motor is housed in an all-metal housing, and the motor's automatic brake stops the blade in only five seconds. It's the only motor brake in the survey worth taking seriously: The Sears and Delta both take twice as long. Unfortunately, the DeWalt sports the same difficult-to-remove blade guard as the Black & Decker. A cast-alloy/cast-iron yoke supports the motor front and rear, and a three-point fitting allows both vertical and horizontal alignment to be adjusted accurately. The carriage rides on four bearings, two of which are eccentric-cam adjusted like the Delta, only harder to adjust from below the arm.

All the setting and locking handles on the DeWalt are big, comfortable to grip and located up front for easy access. The elevation crank, located near the front atop the arm, has embossed marks under the crank to give you a quick elevation reference. One owner told me that the crank's belt drive needs occasional tightening—maintenance that the gear-driven Sears and Delta elevation mechanisms don't need. Bevel, yoke and miter settings are extremely positive, with spring-loaded plunger stops that seat a tapered pin in a machined plate for a solid setting.

The DeWalt performed like a workhorse and did every task with power to spare. With repeatable accuracy, the saw delivered exceptionally smooth and true cuts, with no visible signs of track wander. The arm also felt stiff and hard to deflect. My only criticism is that the carriage feels heavy and requires a

good amount of force to operate, which might get tiresome if you need to do loads of narrow crosscuts. DeWalt does, however, offer an optional automatic blade return—a safety as well as a work-saving device.

Inca 810—The unorthodox design for this radial saw came about in an unusual way. The employees of an Austrian appliance manufacturing company made the prototype of the Inca as a birthday present for their woodworker president. The president decided to put the saw into production, and they make the 810 for Inca. Instead of pivoting the arm on the column as other radials do, the 810's table rotates, making the Inca a "radial table" saw in the truest sense.

The Inca sports a 9-amp appliance-type induction motor that drives a 9-in. blade with a depth of cut comparable to most 10-in. saws. Four rollers support the saw carriage and ride on the out-

Delta's Model 10, shown above fitted with the optional leg set, is the only radial-arm saw tested with an on/off switch next to the handle for convenience and safety.

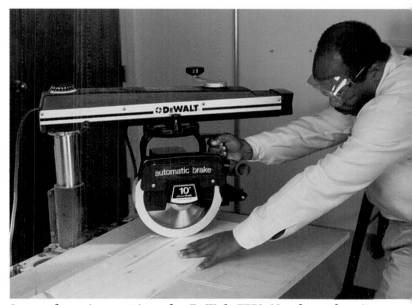

Set up for miter cutting, the DeWalt 7770-10, above, has its elevation crank atop its heavy cast-iron arm and all of its angle-setting controls within reach.

The Inca 810, shown above with the optional extension rail, is capable of crosscutting a 27½-in.-wide, ½-in.-thick panel.

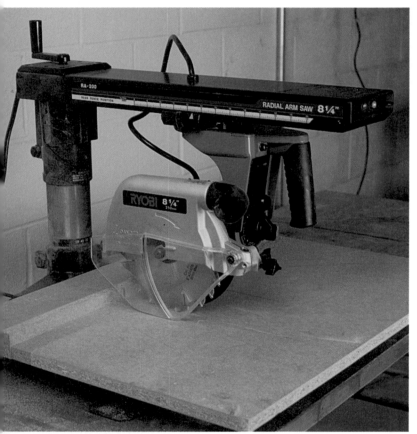

Ryobi's lightweight portable radial-arm saw (model RA200), above, has an 8½-in. blade that's capable of cutting 8/4 stock. The column and arm can be removed from the base for transport. Tapping the high RPMs of the router-type universal motor, the Ryobi is handy for plowing grooves, as shown below, or any other job using a router bit with a ¼-in.-dia. shank.

side of a chrome-plated square steel arm. The entire arm can be replaced with an optional extension arm to give the Inca a 27½-in. crosscut capacity, by far the largest in the survey. The Inca's small laminate-covered table clamps to a square steel beam that also has a sliding support on it, to hold wide workpieces.

Setting the Inca for angled cuts is different than other radials, but generally easy and positive. As mentioned, the table rotates for miter cuts, with stops at 45° in either direction. There's no positive stop for a 90° cut, but the Inca's large protractor scale allows accurate resetting to square. For ripping, the Inca's four track bearings are set so you can remove the entire carriage, rotate it 90° and slide it back on the arm. Setting the bevel angle is a hassle, because four bolts must be loosened and there are no stops to establish square or 45°. Besides being spartan on the stops, the Inca boasts few adjustments. For instance, in lieu of adjustable bearings, the cast-alloy mounting posts for the track bearings spring inwards slightly to provide constant tension between the bearings and the arm beam.

In use, the Inca performed reliably, though when cutting 2-in. maple, the motor seemed on the verge of being underpowered. The saw cut smoothly, but all my cuts showed signs of track wander, even when I tried different machines. The upper/lower blade guard has an unusual kerf splitter that effectively prevents blade binding during crosscutting and ripping. Unfortunately, the spring-loaded lower guard hung up on the workpiece often, and the thumb lever that manually raises the lower guard was awkward to operate. The Inca's arm is very stiff, especially the extension arm that bolts to a vertical bar at the outboard end. However, I found that the arm tended to get out of parallel with the table. This isn't a problem for most crosscuts, but it's deadly for bevel cuts or for plowing grooves. When I tried to cut some rabbets with Inca's optional router carriage, which slides on and off the arm like the saw carriage, I had to shim the table to get the cut the same depth all the way across the stock. Aside from the handy height scale on the column, I didn't like the Inca's elevation mechanism much. The crank is located inconveniently on the side of the column at the rear, and the crank screw had almost two turns of slop. The Inca's open-frame construction allows it to be disassembled and transported easily, and the optional telescoping legs make this bench saw a freestanding machine.

Ryobi RA200—This model is Ryobi's entry into the portable radial-arm saw market, and it's the lightest (53 lbs.) and most compact saw in the survey. Although the Ryobi uses only a 8¼-in. blade, it has enough cutting depth to make 45° bevel cuts in 8/4 stock. Instead of folding, like the Black & Decker, the Ryobi's column lifts out of the base, and the saw transports in two manageable pieces.

The RA200 is powered by an 11-amp universal motor. It's arguable that a universal won't hold up under heavy use as well as the induction motors used in most other radials, but this design gives the Ryobi some truly desirable features. On the arbor end, the motor's 18,000-RPM speed is geared down to 5,000 RPM to run the blade. The other end of the motor shaft directly drives a ¼-in. router collet that's ready to use (see bottom photo this page). The compact motor is supported by the yoke only at the front, but it doesn't seem flimsy because the motor's so light. The radial arm is fabricated from pressed steel, but the track is machined and the steel is heavy gauge (.170 in. thick). The Ryobi is the only saw with a push-button arbor lock, which allows blade or bit changes with only one wrench, and the quick-release blade guard comes off with minimum effort. The lower guard is also the only one I tried that didn't hang up on the work while mitering.

Setting the Ryobi is very positive and simple for all the usual miter, bevel and rip cuts. The spring-loaded stops for miter and bevel work are tight-fitting and accurate. Most of the settings on the Ryobi are "factory set," and the only real user adjustments are to make the table parallel to the arm and square to the blade.

I thought the lack of adjustability was a drawback at first, but the Ryobi cut extremely well and true as it came out of the box. The motor slowed considerably while crosscutting 8/4 oak, but all cuts were smooth and showed no sign of track wander. I was able to repeat all bevel and miter cuts to within ½°—a tolerance I couldn't better with any of the other radials I tried. Routing with the Ryobi is pleasurable, in part because of the motor's high speed

and partially because the carriage feels light and rides extremely smooth. (Most direct-drive accessory shafts are 3,450 RPM—too slow for a clean cut with a router bit.) Two things I didn't like were the noise, much like a screaming router, and the odd choice of blade size that makes replacements hard to come by at a local hardware store. But these are minor complaints considering the Ryobi's versatility and low price tag.

Sears 19825—All the radial saws by Sears are mechanically identical, the only differences being the electronics and the legs or stands. The Sears model I tested features a built-in "electronic

Using a radial-arm saw

I've always had my radial-arm saw built into a long workbench, with auxiliary tables and fences to give long workpieces more support. If you don't have room for a built-in saw, or if you need to take the saw to the job site often, you may opt for a radial with bolt-on legs or a portable model. Take care though: If you move any radial saw, pick it up only by the frame and column; if you lift it by the table or arm, you may throw the saw out of adjustment. Also, avoid using extension cords that can rob the saw of power and cause motor overheating, and never use a cord not rated to handle the amperage of the motor.

Because I use my radial-arm saw mostly for straight cut-off work, I've installed a tape on top of the fence that I use with a clamped stop to get accurate cuts. I zero the tape to the blade after making adjustments or changing blades by loosening the table clamps and sliding the fence back and forth. My clamped stop is a hinged woodblock, so if I need to square a rough end before trimming to final length, the stop pivots up, out of the way.

If the upper guard on your saw has a dust chute, connect it to a vacuum system to keep chips and dust at bay or try fitting a length of flexible hose—the kind used to vent clothes dryers—between the chute and a trash can. The wind from the blade will blow chips through the hose with surprising force. Even with dust collection, take the time to wipe the tracks and carriage rollers clean every day or so. Never lubricate these parts with grease: A light, dry lubricant will prevent dust from sticking and keep things rolling smoothly.

Cutting with a radial: Once a radial saw is correctly adjusted and cutting smoothly, there are a few tricks I've learned that can help the job go more quickly and accurately. First, I prefer pushing the blade through the cut rath-

er than pulling it—the more traditional method. The advantages to push-cutting are that the blade ends up on the other side of the fence after the cut, farther from harms way. Also, pushing prevents the blade from "self feeding" toward you (the tendency of a pulled blade that's climb-cutting) and stalling in the cut or jerking the saw out of adjustment. The disadvantage to push-cutting is that the blade can lift the workpiece, so you must hold the piece down firmly. Also, your crosscutting capacity is diminished, because the blade must clear the stock with the blade at the end of the arm.

Whenever crosscutting a board with a slight bow or cup, keep the hollow edge against the fence or the cup down on the saw table. This will keep the board from rocking and causing the blade to bind in the cut. If a gnarly grained piece binds the blade, try rough-cutting the end, then taking a light trim cut to final length. Also, a little groove on the saw table where it meets the fence will keep sawdust from preventing the workpiece to butt tight and true to the fence.

For miter, bevel or compound-angle cuts, I avoid setting and resetting miter and bevel angles whenever possible. Instead, I use angle jigs that mount on the saw table and change the angle of the workpiece relative to the fence.

The smoothest-cutting carbide blades to use on the radial-arm saws I've tried have a high alternating top bevel (ATB). I've also had success with thin-kerf blades. These are more subject to heat warping though and seem to run better if mounted on the arbor with large blade-stabilizing washers. If you experience splintering on the bottom of your cuts, try lowering the blade ¼ in. to ½ in. below the surface of the saw table.

Fitted with a dado blade, the radial-arm saw is great for cutting dados or rabbets and for joinery. I've often used a wide dado set to waste the cheeks on tenons. Just remember that if the thickness of the material you're cutting changes, the depth of the cut will also change. To set the depth of a groove, reference the blade's height from the top of the workpiece, not the saw table.

Many people have an aversion to rip-

ping on the radial-arm saw, and with good reason: If the work binds on the blade or is fed from the wrong side of the blade, the saw can hurl a board, or worse, yank your hand into the blade. Make sure the carriage is firmly locked on the arm, and always feed the board against the rotation of the blade, with the guard tilted back almost touching the board on the infeed side. On the outfeed side, lower the antikickback pawls and splitter to contact the board, to prevent kickback.

Fancy cutting: The radial-arm saw's multitude of settings can do all sorts of fancy cuts that are difficult or impossible with other saws. For instance, you can cut coves by rotating the yoke so the blade is skewed to the line of cut, or you can actually hollow out a bowl by locking and rotating the carriage with the motor on. Beyond regular blades, there is a plethora of accessories made to fit on the accessory shaft, including sanding drums and discs, chucks for drills or bits, safety planer cutters and even jigsaws. For a thorough exploration of the applications of the radial, consult R.J. De Cristoforo's book *The Magic of Your Radial Arm Saw*, available from Black & Decker Inc., 701 E. Joppa Road, Towson, Md. 21204.

Safety: The radial-arm saw has lots of potential to be dangerous, because since the blade moves through the cut, it can cut you even if you stay still. *Always keep your hands clear of the blade's path, and NEVER reach behind the blade while it's still spinning.* The automatic blade brake found on several saw models is a great safety feature, because even an idling blade can cut you badly. The radial's blade can hurl cutoffs with tremendous velocity, so always wear eye protection and prevent hearing loss by wearing earplugs or earmuffs. Resist the temptation to cut with the blade guard removed, even if only for a few cuts: Unlike the tablesaw, the blade on a radial is completely exposed without its guard. If the lower guard persistently hangs up on your work, try smoothing its leading edges with a file and then waxing them. —*S.N.*

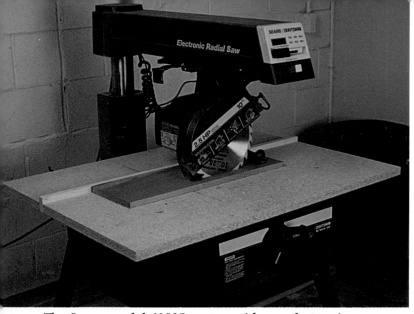

The Sears model 19825 comes with an electronic measurement display that shows the angle and height settings of the saw. The saw is set up in the photo for a rip cut, with the guard and antikickback arm in the correct position.

measurement" device and plain stamped-steel legs. The 10-in. blade is powered by an 11-amp motor housed in plastic and supported from the front only by a cast-alloy yoke, which does allow horizontal heeling to be set. The quick-release blade guard covers the upper blade only, but a lower guard is available as an accessory. The arm on the 19825 is cast alloy, with a replaceable pressed-steel track on which ride four carriage rollers.

All the settings on the Sears are accessible and can be set from the front of the saw. Like the Delta, the elevation crank is just below the table and raises and lowers the saw arm with well-meshed gearing. Because the crank is at groin level, the crank's

handle mercifully folds up out of harms way. Both the miter and yoke stop/lock handles operate positively, unlike the bevel lock, which feels mushy. Most adjustments on the Sears are made with a ⅛-in. Allen wrench, which offers little leverage if the screws are overtight or frozen. The saw does have screws for adjusting horizontal alignment at the rear of the yoke.

Aside from the Ryobi, the Sears is the only radial saw I set up right out of the box, and it took me over half a day to assemble and adjust the saw. The manual is extensive and clearly illustrated, and I didn't run into any assembly problems. I did have some problems adjusting the carriage bearings to ride smoothly. Even with the bearings set tight against the track, I still couldn't get cuts with the Sears that were clean and free from signs of track wander. This is probably due to the non-milled sheet-metal track—a cheap treatment for a part that's so critical to the accuracy of the saw. The arm was also easy to deflect by pulling the carriage to the side while cutting.

I was ready to dismiss the Sears electronic display as a sales gimmick, but in use, I found the distance- and angle-measuring capabilities accurate and well worth the $50 extra. The liquid crystal display (LCD) on the end of the arm gives a readout of the saw's elevation, bevel angle, miter angle and distance of carriage on the arm for ripping. These measurments are fed to the electronic display by four encoders mounted on the saw. By selecting from six buttons, you can monitor any of the measurements while adjusting the saw. All the settings are stored in memory when you turn the battery-powered display off. The system was easy to use, and it gave accurate measurements to .010 in. and angles to ½°— certainly adequate tolerances for most cabinet work. The encoders must be kept clean of sawdust though, to prevent problems. □

Sandor Nagyszalanczy is an assistant editor at Fine Woodworking.

Adjusting the radial-arm saw

by Mark Duginske

Of all the problems the radial-arm saw is prone to, none is more insidious than adjusting and aligning the saw. On a typical saw, this setup can take hours, require several studious readings of the saw's instruction manual and still result in unsatisfactory cutting performance.

It's fairly obvious that for a square cut, a radial's sawblade must be 90° relative to both the table and the fence. What's not obvious is that you can square a blade precisely and the saw may still not cut properly. This is because, in addition to being adjusted for squareness, the blade of a radial saw must also be adjusted for what I'll call "alignment," a more complicated adjustment than squareness. Alignment problems are often called "heeling." Heeling occurs when the leading edge of the blade and the blade's trailing edge, or heel, aren't perfectly lined up with the travel of the saw. The blade goes through the cut on a slight angle and the heel rubs in the kerf, causing splintering. Heeling can also burn the workpiece or be dangerous if the blade's dragging heel

hurls a scrap. To eliminate heeling problems, blade alignment needs to be set in two separate axes: Alignment in the vertical axis, as shown in figure 2 on the facing page, is responsible for heeling problems with the blade square to the saw table. Horizontal-axis alignment affects blade heeling anytime the blade is tilted for a bevel cut, say 45° or more. Vertical alignment can be tricky and is often ignored in many radial owner's manuals.

Besides knowing how to adjust a radial, you must make the adjustments in the right order, because the accuracy of one adjustment is often built on a previous adjustment. The way in which adjustments and alignments are made on different saws varies, but the order in which they should be done is basically the same. I'll go through the basic procedures for setting up a saw, but for a complete treatment, read John Eakes book "Fine Tuning Your Radial Arm Saw," available from Lee Valley Tools Ltd., 2680 Queensview Drive, Ottawa, Ontario, Canada K2B 8H6, and consult your saw manual.

Before starting, you have to unplug the saw and remove the blade guard.

Parallelism: Rotate the motor so the arbor is pointed downward. Check the distance between the saw table and the arbor with a feeler gauge. A gauge .025 in. thick is about right (see top, left photo on the facing page). Then, pivot the arm and slide the carriage over various spots on the table, adjusting the height of the table on its brackets until the feeler-gauge clearance is the same at all points. This makes the table parallel to the arm.

Horizontal alignment: Set the sawblade parallel to the table by tilting the blade down to a 0° bevel. Make a wooden test bar with four square, parallel edges. Lay the bar on the saw table under the blade so it is parallel to the arm, and lower the arm until the blade almost touches the bar. Make sure the bar isn't contacting a sawtooth. Slip a feeler gauge between the bar and blade to see if the gap is the same along the block. If it's not, the adjustment

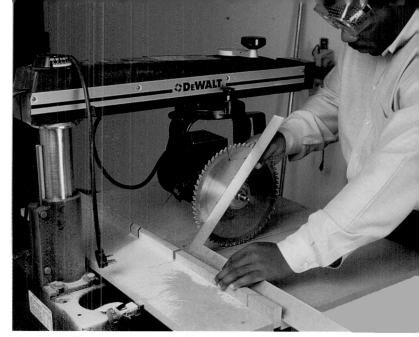

A feeler gauge checks the distance between the vertical motor arbor and the saw table so the table can be adjusted true to the arm.

Vertical alignment is checked, above, with a framing square held at a 45° angle. One leg is against the blade and the other leg sits where the fence and saw table meet.

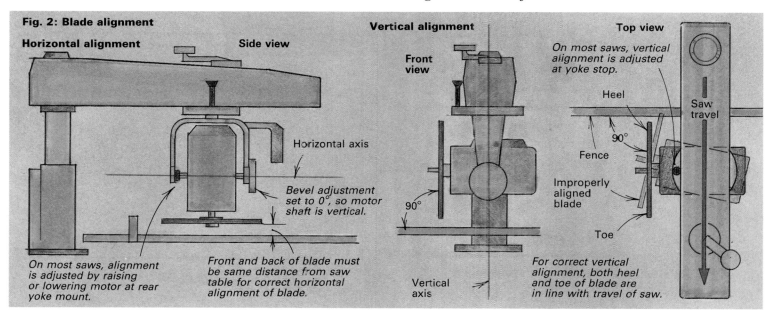

Fig. 2: Blade alignment

Horizontal alignment　　　**Side view**

Horizontal axis

Bevel adjustment set to 0°, so motor shaft is vertical.

On most saws, alignment is made by raising or lowering motor at rear yoke mount.

Front and back of blade must be same distance from saw table for correct horizontal alignment of blade.

Vertical alignment

Front view

90°

Vertical axis

Top view

On most saws, vertical alignment is adjusted at yoke stop.

Heel

Saw travel

90°

Fence

Improperly aligned blade

Toe

For correct vertical alignment, both heel and toe of blade are in line with travel of saw.

on most saws is made where the motor attaches to the rear of the yoke. Some saw yokes, however, don't attach to the motor at the rear and don't allow this adjustment.

Square blade to saw table: Lay one edge of a large square on the saw table, parallel to the fence, and the other against the blade close to the arbor, avoiding the sawteeth. A large plastic drafting square is good for this, especially if you cut out a notch that'll clear the arbor, flange and lock nut. Follow your saw manual and adjust the bevel stop to square.

Square fence to saw table: Place a square flat on the saw table with one edge against the fence. Mark a tooth on the bottom of the blade and push the square over until it just touches the blade. Hold the square down and pull the carriage toward you. If the fence and blade are square, the tooth and the square will keep the same contact. If the

angle is off, the blade will either move away from the square or walk over the square as you pull. Adjust the 90° miter stop on the column.

Vertical alignment: The previous adjustment established that the fence is 90° to the travel of the saw. Now you need to make sure the body of the blade is parallel to this path. Place one edge of the square where the fence and table meet, and raise the other edge so it's against the blade (avoid the teeth). If the square contacts the blade unevenly, the blade is heeling. Adjust the stop for carriage rotation according to your saw manual.

After you make the above adjustments and alignments, check them by cutting a few test pieces. To check the saw's blade-to-table squareness, start with a piece of plywood that's ¾x6x30 in. Mark the ends A and B, and draw a big X in the middle of the board. Now cut the test piece in half, flip one side over and put

the cut ends in contact. Any deviation from a 90° bevel will be doubled and can be seen clearly. By placing the same piece up against the fence, any error in the fence-blade squareness will be doubled. Readjust the saw as necessary and repeat the test cuts until the saw cuts true and square.

Getting an adjustment perfect can be tough, especially when delicate adjusting screws have been overtightened. Instead, I get the adjustment as close as I can and use paper shims to change it a hair at a time. I use shims between the fence and saw table to fine-tune square cuts.

Once a radial-arm saw is properly adjusted, the alignment settings should stay secure for a long time if the saw isn't abused or moved. Adjustments for squareness should be checked and corrected periodically.　□

Mark Duginske is an author and cabinetmaker in Wausau, Wis.

Choosing a Tablesaw

How to find the one that fits your needs

by Rich Preiss

I have pushed wood over a lot of tablesaws during my years as student, furnituremaker and teacher, and one thing I've learned is that there is no single "best" tablesaw. Nor do you need the finest machine money can buy to accomplish the highest level of workmanship. The goal in choosing a tablesaw should be to first decide what you really need for your work (this is not to be confused with what you merely want) then to select the most appropriate tool and use it to your maximum ability. A machine larger and more expensive than you need will, at best, wind up as inappropriate in your shop and could rob the resources necessary to purchase other needed equipment.

In support of this, I would like to relate a short tale. After graduating from school, I was faced with the furnituremakers' nightmare—I no longer had access to a shop. My landlord was doing some remodeling and had brought in an older-style 10-in. Sears tablesaw to help with the work. I was taken by the simple, rugged design that had enabled it to survive for so many years.

I decided to try making a run of small, decorative boxes completely on what had been, up to now, a rough-use contractors' saw. With the help of a sharp sawblade, I was able to resaw the boxes' 5-in.-wide boards with over/under cuts. I next devised a mini sliding-table jig for crosscutting, and ultimately machined delicate splined miters for the corners. By the end of the project my illusions of dependency on ever-fancier machine tools were shattered. True, if I'd had a better saw I would have used it, but the final solution wasn't in the machine, it was in me.

Types of tablesaws—As I see it, there are four categories of saws: the fully-enclosed stationary saw, the open-based contractors' saw, the specialty saw, and the benchtop saw, which is often "motorized" (direct drive) and frequently has only a ½-in.-dia. arbor. Stationary saws weigh-in at upwards of 300 lb., contractors' saws (designed to be moved around a lot) might be 50 lb. to 100 lb. lighter, and benchtop saws can be hauled around easily by one person. Specialty saws, as we shall see, can be anything.

Though all saws are expected to do roughly the same tasks, their performance varies greatly depending on their construction, power, and features. Tablesaws rip, crosscut, resaw, mold, miter, rabbet and dado, and they are often called upon to cut many types of joints. Many saws have add-ons such as extension tables for handling full plywood sheets, extension rails and dust-collection gear. These accessories are standard on some saws and optional on others. This article won't attempt to evaluate accessories, but rather the basic tablesaw.

A series of boxes specifically describes and compares three very different machines—the Unisaw, Inca and Sears—that I've

been testing in my own shop. I'll talk briefly about specialty saws, and on pp. 48-49 a chart lists the sorts of saws available from as many manufacturers and importers as I could find. The job of comparing each tablesaw head-to-head with its competition is not something I can attempt, mostly because everyone expects different things from machines. But this article should get you on the way to being able to pick and compare for yourself. To keep the chart reasonable in size, I've set the cut-off point at saws that will accept a 12-in.-dia. blade. It is common to run 10-in. blades on such saws, though some saw models have arbors larger than ⅝ in. and won't take the usual blade.

Start by considering just what type of woodworker you are. Do you need a saw for rough work only, or is accuracy most important? Many professionals need a light-industrial tablesaw that will work all day, every day, often under adverse conditions of repetition and dust. Other shops may be able to get by with an open-base contractors' saw, which will saw a lot of 4/4 lumber satisfactorily, while still allowing for heavier jobs from time to time.

If you are a hobbyist, you don't need what the professional needs, and probably don't want to pay for it. By this I don't mean that a hobbyist's woodworking is necessarily inferior, in fact the opposite may well be true. But if you're an amateur, you're not under the same pressures of production as a professional. You can buy a lighter-duty saw entirely adequate for your needs and have money left over to invest in some decent sawblades.

When you begin shopping for a tablesaw, you should be familiar with its basic operation. The heart is a sawblade mounted to a rigid arbor rotating at a precise speed. The arbor might be the motor shaft itself, or power can be transferred from a separate motor by means of belts and pulleys, or even a flexible shaft, as in the Sears saw I tested (see p. 47). In general, better saws have more than one belt, and the shorter the belts are, the better. Once locked to the arbor, the blade should adjust vertically, and its angle to a flat table should be variable through 45°. Most machines today accomplish the adjustment by tilting the motor and arbor, while some older ones (and the Inca) have a tilting table.

A tablesaw requires an adjustable fence that can be locked parallel to the blade for ripping, and a means to direct a guide perpendicular to the blade for crosscutting and mitering. The whole system must be rigid, as free of vibration as possible and sturdy enough to be banged about by materials and mishaps alike.

Blade sizes and arbors—A saw will initially be rated by the diameter of its maximum sawblade, which bears directly on the depth of cut, both at 90° and at 45°. Be sure that the 45° depth of cut is sufficient to cut through the thickest stock you want to

From *Fine Woodworking* magazine (January 1986) 56:50-57

Unisaw

The Delta Unisaw is probably the most popular tablesaw of all time. With its fully-enclosed base and predominance of cast-iron parts, it has been standard in small commercial, vocational and private shops since it was first introduced in 1939. The particular Unisaw I tested was 3-HP, 220-volt, single-phase model #34-756 with the standard "see thru" splitter-mounted blade guard. My saw was bought in 1982, just before the Rockwell name became Delta again, but is the same as the machines currently sold.

Uncrating and assembly were quick and easy. The two cast-iron table extensions had to be bolted on and aligned, and the one-piece splitter/anti-kickback safety shield had to be mounted and aligned. All that remained was to screw on the fence bars, mount the magnetic on/off switch, clean off the table and plug it in.

The construction of the Unisaw is mostly cast iron, with the base enclosure being folded heavy-gauge sheet steel. The table surfaces still show the swirl marks left by a Blanchard grinder, though they are good and flat, and showed no eroded edges top or bottom. The T-slot table grooves were cut clean and square, though the table did require minor adjustment to bring the grooves parallel with the blade.

The arbor on the Unisaw tilts to the right, and is securely supported by a cast-iron bracket and 2¼-in. O.D. sealed ball bearings. Power is transferred to the arbor by three short V-belts, from a motor specially bracketed for this machine. The whole arrangement sits firmly on a four-part series of cast-iron brackets and trunnions. Arbor runout measured 0.0015 in., which is perfectly acceptable and half that of the Sears saw I tested.

I like the straightforward operation of the Unisaw. The control handles for raising and inclining the blade are 7-in.-dia. cast-iron wheels with threaded locking pins in the center. Both the tilt and elevation shafts function by means of a short, fixed worm gear section that must be kept clean for the system to work smoothly. It takes 31 turns of the wheel to reach 45°, and only 13 quick cranks from minimum to maximum elevation. Factory-set limit stops required no adjustment to work perfectly. The system is comfortable and functional, although if you overtighten the locking pins or crank hard past the fixed stops, the controls will lock up and can be difficult to free.

Changing the blade and other common maintenance procedures are very simple. With a little pressure on the far end, the metal throat plate pops right up to expose the arbor nut and also provide enough access for general lubrication of the ways. The throat plate is sturdy enough and ribbed so that it doesn't flex, and its height is adjustable with four Allen set screws. I wish they would provide better wrenches and an arbor lock button for changing

Fully-enclosed stationary saws, such as the Delta Unisaw shown here, are light-industrial machines that won't complain when asked to do hard work at a steady pace. The extension table, an optional accessory that most tablesaw manufacturers allow for, is great for handling plywood sheets. But if you don't work a lot of plywood, such a setup may be a mixed blessing, taking up more room in your shop than you have to spare.

blades, to make a good system even better.

Turning the machine on requires groping under the table for the control or actually stooping to locate the switch. Once running, however, performance is strong and vibration free, and other functions are convenient to control. The 3-HP motor feels like a middle-of-the-road selection for this machine. I think 1.5 HP would not be enough and 5 HP would be even more to my liking. When ripping 2-in.-thick oak and maple, the machine had to work, but it never bogged down or required an unusually slow feed rate. There are no particular provisions for dust collection, other than a covered 3-in. by 5-in. opening in the base ring of the saw. A motor cover, to cut down dramatically on dust, can be purchased from Delta or made up of plywood and fastened through the pre-drilled holes.

The rip fence and miter gauge that come standard with the Unisaw work adequately. It's difficult to say anything too good or too bad about either. The rip fence locks to the bars simultaneously with an eccentric cam on the near side and a J-shaped hook on the other. After a time, drift can become a problem. In the shop at school, we've broken at least two of the flimsy levers that

With 3 HP, the Unisaw effortlessly gobbles up 8/4 stock. Preiss replaced the standard fence with a Biesemeyer.

activate the J-hook. The tubular bars remind you when they need waxing by grabbing the fence when you release the lock or causing it to rack instead of glide smoothly between settings. The miter gauge has a single locking knob (no hold-down), is very sturdy and designed to support a bolt-on wooden fence extension. It has adjustable limit stops (with a screw and lock nut) at 45° and 90°, and a solid 18-in.-long guide bar that fits the T-slots in the table just right.

Basic safety features on this Unisaw are minimal and awkward. Alignment of the metal splitting plate never seems completely right, and it blocks your line of sight almost completely after the cut. The standard blade guard does not encourage even the creative user. The plastic blade cover jiggles around a lot and can't sustain itself perched up and out of the way if you want to measure for a cut. The built-in electrical motor brake, however, is a real plus that takes no time at all to get used to.

I wouldn't rush out to buy a 3-HP Unisaw at its "suggested list price" of $1,871. But if you are more than a casual user and can deal your way down $300 and use the savings for optional attachments, the Unisaw is a good buy. It's a durable, consistent, light-industrial machine with quality components that can be replaced readily, if need be. I believe it's worthwhile to upgrade to a "Uniguard." When equipped with one of the optional 50-in. fences, the Unisaw's realm increases greatly and, having come this far, it's worth it to convert a good machine into a great one.

Delta's Contractors' saw is also worth mention. This saw intends to be a light-weight version of the Unisaw, with open stand, 1½-HP motor, plastic control wheels, stamped-steel table extensions and a steel-tube trunnion. It has many of the Unisaw's features at about half the price. This type of saw would be good for somebody who didn't expect to push it too hard. Compare it with other models of about the same power and weight in the chart. A saw in this category might be just what a hobbiest needs. —R.P.

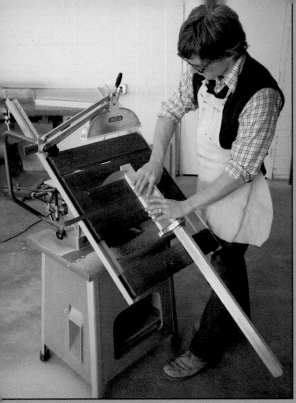

Inca Major

The Inca Major is a specialty circular saw manufactured in Switzerland by the INCA Injecta Company. It's sold in this country through numerous regional distributors for about $1,400 when fitted with the mortising attachment, base and standard 1½-HP motor. This design is most notable for its tilting table, pressure die-cast aluminum parts, and unflagging accuracy.

The Inca is an accurate, carefully made tool that is an enjoyable machine to own. It could not possibly function as the only tablesaw in any production woodshop, but that's not what this machine was designed to do. The Inca seems geared especially to the small cabinetmaker, instrument builder, or any hobbiest doing fine furniture woodworking. Its lightweight, compact design (the base is about as heavy as the saw itself) and versatile operation make it possible to take this saw to a jobsite for furniture-quality finishing work, or easily move it out of the way in a small workshop.

It doesn't take very long to assemble. The first thing you discover is that this is a tilting-table, and not a tilting-arbor saw. By fixing the arbor, a lot of the bulk and potential vibrations inherent in tilting-arbor saws are eliminated. By combining this concept with precision components, the Inca is able to perform smoothly and accurately without great mass. The trade-off for this apparent windfall comes when mitering wide, long pieces, such as cabinet sides and tops. They want to fall off the table and can cause the miter gauge to bind and sometimes bow. It takes longer to set angles, and I have yet to comfortably adapt to working on an inclined surface.

Precision is evident throughout this machine, even including the base. The table, though small, is finished smooth and flat, and the closely-ribbed undersurface is also extremely clean. The pressure die-cast aluminum has a dark gray color throughout and appears very unlike the slightly harder surfaces of cast iron. Deep scratches tend to stand out as silver streaks. The miter gauge grooves are not T-slotted, though the fit of the guide bar is so exact it doesn't seem to matter. So, too, is the fit of the assorted throat plates that screw into perfect position in their opening. Optional extension tables lock securely and level via a sliding dovetail arrangement and can increase the work surface as much as you want. The base is very sturdy, thanks to a snug fit between its metal legs and particleboard sides. There is even a built-in dust chute that really helps channel dust and chips.

Though parts can quickly be mail ordered, I have found, in six years of use, maintenance on the Inca Major has been

The Inca, conservatively rated at 1½ HP, passed all the precision tests with ease, but this unusual machine has what many consider to be three main drawbacks: The arbor is non-standard size, a 10-in. blade won't fully retract beneath the table surface, and the table has to be tilted for angled cuts, as shown.

---

miter in one pass. If you decide that ripping 3-in.-thick boards is integral to your work, then a 10-in. saw will be the minimum size needed. In contrast, an 8-in. saw will average a 2⅜-in. depth of cut. This won't preclude ripping thicker lumber—you can cut halfway through from one side, then flip the work over to finish the cut—but the saw will probably be underpowered if it has to do this job often. I have included a number of small-blade saws in the chart. I won't tell you never to buy such a saw—it might be just what you need—but I will tell you that in builders' and contractors' slang, any saw that draws less than 10 amps is considered a "throwaway."

The blade arbor should have at least a ⅝-in. diameter to minimize the chances of wobble and to accept most commonly available blades, and you'll probably want an arbor length that can take a ¾-in. stacked dado. Many foreign machines, such as the Inca, have a metric-scaled arbor and require special sawblades.

The nominal arbor size is only part of the story. Many ⅝-in. arbors are ⅝ in. clear through the bearings. The Inca, however is stepped up to about 30 mm (about 1¼ in.) through the bearings, making it a true heavy-duty saw despite its light weight and small size. If you need beef, this is the sort of thing to look for.

What about the motor?—As the cutting capacity increases, so too should the horsepower. I would always opt for the largest motor possible, with 1.5 HP being the minimum for any saw with an 8-in. blade capacity or larger. For a 10-in. saw, 3 HP is appropriate, and for a 12-in. machine, 5 HP or 7 HP will be required.

These figures may at first seem like overkill, but think about it. With less power you won't be able to make rip cuts in thick stock without severely straining the motor. If your current saw is underpowered, you know already that one way around burning

out the motor is to rip in a series of 1-in.-high increments, but it's nasty and frustrating work to pass a piece of wood over the saw three times when once should do the job.

Be aware of inflated peak horsepower ratings. Many motors can supply spurts of peak horsepower, but it's the continuous-load performance that will endure, especially under heavy daily use. One way to judge whether the rated horsepower of a motor is honest is to check the motor plate for the amperage that the motor draws—an honest, continuous 1.5 HP motor should draw about 14 amps at 115 volts, or half that at 230 volts. By extension, a 3-HP motor run at 230 volts should draw 14 or 15 amps.

A totally enclosed fan-cooled (TEFC) induction motor is the best. All-ball bearings and self-contained overload protections are not luxuries, but necessities for a healthy motor life. Don't assume that all motors are thermally protected or equipped with all-ball bearings. Check the motor plate carefully and ask your distributor to spell out these features.

Despite the recent introduction of small but powerful universal motors on many imported machines, I still favor the proven endurance and quieter operation of the induction motor.

Look carefully at the motor mount setup. Are the mounts accessible with a wrench and ratchet? Universal mounts, though arguably less rigid than integral housing mounts, are much more versatile. If your motor dies, integral mounts require you to replace the motor with a "factory only" replacement, at a "factory only" price. The same holds true for belt drive versus direct drive. Look for a multiple, short belt drive system for maximum performance, safety and maintenance flexibility.

Be sure that your electrical system can supply enough current. Low fluctuations in current can greatly reduce your motor's efficiency and shorten its life. Low voltage conditions can occur for minimal. The arbor runs on two good-sized sealed ball bearings and is driven by a single V-belt and pulley arrangement. I feel my saw to be slightly underpowered at 1.5 HP, and could bolt on a larger 3,450-RPM motor with little difficulty. (There's an optional 2-HP motor.) Little lubrication is required as long as the tilting-table ways are kept clean. It has been a few years since my saw was new, but even so, when I measured for this review, arbor runout was still an almost non-existent 0.0005 in., one-third that of my Unisaw.

Like any machine, the Inca takes a little bit of getting used to. The table raises and lowers on vertical dovetail ways by means of a pivoting bracket, screw, and 3-in. handwheel. This is very slow, but accurate. The table locks function well, though the lever handles on my saw no longer fit as positively, and in some positions will conflict with other controls. Space under the table can get very close for big hands. When fitted with a 10-in. blade, there will always be at least ½ in. of blade projecting above the table, so I use 8-in. blades on the machine almost all of the time. Cutting 2-in.-thick hardwoods in any direction requires a really slow feed rate, but the saw doesn't hesitate and the belt has never slipped.

I like the accessories for this machine very much and rely on their accuracy, especially for small work. The rip fence only locks on one end, so I have had to add a maple extension to be able to guarantee rigidity. When used in conjunction with the vernier adjustment device, it's possible to make micro-fine adjustments or even find your way back to a previous exact position.

The miter gauge can be purchased with a choice of optional aluminum extensions in various lengths, but comes standard with a 16-in. fence and a locking tailstop. Missing are any pre-set limits, even at 45° and 90°. The long, 22-in. bar really comes in handy and offsets some of the short crosscutting distance in front of the blade. Most other accessories, especially the tenoning jig, are equally well considered and extremely easy to use. I have also tried Inca's optional sliding table, which is well made, though I consider such an addition somewhat contrary to the machine's compact nature.

The arbor size is 20 mm, about ⅛ in. larger than the ⅝-in. arbors most of us are used to. If you buy an Inca, your old sawblades won't be compatible with it unless you have them bored out. Inca does sell a wide range of blades at reasonable prices, though, carbide as well as steel.

The Inca's optional built-in mortising table is at the right side of the saw. If you don't have a horizontal mortiser, it will do the job, but I don't find that I use mine very much—it's too slow.

I have found that the safety devices on

Precisely machined parts and fine adjustments remind the author of Swiss watches.

the Inca get left in place more than on other tablesaws. Because the blade always remains in one position and because the splitter is independent of the saw guard, it seems to stay in line very well. The blade guard is suspended from a mostly unobtrusive and retractable U-shaped bar. Though not transparent (it is made of aluminum) the guard can be positioned to hover over any thickness of cut, thereby leaving the line of sight open at all times.

Like Swiss watches and German cars, the Inca may seem relatively costly for it's size, but in the long run I think it returns every bit of what you pay for it. —R.P.

a variety of reasons—one common mistake is to run a saw at the end of a long extension cord, another is to have two heavy machines running on the same circuit. The total amperage of machines in operation at any one time should not exceed 80% of your system's maximum load capacity.

No matter what type of electric motor you run, and what type of current you run it on, without a good magnetic on/off control, the risk still exists that you will damage your motor. A magnetic control will automatically disconnect if the fluctuation approaches a significant danger level. Like any good insurance, it's worth the additional cost. All the stationary tools in my shop are equipped with magnetic controls.

Rip fence—A woodworker who expects to handle 4x8 panels regularly needs a minimum rip capacity of 24 in. If the lowest edge of the rip fence does not kiss the table surface and you need to cut Formica or thin stock, be sure to allow for the thickness of an auxiliary fence plate and refigure the maximum rip. As mentioned earlier, 50-in. extension bars (and longer) are readily available for many 10-in. saws and can be simply bolted on at any time. But don't let your "wish list" run away with you Though sliding extension tables and extended rip bars are nice options, they take up a lot of shop room—a smaller capacity tablesaw, in combination with a hand-held circular saw and a good straightedge, might be your best bet. For professional use or daily cutting, upright panel saws offer another alternative to purchasing oversized attachments solely for sizing 4x8s.

A precise, hassle-free rip fence is a must. If the fence cannot be brought smoothly into position, lock itself automatically square, and hold that setting without flex or drift, then it will drive you crazy every time you use it. A fence should move without jerking or racking and reasonable amounts of chips and dust shouldn't cause it to bind. The lower edge should ride close and parallel to the table surface. A fence that locks on both the inboard and outboard ends, whether simultaneously with a single lever or with a screw lock, will be less apt to deviate under feed pressure. Whatever type of mechanism is used, the fence should be easily adjustable for both locking pressure and parallel alignment. For two years I have been working with a Biesemeyer fence on my Unisaw, and despite the fact that it has no lock on the far end, it is mounted to a bracket that is rigid enough and triangulated over a large enough area that it overcomes the need for a second lock. The same is true for the Delta Unifence.

On the tablesaw, I prefer a full-length fence to the European-style half fence for the support it provides larger work after the cut. If the rip fence happens not to be 100% in alignment, or your work is pulling slightly away, it's an advantage to have the full fence to help keep the cut going straight. My Inca came with a short fence that locks square and feels sturdy, yet even so I have added a full-length maple extension that allows me to clamp the fence outboard for production work.

Miter gauge—The length of table in front of the sawblade will determine the maximum width of stock that can be crosscut with the miter gauge. This capacity is somewhat variable, however, depending on the length of the miter gauge bar, and, more important, whether the table groove is T-slot or rectangular. Though marginally more awkward to insert and remove, a T-slot will enable you to draw the miter gauge ahead and off the table surface, thereby extending the range for crosscuts beyond mere table limits. It is common practice to do this with rectangular-bar gauges as well, but it really isn't safe—better to insert the gauge

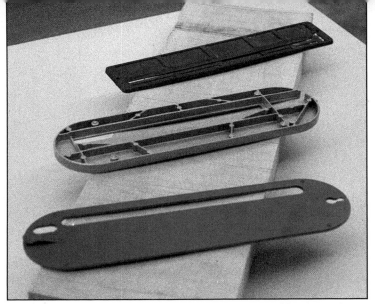

Table inserts give a clue to overall saw quality. The Sears insert (front) is unribbed and flexes under load. The Unisaw's (center), a drop-in type, is well ribbed and has height-adjustment screws. The Inca's (rear) is stiff, and screws rigidly to the table.

facing backwards, so that the leading edge of the work can bear against it to start the cut. If necessary, you can then stop the saw in the middle of the cut and transfer the gauge to its normal position to finish up. Shorter distances in front of the blade can also be overcome by constructing a sliding-table jig.

The miter gauge itself needs to be constructed of sturdy materials to endure typical mishaps such as dropping. This is especially true for the locking mechanism and the pre-set angle stops. Small plastic handles and parts are insufficient, as are stamped metal guide bars, and bodies whose faces are too thin to sustain shopmade extensions. A built-in hold-down is handy if the gauge itself is up to par. My own gauges have shopmade wooden fence extensions with movable tail stops.

Heavy metal—The best stationary machines I've seen are constructed primarily of cast iron. A well-designed casting, with careful ribbing that has been adequately destressed and accurately machined, provides guaranteed trueness and long life. The inherent mass endows the tool with vibration dampening and maximum stability. The more good cast-iron components that are incorporated into a saw, right on down to control wheels, fence parts, etc., the more likely it will interest me. Cast-iron trunnions and arbor-support housing with rack-and-worm-gear elevation and tilting mechanisms score well with me. Look out for lightweight sheet metal at any stress points, especially under the table in the arbor-tilting and height mechanisms.

Check with a straightedge that the table and wings are flat and true. Reputable manufacturers allow a delay between casting and final machining. This "destressing" can take a year before internal stresses neutralize. If a rough casting doesn't get sufficient time in the "bone yard," distortions such as twists in what were intended to be flat surfaces can appear later. As a consumer, it's impossible to know the history of a machine's components until it is too late—you have to trust the manufacturer's reputation.

Die-cast aluminum has become a more common and competitive material, making possible lightweight machines that are also rustproof. Although tables require a denser ribbing system to ensure flatness, they are still a lot lighter than cast iron. The traditional mass value of cast iron has been seemingly offset by sound overall designs that minimize vibration in the first place, and by the sort of advances in processing and casting aluminum that now allow it to be used for such highly stressed (and precise) parts as automobile engine blocks.

Safety—All exposed moving parts should be guarded. The blade guard should be as rigid and unobtrusive as possible, so as to interfere minimally with the work and provide maximum visibility. The blade guard, splitter, and anti-kickback assembly should be easy to remove and install so as to encourage use—a guard is no good at all if you've removed it to get it out of the way. Unfortunately, no saw combines all these criteria into one system.

Most guards are variations of two basic ideas: One mounts behind the blade—either to the splitter or behind the table—then pivots up and down. This type of guard must be removed for certain molding and ripping cuts where the fence must be very close to the blade; then it must be reinstalled before going on to other work. The temptation is not to reinstall it. The other type of guard pivots on a long arm mounted off to the side. It takes only a moment to position it over the blade, but this type of guard sometimes does not have anti-kickback protection.

Controls, especially the "off" button, need to be readily accessible and housed in such a way as to prevent accidental start-up. Switches that have different height on/off buttons, or isolate the "on" switch with a specific enclosure, accomplish this very well. Lockable controls, such as on the Sears saws, or wall-mounted disconnects are the sure way to child-proof your machines. As further operator protection, many new machines come standard with a motor brake—either automatic or activated by foot pressure—to stop a free-spinning blade quickly. You can add a motor brake to an existing 3-phase tablesaw to accomplish the same thing, though the $200 cost is high for the small shop. Blade height and tilt controls should have enough clearance around them to leave the skin on your knuckles intact and should lock firmly.

Before purchasing a particular tablesaw, take careful account of available shop area—you have to have enough room so you won't be bumping into or tripping over one machine while working on another. Optimum use of the stationary machine would have it fixed in place and surrounded by carefully positioned outfeed and side tables. For extra versatility, an old hospital gurney or rolling bed table with a plywood top makes an excellent, adjustable-height support table.

Specialty saws—There are some unusual tablesaws worth considering. For example, Delta makes a 10-in. Scoring Saw, actually a 12-in.-capacity saw with an extra arbor in front of the main blade. The front arbor carries a small scoring blade that pre-kerfs the surface of the stock to eliminate chipping on hard-to-cut panels such as plastics and brittle veneers.

The Vega tablesaw features a rolling table to the left of the blade. This is not to be confused with the extension tables for handling plywood. In the Vega saw the entire table surface to the left of the blade moves. A crosscut fence attached to the rolling table holds the work, then the table is pushed past the blade. All ripping is done to the right of the blade, on the stationary part of the table. Ulmia makes a true sliding-table saw as well.

I'd compare the Erika and the Henniker to upside-down radial-arm saws. Unwieldy work is simply clamped to the table, then the motor and blade are pulled through to make the cut.

I don't have enough work experience with any of these machines to say much about them, although I can imagine that they would be very attractive for certain jobs. I would be interested to hear from readers about the subject.

The chart—The chart is not the dizzying, spec-heavy compilation I first set up. In the process of listing every dimension and feature of more than 50 tablesaws, it became apparent that saws

Sears

If you have a tight budget, then you'll need to look at the Sears Craftsman 10-in. tablesaws, which come in several versions. The one that I tested was the 10-in. Deluxe Flex Drive tilting-arbor saw, priced in the catalog at $590. It is not as ruggedly constructed as many of the older model Craftsman saws that I have tried, but it does aspire to the same concept of functional simplicity at an affordable price. This saw should not be purchased for any heavy-duty work, as it is in no way a light-industrial machine. With some modification, however, this Craftsman saw could be elevated to an operating level sufficient to satisfy most sawing chores encountered in the home workshop.

The cast-iron tables are good and flat, amply large, and hefty. As on many contractors' saws, the extension wings are cast in an open grid, which helps to save on weight. Slots for the miter gauge are squarely milled, and there is even a special plastic spot set into the table to mark the exact location of the saw cut (but the kerf width is likely to be different with each blade change, so the gauge line won't always be accurate). Two cleverly concealed Allen screws, for easy adjustment of the tilt-angle stops, are also set into the table. Unfortunately, the throat plate is awkward to remove and will deflect under pressure.

The most unusual component of this machine is the flex shaft drive. Because there are no exposed belts or pulleys, the system seems very safe. In practical terms, however, the power transmission is insufficient, especially when the saw comes with only a $1\frac{1}{16}$-HP motor. (Specs say the motor will develop a peak of $2\frac{1}{8}$ HP). When the arbor is tilted to 45°, the resulting compound bend in the shaft causes the blade to jerk when started and stopped, and the shaft itself heats up considerably. Whether caused by inadequate power or design problems with the drive, the net result is that feed rates, even through 1-in. hardwoods, are distinctly slow, and I was able to virtually stop the rotation with any 8/4 material.

Time and again I was bugged by a missing sense of positive control while working with this Craftsman saw. The open base is bolted to four legs that seemed to want to

Preiss feels that the Sears shaft drive is the saw's Achilles Heel—it gets uncomfortably hot to touch and if the blade is tilted, the saw starts and stops with a jerk.

twist and rack no matter how much I tried to stabilize the saw. The blade-raising and tilting controls feel very mushy, and the arbor-lock handle wants to tighten forever. It's tucked *right* up under the table and the handle has to be constantly repositioned on the screw head to get the job accomplished (and if you don't set the lock, the blade creeps). When resetting the blade angle, it tends to lock in a position slightly different than where you set the crank, which can get frustrating after a very short while. The 5-in. plastic control wheels for the arbor settings both require 45 turns to go from lock to lock, enough to try anyone's patience. The arbor runout on the machine I tested registered at a loose 0.003 in.

I like the miter gauge design very much, though the rip fence seems neither sturdy enough nor rigid enough to guarantee continued reliable performance. The miter gauge has a large, comfortable handle with a quick-action hold-down that makes quick and accurate crosscuts a breeze. However, its pre-set stops are controlled by a spring-loaded pin that is not adjustable. The rip fence is supposed to lock on both ends when you tighten the single control lever, but it requires perfectly aligned support bars if it is to do so along its entire length, and it's difficult to accomplish this. Also, there is enough play in the fence so that if the bars are not perfect and there happens to be some dirt on the table, the fence will rack its way from one setting to another. Despite being able to see the Metric/English scale easily, I could not rely on it for consistent or accurate settings.

The safety features are very similar to those of the Unisaw, with a few small differences. Unlike the Delta, the see-thru blade guard can be pivoted up and out of the way, although it balances very precariously and tends to crash down at inopportune moments. Aligning the splitter takes some doing, and even after you get it right, it flexes out of position when the saw is tilted because it is forced to support the

angled weight of the blade guard.

The on/off switch is easy to operate and is located perfectly, right up near the table. It is a simple switch without magnetic protection, but it does have one nice feature that might be a real asset to some woodworkers—there's a built-in key for childproofing. Dust collection is not accounted for at all, though a bag or sheet metal chute set under the base would probably work.

The Craftsman Flex Drive tablesaw appears to have all the capacities associated with any 10-in. machine, without the necessary power or beef to back it up. By upgrading to a larger motor, or even adding an aftermarket rip fence, it might be possible to substantially increase this machine's performance, though it could add as much as $350 to the cost. Before I purchased this machine new, I would look around for a used, older style Craftsman—the older the better—with a belt and pulley drive. Many of these saws appear able to last forever. In a friend's home shop, I checked out a Craftsman 10-in. saw that had been purchased by his grandfather and had been used in family workshops for three generations. The basic design is similar to today's models, but part for part everything has more meat, is cast iron instead of aluminum or plastic, and, above all, all the original parts are still functioning. The fence never locks parallel, I was told, but that's not hard to explain after so many years of service.

I also visted an architectural model shop that employs both a Craftsman belt-driven saw and one of the newer 9-in. "motorized" saws. Everyone I spoke with preferred the 9-in. saw for its quieter direct drive and more manageable size. It retails for $290.

There's a saying that people on a low budget usually have to buy everything twice. Of course, you can get a Craftsman saw on credit, and you don't have to shell out a thousand dollars for one tool. But for twice the money you can get lots more than twice the saw.
—R.P.

A study in patience: The Sears flexible shaft drive tablesaw will rip 8/4 stock, but at a pace that tends to put the operator to sleep. Preiss prefers the older, belt-drive models.

Manufacturer/ Distributor		Andreou	Black & Decker	Bratton	Delta	Erika	Foley-Belsaw	General	Grizzly	Henniker	Hitachi	
Number of models		6	6	2	6	1	1	1	2	1	1	
Country of origin		Taiwan	U.S.A.	Taiwan	U.S.A.	Germany	U.S.A.	Canada	Taiwan	U.S.A.	Japan	
Blade diameter	8		●									
	9				●							
	10	●	●	●	●	11	●	●	●			
	12	●		●	●					●	●	
Weight in pounds	Benchtop		●		●	●						
	100+		●		●	●						
	200+	●			●				●	●		
	300+	●			●		●				●	
	400+	●		●	●			●	●			
Continuous horsepower (estimated according to amperage)	1 HP (+ or −)		●		●							
	1.5 HP				●		●	●	●		●	
	2 HP	●			●	●				●	●	
	3 HP	●		●	●			●	●	●	●	
	5 HP +	●		●	●			●				
Tilt table												
Rolling table												
Traveling arbor						●				●		
Price range— rounded off		$325–$1400	$150–$525	$900–$3000	$150–$3000	$975–$1125	$700–$1000	$1200–$1400	$325–$800	$2000–$2500	$1850–$2150	

with similar power and weight were similar in most other respects as well. As I compared a long string of numbers about one saw with a long string of numbers about another, I realized how little such information really meant. For example, once past a certain weight, almost all trunnions, tables and wings are cast iron, and that's all a chart can tell you, not the quality. Even weight can be deceptive: one casting might outweigh another one but it could warp, have an ugly surface and even be flawed with air bubbles and voids. You have to look for yourself. I check for thin spots and for cracks, and I'm suspicious of any castings with heavy, possibly fault-concealing, coats of paint. Yet my impressions are subjective, and I admit to being slightly spoiled by having had lots of work time on machines of excellent quality. The guy standing next to me might feel happy with a machine I wouldn't let into my shop.

Prices are somewhat deceptive as well, so I deliberately made them approximate. Suggested retail isn't meaningful in the first place, and you can get all the better saws with a variety of options that will swing the price many hundreds of dollars. Consider shipping costs and other factors that may influence price. Some manufacturers give a trade-in allowance, for example. Ask.

The best advice I can give is to make up your mind about what you need, then write for brochures. If possible, visit a showroom—read the motor plate and work the fence and the controls, try all the adjustments, push on the throat plate. Better yet, find somebody in your neighborhood who owns the machine and get an evaluation of what it's really like. There's nothing like living with a saw for a while to show up its pros and cons. But keep in mind that owner loyalty can have its blind spots.

The tests—I'm not intending the tests to be an endorsement of any particular brand of tablesaw, but rather a sampling of what you can expect from a saw in the various categories. I know people, for example, who prefer Powermatic to the Unisaw, but when you get into this class of tablesaw, I don't think there are really any differences worth arguing about seriously.

For some woodworkers, even the range of saws described here won't be enough. I know of a custom-door and window maker who regularly has to rip 8/4 oak, and a lot of it. He ended up with a used Beech tablesaw—18-in. blade capacity, 5-HP, 3-PH motor (direct drive, no belts), and an arbor the size of your arm. For him, it's just the right saw. If you think you could use a piece of equipment in this category, just be sure your shop floor will be able to support its weight.

Conversely, lots of people build furniture with a Sears saw and swear by it. In the long run, what you need from your tablesaw and what you expect of yourself are the two main parts of the woodworking equation. When these factors are in pleasant balance, all is well. □

Rich Preiss supervises the architectural woodworking shop at the University of North Carolina at Charlotte.

Inca	Jet	Makita	Davis & Wells	Power-matic	Sears	Ulmia	Vega	Wilke	AMT	Skil	Fine Tool Shops
1	5	1	1	4	6	3	1	1	4	1	3
Switzerland	Taiwan	Japan	U.S.A.	U.S.A.	U.S.A.	Germany	U.S.A.	Taiwan	U.S.A.	U.S.A.	Taiwan
		●							●	●	
					●						
	●			●	●	●					●
	●		●	●	●	●	●	●			●
		●			●				●	●	●
●					●						
	●						●				●
	●		●	●	●	●	●				●
		●			●				●	●	●
●	●				●				●		●
●			●	●	●			●			●
	●		●	●		●	●				
	●		●	●		●	●				
●											
						●	●				
$1100–$1600	$475–$2500	$325	$3000–$3400	$1700–$3500	$300–$700	$3350–$5950	$2425–$2700	$300–$450	$50–$125	$184	$190–$1100

Sources of supply

American Machine & Tool, Fourth and Spring Sts., Royersford, PA 19468, (215) 948-0400.

Andreou Industries, 22-69 23rd St., Astoria, NY 11105, (718) 278-9528.

Black & Decker U.S. Inc., 626 Hanover Pike, Hampstead, MD 21074, (301) 239-5122.

Grizzly Imports, Box 2069, Bellingham, WA 98227 (206) 647-0801.

Davis & Wells: PAL Industries, 11090 S. Alameda St., Lynwood, CA 90262, (213) 636-0621.

Delta International Machinery, 246 Alpha Drive. Pittsburgh, PA 15238, (412) 963-2400, (800) 438-2486, (800) 438-2487 (PA).

Erika: MaFell North America, Box 363, Lockport, NY 14094, (716) 434-5574.

Fine Tool Shops, Inc., 20 Backus Ave., Box 1262, Danbury, CT 06810, (203) 797-0772, (800) 243-1037.

Foley-Belsaw, 6301 Equitable Rd., Kansas City, MO 64120, (816) 483-4200, (800) 468-4449, (800) 892-8789 (MO).

General: J. Philip Humfrey Ltd., 3241 Kennedy Rd., Unit 7, Scarborough, Ontario, Canada M1V 2J9, (416) 293-8624, (800) 387-9789.

Bratton Machinery, 1015 Commercial St., Box 20408, Tallahassee, FL 32316, (904) 222-4842, (800) 874-8160, (800) 342-2641 (FL).

Henniker: The Versatile Saw Corp., Box 716, Henniker, NH 03242. (603) 428-3258.

Hitachi Power Tools USA Ltd., 7490 Lampson Ave, Garden Grove, CA 92641, (714) 891-5330.

Inca: Garrett Wade Co., 161 Avenue of the Americas, New York, NY 10013, (212) 807-1155.

Jet Equipment and Tools, Box 1477, Tacoma, WA 98401, (206) 572-5000.

Makita USA Inc., 12590 E. Alondra Blvd , Cerritos, CA 90701, (213) 926-8775.

Powermatic Corporation, McMinnville, TN 37110, (615) 473-5551.

Sears Roebuck and Co., Michael Mangan, Dept. 703, 40th Floor, Sears Tower, Chicago, IL 60684.

Skil Corporation, 4801 W. Peterson, Chicago, IL 60646.

Ulmia, Mahogany Masterpieces, Suncook, NH 03275, (603) 736-8227.

Vega Enterprises Inc., Box 300 B, Rt. 3, Decatur, IL 62526, (217) 963-2232.

Wilke Machinery Co./Bridgewood, 120 Derry Ct., York, PA 17402, (717) 846-2800.

Carbide Sawblades

Compromises in quality make for affordable cuts

by Jim Cummins

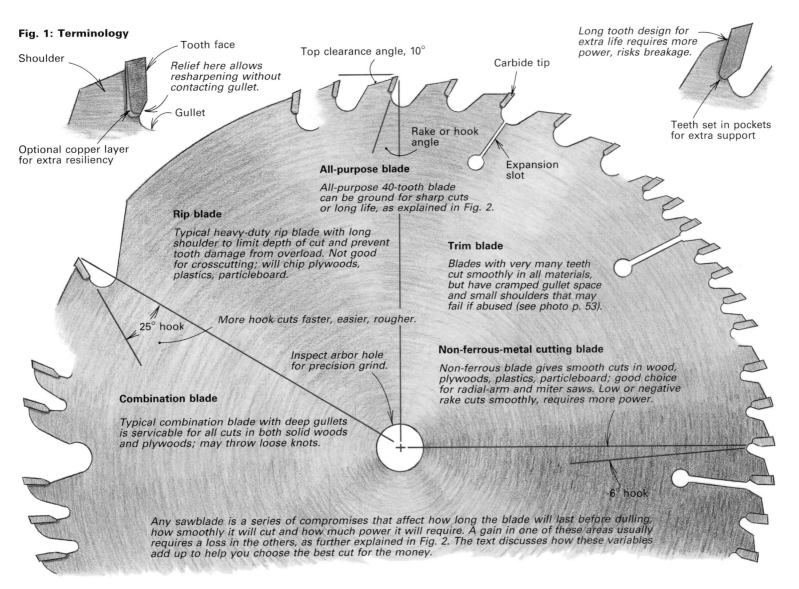

Fig. 1: Terminology

Shoulder

Tooth face

Relief here allows resharpening without contacting gullet.

Gullet

Optional copper layer for extra resiliency

Top clearance angle, 10°

Carbide tip

Rake or hook angle

Expansion slot

Long tooth design for extra life requires more power, risks breakage.

Teeth set in pockets for extra support

All-purpose blade

All-purpose 40-tooth blade can be ground for sharp cuts or long life, as explained in Fig. 2.

Rip blade

Typical heavy-duty rip blade with long shoulder to limit depth of cut and prevent tooth damage from overload. Not good for crosscutting; will chip plywoods, plastics, particleboard.

Trim blade

Blades with very many teeth cut smoothly in all materials, but have cramped gullet space and small shoulders that may fail if abused (see photo p. 53).

25° hook

More hook cuts faster, easier, rougher.

Inspect arbor hole for precision grind.

Non-ferrous-metal cutting blade

Non-ferrous blade gives smooth cuts in wood, plywoods, plastics, particleboard; good choice for radial-arm and miter saws. Low or negative rake cuts smoothly, requires more power.

Combination blade

Typical combination blade with deep gullets is servicable for all cuts in both solid woods and plywoods; may throw loose knots.

-6° hook

Any sawblade is a series of compromises that affect how long the blade will last before dulling, how smoothly it will cut and how much power it will require. A gain in one of these areas usually requires a loss in the others, as further explained in Fig. 2. The text discusses how these variables add up to help you choose the best cut for the money.

A top-of-the-line carbide tablesaw blade costs more than some motorized 10-in. tablesaws. Does it make sense for a woodworker to shell out $100-plus for such a blade? There's no single answer, but after researching this article, I formulated a two-part rule of thumb: First, don't spend more than 15% of the cost of your tablesaw on any one blade; second, figure on spending from 25% to 50% of the saw's cost on three or four special-purpose blades that will let you cut just about anything. While this may sound arbitrary, it's based on careful observations.

No sawblade can be better than the tablesaw powering it. In fact, I spent about $900 on sawblades for my Sears saw in the first five years I ran my shop, ignorantly buying toothier blades each time in hopes of finding one that would cut both smoothly and at an economical rate. It wasn't until I bought a Rockwell/Delta Contractors Saw with about 50% more horsepower that I found out I had some real winners. Four of these are in constant use today, while the rest of my investment mostly hangs on the wall.

I'll tell you what my old favorites are, but I'm convinced that the most significant part of my list is the *type* of blade, not the manufacturer: a 10-tooth ripping blade (Winchester), which can slog through full-depth cuts on anything I've ever fed it; a 40-tooth combination blade (Freud) that's on the saw 95% of the

From *Fine Woodworking* magazine (May 1988) 70:36-41

time; an 80-tooth, thin-kerf plywood blade (Freud); and a 120-tooth no-set steel blade (Simonds), which I use for cutting aluminum picture-frame molding, but which can give me a glassy surface on wood on the few days a year I want it. At one time, all my blades were steel. I switched to carbide because my steel blades dulled too quickly, especially in abrasive, man-made materials. One saw-blade manufacturer I talked with mentioned an informal test his company had done comparing two types of carbide blades with a steel blade. One carbide blade cut 12,000 linear ft. of particle-board; the other cut 9,000 ft.; the steel blade was hopelessly dull after 300 ft.

My saw is now about 10 years old, and while it's in pretty good tune and a darn nice machine for the money, it's incapable of showing up noticeable differences in blades that cost more than about $55. But when I tried the same expensive sawblades on a new, fine-tuned, General tablesaw, their special qualities became apparent. The owner of the saw, Jim Van Etten of Perkasie, N.J., had recently spent three hours getting the blade perfectly parallel with the miter slots, aligning his Biesemeyer fence and adjusting his shopmade sliding tables. This attention is critical for smooth, splinter-free cuts. One easy day-to-day test for proper fence alignment is that both sides of the cut should show an X-pattern resulting from the front teeth cutting down and the back teeth cutting up. For some applications, the back of the fence can be canted a hair away from the blade. This will give a smoother cut on the fence side of the blade, but on the offcut, the teeth at the back of the blade will cause a rough cut and surface tearout.

For this article, I interviewed major sawblade manufacturers, as well as some small saw shops. I called woodworkers around the country for their opinions. I bought, and borrowed, about four dozen blades, tried them in my shop and persuaded other wood-workers to try them in theirs. Taking a look at this assortment is by no means a "test." That would require subjecting perhaps three dozen blades of each design from each manufacturer to test cuts until they were dull. Without such rigor, results are bound to be subjective, although some clear patterns did emerge: Saw-blades do work best cutting the materials the manufacturers say they should cut and, yes, you get what you pay for. When I counted last, I owned 28 sawblades; the ones that I prefer to use are the most expensive in each category. This doesn't mean, however, that you have to pay big bucks for good cuts.

Grades and tolerances—Most manufacturers make several grades of blades, aimed at three broad markets. The top line is for industrial use. The middle line is for contractors. The bottom line is for "consumers."

Industry needs sawblades so uniform they can be ganged up 10 or more at a time on an arbor, then run at high horsepower and feed rates. Ten-inch industrial blades sell in the range from $75 to $200, depending on the number of teeth. Even so, a large part of the blade's cost is the plate—the alloy-steel disc the teeth are brazed to. Both the initial cost of the plate and the cost of the manufacturing steps to bring it to close tolerances can make an expensive blade even more costly.

Contractors don't need industrial-quality blades and are more likely to be concerned with the most cut for the dollar. By relaxing tolerances a little and automating, manufacturers can sell very good blades between $35 and $60. Special promotions can yield incredible values—Freud's new version of my old combination blade, for example, costs less than half, from today's discounters, of what I paid retail. Similar values from U.S. Saw, DML, SystiMatic, Delta, Amana, FS Tool, Forrest and all the others competing for your dollar make carbide blades real bargains.

Two setups for checking blade/arbor runout. If you don't have a dial indicator, you can make do with an engineers' rule clamped to the miter gauge and an automotive feeler gauge to check the gaps. The masking tape on this blade indicates high spots—initial runout was 0.007 in.—yet by reorienting the blade on the arbor, it was made to run true.

Industry thinks "consumers" just want to get the job done as cheaply as possible. Tolerances are so loose in this part of the market that it's safe to generalize: Good blades don't come in blister packs; the flashier the packaging, the cheaper the blade.

The technology to make the best sawblade in the world is available to anyone who wants to use it. The few proprietary patents and new tooth designs don't amount to all that much. In fact, any carbide sawblade you pick up is likely to be worth the money, provided you buy it on sale. There are many ways to get sawblades into an attractive price range for contractors and homeowners. It's a benefit, when making up your mind to buy, to be able to discern where the cost cutting was done. First, let's consider the saw plate.

The plate—The plate should be alloy steel that's tempered to an appropriate hardness. Standards range anywhere from 30Rc (Rockwell C scale) to 46Rc or even 48Rc. Most plates on industrial blades range from 38Rc to 44Rc. The higher the plate hardness, the more the blade can be deflected and twisted without permanent deformation. Some manufacturers talk about plate hardness in their ads, and you can always ask the ones who don't. For the average woodworker feeding the saw by hand, plate hardness is not as important as it is in industry, where feed rates can approach 300 ft. per minute.

What is important is that the plate is the reference for all sharpening. The arbor hole in the plate should be as snug as possible on the arbor. It is the reference for the concentricity of the teeth; the plate surface just below the teeth is the reference for top, face and side grinding. Two ways of checking plate flatness, or runout, are shown in the photo above. Holding a backlit straightedge against the plate will also show runout. A plate that is not flat will be forced flat as each tooth is sharpened, then will spring back, leaving the teeth out of line. A blade that is not concentric because of a loose-fitting arbor hole, or that has teeth out of line, will not only be less efficient and less smooth cutting, but will require more frequent sharpenings, at $10 to $20 a shot.

Cheap plates are merely punched out—as if using a cookie cutter—then polished to look good in the store. The dividing line seems to be about $25, discount price. Such a blade might be an excellent value if you plan to rough-cut cheap stock and discard the blade after a sharpening or two.

Better plates are flattened by sanding or grinding. A sanded plate will show grind marks that spiral out noticeably toward the rim; ground plates, which can be made more precisely, will show marks that are concentric. The finer the grind marks, generally, the more careful the manufacturer was. A plate can lose its flatness through abuse. Sticking a screwdriver in an expansion slot to loosen the arbor nut is not wise—as little as 0.001-in. abrupt runout makes for a noticeably scratchy cut. Heat buildup from hard running or forcing an overdull blade can also distort the plate.

Manufacturers go to great lengths to make sawblades look good, but one thing that hasn't occurred to them yet is that you can look into the arbor hole and tell a lot about how carefully a blade was made. Cheap arbor holes are simply punched to size, and this is obvious to the eye. The edges of the hole will be bent in, and there will be a fracture line within the hole showing where the center popped loose. Better arbor holes are at first cut or punched to a rough diameter, then brought to true round by reaming or grinding. Reaming is fast and leaves a smooth surface with minor, intermittent scoring and chatter marks. Grinding is better, but bad grinding is done fast, leaving slag and rough score marks. Manufacturers who skimp on arbor-hole machining tend to make the hole oversize, on the theory that if a blade fits loosely, it's better than if it doesn't fit at all. But if a blade fits loosely, it's only by luck that you'll ever get it to run true.

The other quality affecting the plate is its tensioning. Tension-

Fig. 2: Grinds

Blades can be designed to work best in particular materials by choosing the appropriate combination of hook angle, grind type, grind angles and number of teeth. Some of the necessary compromises are noted below.

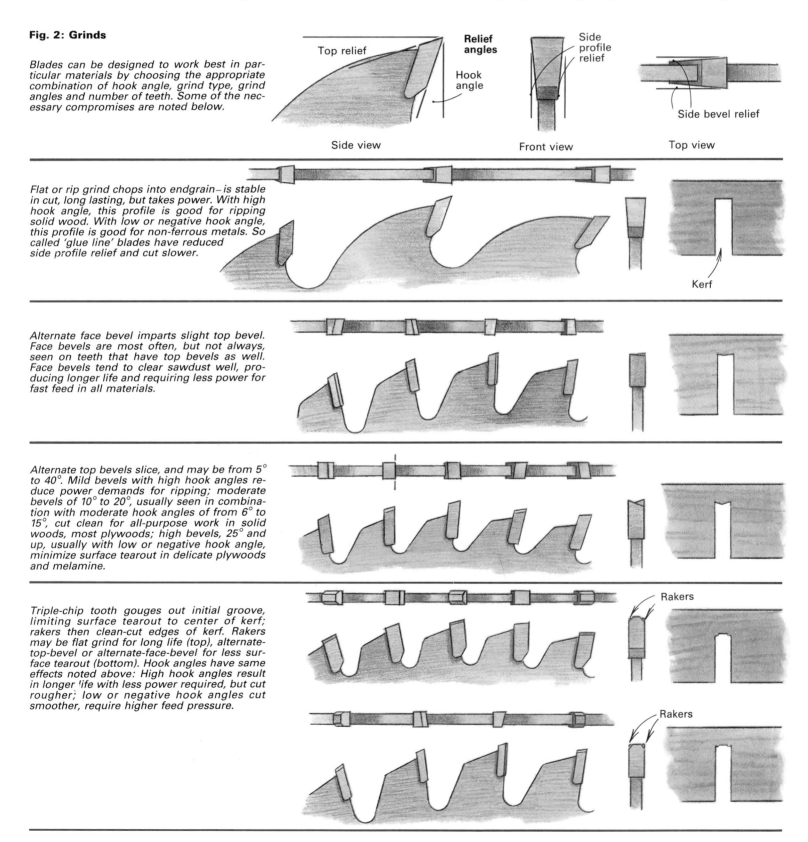

Flat or rip grind chops into endgrain—is stable in cut, long lasting, but takes power. With high hook angle, this profile is good for ripping solid wood. With low or negative hook angle, this profile is good for non-ferrous metals. So called 'glue line' blades have reduced side profile relief and cut slower.

Alternate face bevel imparts slight top bevel. Face bevels are most often, but not always, seen on teeth that have top bevels as well. Face bevels tend to clear sawdust well, producing longer life and requiring less power for fast feed in all materials.

Alternate top bevels slice, and may be from 5° to 40°. Mild bevels with high hook angles reduce power demands for ripping; moderate bevels of 10° to 20°, usually seen in combination with moderate hook angles of from 6° to 15°, cut clean for all-purpose work in solid woods, most plywoods; high bevels, 25° and up, usually with low or negative hook angle, minimize surface tearout in delicate plywoods and melamine.

Triple-chip tooth gouges out initial groove, limiting surface tearout to center of kerf; rakers then clean-cut edges of kerf. Rakers may be flat grind for long life (top), alternate-top-bevel or alternate-face-bevel for less surface tearout (bottom). Hook angles have same effects noted above: High hook angles result in longer life with less power required, but cut rougher; low or negative hook angles cut smoother, require higher feed pressure.

ing is pre-distorting the saw plate by means of hammering or roller pressure. This leaves stresses in the steel that tend to push the blade's rim out when the blade is at rest. When the blade is running, centrifugal force at the rim balances the tensioning and lets the plate run true. Tensioning also allows for some rim expansion from heat buildup. To a major extent, the blade's expansion slots leave room for this, and I believe that tensioning of a 10-in. blade in average use is less important than its flatness. Runout, or blade wobble, should be no more than 0.004 in., and a gradual runout affecting many teeth is better than an abrupt one.

Plates can be made in various thicknesses. Some Japanese plates are so thin that they cut kerfs barely more than ¹⁄₁₆ in. wide, while some rip blades clear a kerf of almost ³⁄₁₆ in., and a number of blades have thin-rim designs that feature a heavy plate in the center with a thinner edge. Standard plate thickness is about 0.085 in., which seems good for most work. My favorite rip blade's plate is 0.095 in. thick. I like the heavy plate on this blade for several reasons: Its mass keeps it turning when a thin plate might bind and helps damp out shock from hitting knots or contrary grain. And it's also almost deflection-free.

A good case can be made for thin-kerf blades, provided they are not misused. On tablesaws that bog down frequently, a blade with a narrower kerf has the advantage of needing less power because it is removing less wood. The main problem with thin-kerf blades is vibration in the cut, causing deep gouging that has to be planed or sanded away. It is a good idea not to force thin-kerf blades so that they slow down from normal speed range—the blade's natural vibration frequency will become excited and amplified by vibrations generated in cutting, causing the blade to flutter. Also, don't feed too slowly, as heat buildup may distort the plate. I have not found that stiffeners or dampeners are necessary to get good cuts on my saw, but on a more powerful saw allowing faster feed rates, they may prove beneficial. It is a good idea to save thin-kerf blades for cutting top-grade stock that's not likely to warp or twist. As one woodworker I talked with put it: "When you're cutting a $200 claro walnut board or a $100 sheet of plywood, a thin-kerf blade can mean the difference between a usable offcut and a piece of scrap." Smaller diameters of the thin-kerf family make admirable blades for hand-held circular saws, because their free-cutting action greatly reduces fatigue.

Here's a tip from the experts: After you tighten the arbor nut, give the saw a short power bump, then watch for runout as the blade winds down. If there's any runout visible, change the blade's orientation on the arbor and try again until it runs true. If using stabilizers or a dampener, rotate these to various orientations as well. While checking one sawblade with a dial indicator, I was able to reduce a runout of 0.007 in. to nothing—a freak occurrence where my arbor and plate runout exactly cancelled each other.

The carbide—Carbide is composed of fine grains of extremely hard tungsten-carbon particles cemented together with cobalt as a binder in a process called sintering, which involves pressing powders together, while applying heat below melting temperature, to produce a coherent mass. Carbide is usually rated on a hardness scale from C1 (soft and tough, with up to 8% cobalt) to C4 (hard and brittle, with as little as 2% cobalt). I would not make a big deal about which carbide grade the manufacturer uses, because C1 carbide is about 89Rc, and C4 is about 94Rc (diamond is 100Rc). Also, the "C" rating does not define the material—carbide grains may be coarse, fine or mixed; binder alloys vary; homogeneity within each tooth can vary. Cheap carbide may be so full of voids that the cutting edge simply flakes away, but good carbide is pretty much all good. I found no bad carbide

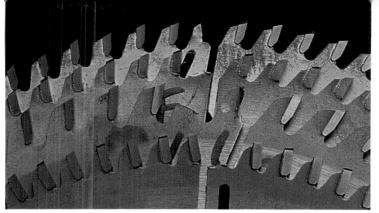

Blades with a lot of teeth don't have much room for shoulders. Here are a few that failed—most likely while cutting aluminum—and were returned as 'defective' to the dealer.

on any blade except a Sears 20-tooth all-purpose ($25), which had seven teeth chipped or pitted, as shown in the photo on p. 55.

To make a tooth, the mixture of carbon and cobalt is pressed together in a mold and sintered into solid form in an oven. Teeth can be molded so close to final size that, on cheap blades, the tops alone are ground, with the faces and sides retaining the dull gray, matte finish from the mold. Avoid these. Some design approaches to shape are shown in the drawings, but I feel normal, moderate-sized teeth up to about ¼ in. long are the best bet. The photos on p. 55 show nearly 20 years of grinding on my first carbide blade from Sears ($35 then, $55 now), and there's a little more life in it yet. Big teeth may promise a few more sharpenings, but you'll use a lot of power and time over the life of the blade, dragging them through the cut.

The carbide chunks are brazed into pockets on the plate's shoulders, which were cut, along with the gullets, when the plate was made. Teeth brazed directly to the front of a blade without being pocketed used to be the sign of a really cheap blade, but I found none of these. Also, I did not find bad brazing on any of the sawblades I considered for this article, so I will not dwell on the things that can go wrong—shoulders losing temper and being softened by too much heat, lack of adhesion from too little heat, serious voids, etc. It seems these are problems of the past, but that's not to say you shouldn't keep your eyes open.

The number of teeth—There's something immediately appealing about a blade with a lot of teeth. The truth is, however, that you are best off with the *fewest* teeth you can get away with for the job. The rule is that there should be at least two, but not more than four, teeth in the cut at any one time. For extended blade life, it pays to raise your sawblade high when smoothness is not important. Use the guard, of course. Lower the blade to get more teeth in the material for smoother cuts.

The more teeth, the faster the blade dulls, for three reasons: First, when there are a lot of teeth, each tooth takes small chips, which gives a smooth surface with little breakout and chipping, but each tooth hits the wood more often and the initial impact against the wood is a serious dulling factor. Second, when there are a lot of teeth, blades tend to recut the chips, in effect doing much more work than is necessary. A third factor is chip size. Good-sized chips carry away much of the heat from cutting; small chips don't. Blades with a lot of teeth run hot and cut slow.

Another factor working against high tooth numbers is geometry. There's only about 30 in. around the rim of a 10-in. sawblade, and each tooth needs room for the carbide chunk, for the gullet and for the shoulder. An 80-tooth blade needs three times 80 divisions, or approximately ⅛ in. for carbide, ⅛ in. for gullet, and ⅛ in for shoulder. Take a look at the damaged high-tooth blades shown in the photo above. If such a blade flutters a little,

Fig. 3: New faces

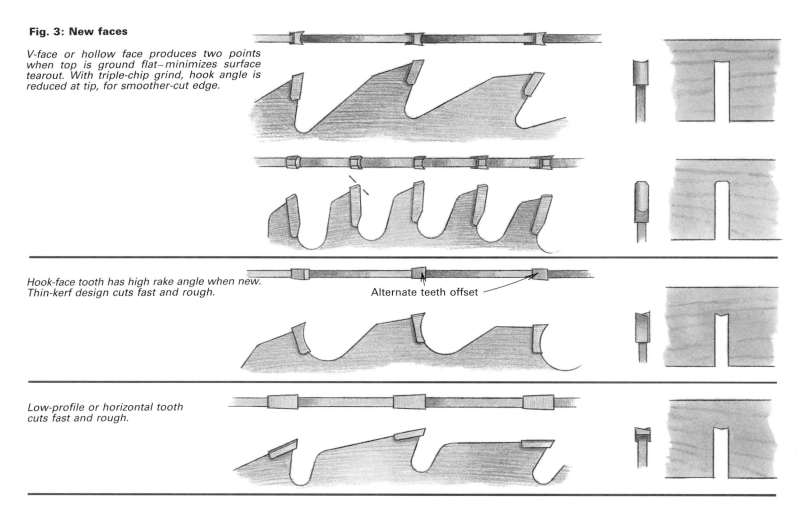

V-face or hollow face produces two points when top is ground flat—minimizes surface tearout. With triple-chip grind, hook angle is reduced at tip, for smoother-cut edge.

Hook-face tooth has high rake angle when new. Thin-kerf design cuts fast and rough.

Alternate teeth offset

Low-profile or horizontal tooth cuts fast and rough.

or catches an offcut or a loose knot, a tooth can find itself taking three times the impact load for which it was designed, which will break either the braze, the tooth or the shoulder. This is a particularly serious problem if you are trying to cut aluminum in a miter saw. Don't do it.

Hook angles, as shown in figure 1, are built into a blade when the plate is cut. The higher the hook angle, the more aggressive, and rougher, the cut. The lower the hook angle, the more the tooth acts as a scraper. Let's say a "normal" hook angle is 10°. A higher hook angle makes a blade act as if it had fewer teeth—it will cut faster and require less power. A lower hook angle, particularly a negative hook angle, makes a blade act as if it had more teeth. Blades with lots of teeth and low hook angles may excel on a miter saw or a radial-arm saw, where cuts are relatively short and feed pressure not too important. But if they are used on the tablesaw, they may require objectionally high feed pressure and may heat up too much on long cuts, burning the work and possibly warping the plate.

The advice to use as few teeth as possible depends on the cutting job. All else being equal, the more teeth, the smoother the cut. Rip blades usually run from 10 teeth to 40 teeth. If you have to surface the sawn edge anyway, it makes little sense to choose a rip blade with more than 20 teeth. Blades with more than 50 teeth are usually designed to crosscut wood or to saw plywoods, non-ferrous metals, particleboard and plastics, where smoothness of the cut is more important than speed and blade life.

The grind—Every cutting edge needs some elementary clearances, or relief angles, which are shown in figure 2. These allow the cutting edge to bite into the work without friction from the top and sides of the tooth. Top and side clearances are fairly standard, and there's not much to be said about them except that

blades should be cleaned when pitch starts to build up in these areas. Typical cleaners include kerosene, alcohol, ammonia or oven cleaner.

Clearance between the sides of the plate and the work being cut is provided by making the teeth wider than the plate. In addition, there is usually a radial (or side-profile) clearance of typically 0.007 in. to 0.010 in. from the tip of the tooth down to the bottom of the tooth. Some planer-type blades have radial clearances of 0.001 in. and less for an especially smooth cut, rivaling hollow-ground steel blades. The two best-known contenders for an ultimately smooth cut, Forrest's Woodworker I and Freud's LU85M, take different approaches toward the goal. Forrest grinds little or no radial clearance and uses a thin plate machined to very precise tolerances to provide sufficient plate clearance. Freud's LU85M is designed to have as little plate clearance as possible, on the theory that if a tooth doesn't stick out far, it can't scratch much. The blade is therefore coated with Teflon, because in most cutting, the plate will rub. Freud includes special sharpening instructions, because if this blade is sharpened normally, all plate clearance can be lost and the blade may start to smoke. While this design approach may have its drawbacks, it makes the blade particularly appropriate for vibration-prone machinery—miter saws, radial-arm saws and tablesaws with lumpy belts, arbor run-out, out-of-round pulleys, unbalanced motors or other flaws—provided there's enough power to keep it turning.

With these obligatory clearances in mind, the simplest grind is a flat-top, flat-face rip tooth. It works like a chisel with the grain, chopping in, then popping out hefty chips. The whole edge cuts, so the blade requires considerable power, but wear is slow because it's spread across the whole cutting edge. Square teeth have a stable cutting geometry. This is offset somewhat by typically high hook angles that follow changes in grain direction, leading

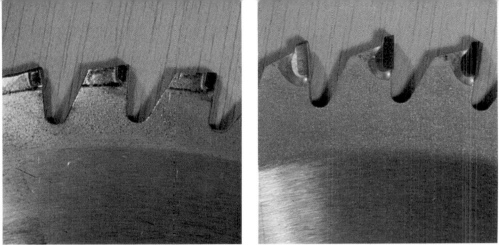

This old Sears blade (left) has been resharpened many times. Although there's hardly any carbide left, the blade cuts smoother than the new one at right because it was sharpened more carefully. It also cuts easier, because the teeth have become smaller and thinner, so less carbide has to be dragged through the cut.

It's worth inspecting blades before you buy. On this Sears combination blade (about $25), seven of the 20 teeth were chipped or had pitting and inclusions. Even on costly blades, magnification may show similar sharpening damage.

to rough cuts. Like a chisel, a rip tooth cuts poorly cross-grain.

A cure for the rough cut, while keeping balance, is the triple-chip design. A leading tooth has its corners ground off so it plows a center groove, which is then cleaned up by one or more rip teeth, called rakers, that follow it. These blades are effective in particleboard or other materials that have uniform tough structure. A triple-chip blade with square rakers and a low or negative hook angle is good for non-ferrous metals, but not for cross-grain cutting in splintery plywoods. Where surface splintering is a problem, you need teeth with sharp corners to sever the work.

There are a few ways to grind points onto teeth. If a rip tooth's face is beveled, a mild point on one corner of the tooth will result because of the way the face bevel intersects the top clearance angle. Points can be put onto teeth by such exotic grinds as V-top grinds, hollow faces or concave faces, but by far, the most common tactic is to alternately bevel the tops of the teeth. This bevel can be as mild as 5° or as steep as 40°. The higher the bevel angle, the sharper and more fragile the tooth.

For cutting splintery plywoods, a triple-chip tooth may be followed by two or more alternate-top-bevel teeth. Such a blade with mild top bevels will be more stable in the cut than one with high top bevels. The tradeoff in triple-chip blades is that one with square rakers may splinter the veneer, but will produce a smoother-cut edge. One with high alternate top bevels will produce a scratchier-cut edge but with no tearout, and is best for veneer, laminate or melamine. If the tearout problem is paramount, you want a blade with top bevels of between 30° and 40°. Such a blade will dull fast, but the long point will still give a splinter-free cut for a longer time than a shallow-bevel blade that is in fact sharper.

Triple-chip blades are designed for man-made materials, but if they have moderate alternate-top-bevel rakers, they can be used on solid woods as well, making them something of a jack-of-all-trades. Another good all-around blade would be a 40-tooth with alternate top bevels between 15° and 20°. Spokesmen throughout the industry recommend this type of blade for general-purpose cutting in the average shop. It can smoothly crosscut solid woods, plywoods, particleboard and laminates, and if not pushed too hard, can rip up to 2-in.-thick hardwoods.

The last candidate for all-purpose work is a combination blade like my old Freud, with groups of teeth consisting of four alternate-top-bevel teeth followed by a flat-top raker ground a little lower. The usual number of teeth is 50, ten groups separated by deep gullets. Because of their popularity, everybody makes a blade of this design—I tried half a dozen and thought they were all excellent—but the consensus is that you are better off buying separate blades more specifically designed for the work at hand.

Figure 3 shows a few new tooth shapes. The V-top and hollow-face grinds can be found on some very good sawblades indeed, and produce chip-free cuts in difficult plywoods and melamine. But fancy teeth on cheap blades seem aimed for the consumer market, and the generally loose tolerances necessitated by this price range mean you might get a very good blade for the money, but you might also not. A V-tooth gives a smoother cut than the number of teeth would suggest, but requires high feed pressure. The hook tooth and the horizontal tooth both cut very fast, but I wouldn't call either cut smooth.

The polish—With the grind geometry established, the next consideration is how well the carbide has been sharpened. Carbide must be ground with diamond wheels. Some shops use as coarse as 180-grit wheels, but the best shops finish with up to 600 grit. Diamond of 400 grit leaves a finish on carbide comparable to what an 80-grit aluminum-oxide grinding wheel leaves on steel. The surface depends not only on the grit size, but on the slowness of the pass, the lubricant used and the condition of the wheel. Contrary to general opinion, silicon-carbide "green wheels" do not sharpen carbide, but merely remove the cobalt binder material. They can be used to rough-shape carbide, but will not leave a true sharp edge.

A rough grind on the face, sides and top indicates that the cutting edge is ragged, and there is a good chance that the points of many teeth will be missing. Any manufacturer can have a bad day in this regard and it doesn't necessarily mean that the blade is inferior. Provided the plate is good, you'll get many years' work from it, and a good sharpening service can make the blade better than new indefinitely. A highly polished carbide surface, on the other hand, does not necessarily indicate a sharp cutting edge. It may be the result of a glazed, clogged and worn diamond wheel that has overheated the cutting edge, leaving it weak and fractured—you'll be more likely to see this on a resharpening rather than on the original grind, and I'd worry about it. The true test of a good grind is to inspect the cutting edge under magnification. You can verify this yourself very easily. Take a carbide blade that has seen some service and look for a tooth that has picked up more than its share of pitch on the top or face. I'll bet that even under low magnification, you will find the tooth's corners chipped off. By examining teeth under higher magnification, say 20X or 30X, you can tell a lot about how a blade will cut even before you mount it on the saw. □

Jim Cummins is an associate editor of Fine Woodworking.

Power Primer

Electric motors in the woodshop

by Edward J. Cowern

Fig. 1: Induction Motor Anatomy

Capacitor start induction run motor (single phase, totally enclosed, fan cooled)

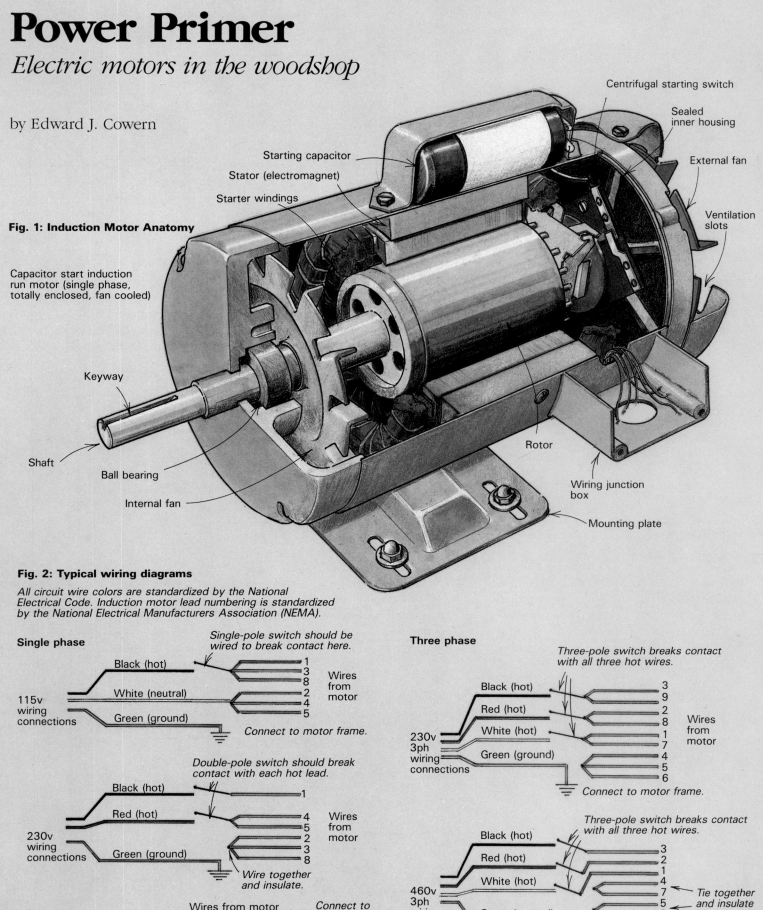

Starting capacitor

Stator (electromagnet)

Starter windings

Centrifugal starting switch

Sealed inner housing

External fan

Ventilation slots

Rotor

Wiring junction box

Mounting plate

Keyway

Shaft

Ball bearing

Internal fan

Fig. 2: Typical wiring diagrams

All circuit wire colors are standardized by the National Electrical Code. Induction motor lead numbering is standardized by the National Electrical Manufacturers Association (NEMA).

Single phase

Single-pole switch should be wired to break contact here.

Black (hot)

115v wiring connections

White (neutral)

Green (ground)

1
3
8
2
4
5

Wires from motor

Connect to motor frame.

Double-pole switch should break contact with each hot lead.

Black (hot)

Red (hot)

230v wiring connections

Green (ground)

1
4
5
2
3
8

Wires from motor

Wire together and insulate.

Rotation reversing switch

Wires from motor

Connect to circuit wires as shown above.

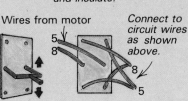

5
8

8
5

Double-pole, double-throw (DPDT) switch interchanges connection of wires 8 and 5 to reverse motor rotation.

Three phase

Three-pole switch breaks contact with all three hot wires.

Black (hot)

Red (hot)

White (hot)

230v 3ph wiring connections

Green (ground)

3
9
2
8
1
7
4
5
6

Wires from motor

Connect to motor frame.

Three-pole switch breaks contact with all three hot wires.

Black (hot)

Red (hot)

White (hot)

460v 3ph wiring connections

Green (ground)

3
2
1
4
7
5
8
6
9

Tie together and insulate each group separately.

Connect to motor frame.

To reverse rotation of motor, interchange connection of any two motor leads.

There was a time not too long ago when a woodworker had to open a sluice gate to a waterwheel or stoke the fire beneath a steam engine's boiler before any powered machinery in the shop could be operated. Nowadays, the relative luxury of just flipping a switch makes electric motors an essential part of the woodshop.

In this article, I'll explain a bit about how electric motors work, why they might stop working and how you can intelligently choose new motors to use as replacements or incorporate in the machines you build. I won't attempt to entirely demystify motor theory, but I can convey enough knowledge to help you make sensible, safe decisions when choosing, connecting and operating electric motors in your workshop.

Motor types—Broadly speaking, two major types of motors are commonly used by woodworkers: induction motors for stationary power tools, and universal motors for portable tools. A third type, the direct-current permanent-magnet motor, is becoming popular for battery-operated cordless tools and in applications where controlled speed is important. However, I'll deal only with induction motors (see figure 1), the basic workhorse found on most stationary equipment—tablesaws, lathes, shapers, jointers, drill presses, etc.

This type of motor converts electricity into rotary motion by taking advantage of the fact that alternating current (AC) reverses its direction of flow 60 times per second. Inside the motor, these alternating electric impulses reverse the polarity of a fixed electromagnet, the stator, around a cylindrical drum called a rotor. These current reversals actually produce a rotating magnetic field inside the stator which, in turn, induces currents inside the rotor, producing a strong magnetic field in the rotor. The interaction of these two magnetic fields causes the rotor to spin as it attempts to match the speed of the stator's rotating field.

Since electrical power is available in either single or three phase, induction motors are designed specifically to operate on one or the other. "Phase" refers to the number of pulses of power delivered during one cycle ($\frac{1}{60}$ of a second for 60-cycle power). Therefore, three-phase electricity delivers six pulses of power in the same time that single-phase electricity produces only two.

Whether you choose single- or 3-phase induction motors may depend on what kind of power is available to your shop. When 3-phase power is available, usually in industrial areas, use 3-phase motors if you can. They are simpler and have longer service lives than their single-phase equivalents, and they are more efficient to operate. It's possible to use 3-phase motors on single-phase power, but you'll need to provide your own third phase. There are several ways of doing this. The rotary-type phase converter is durable and efficient: basically a large, 3-phase motor, used like a generator, it puts out the same voltage that's fed into it.

The best all-around quick-starting single-phase induction motors are either capacitor start/induction run (⅙ HP through 1½ HP) or capacitor start/capacitor run (2 HP through 10 HP). Both types depend on an electrolytic capacitor to energize a starter winding to get the motor spinning (see figure 1). Capacitor-start types use a centrifugal switch to disconnect the starter winding once the motor comes up to speed, while two-value capacitor motors have a separate, oil-filled capacitor that remains connected to the starter winding to provide useful power output after the motor has started. Split-phase motors—a third type—lack starting capacitors entirely and are found on machines that don't require much start-up torque, such as bench grinders.

Most capacitor-start induction motors can be wired to operate on either 115v or 230v and can be made to rotate in either direction. Normally, 115v operation is adequate for motors through ¾ HP, but when possible, 230v should be used for motors 1 HP and larger. This is because amperage halves as voltage doubles, so a 2-HP motor requiring 13 amps at 220v would need 26 amps at 115v. Most household wiring is not capable of delivering that much current without a significant voltage drop at the motor terminals, a condition which substantially reduces motor performance.

Establishing the correct direction of rotation is simply a matter of wiring. Figure 2 shows standard wiring diagrams for both single- and 3-phase motors. If you wish to reverse a motor's rotation, say on a shaper or disc sander, you can wire in a reversing switch that reconnects the starter winding wires while leaving other connections intact. *Avoid using reversing switches on tools with threaded arbors, since the reversed direction could unscrew a blade's locknut or release the faceplate on a lathe.*

The major shortcoming of the induction motor—either single- or 3-phase—is its operating speed, which is fixed by the frequency of the power source and the number of magnetic poles designed into the motor. For example, on 60-cycle power, a two-pole motor will run at a maximum no-load speed of 3,600 RPM. As the load increases during operation, the motor will slow down to a full-load speed of approximately 3,450 RPM. Similarly, a motor with four poles will have a no-load speed of 1,800 RPM and a full-load speed of about 1,725 RPM.

Since most induction motors used in the shop are either 3,450 RPM or 1,725 RPM, speed adjustments must be made mechanically. By varying the diameters of the drive and driven pulleys, the speed of a blade or cutter can be made faster or slower than the speed of the motor. On certain machines where variable speeds are desirable, such as lathes, drill presses and shapers, multi-step pulleys offer a choice of a few preset speeds. Alternately, a mechanical adjustable-speed drive can provide a continuously adjustable range of speeds.

Enclosure types—Modern industrial-duty induction motors are available in three enclosure types. The open drip-proof motor (top left photo, next page) is the least expensive. Its louvered end brackets allow cooling air to freely circulate inside, while preventing water from dripping in directly. It's a fine motor for many applications where relatively clean and dry operating conditions exist, such as an air compressor located in an area of the shop unaffected by sawdust, or a drill press with its motor mounted high and away from the chips generated by the machine.

The second type, the totally enclosed fan-cooled (TEFC) motor, was originally developed for the metalworking industry where oil mist and metal chips are present. Its internal housing is completely closed (bottom left photo, next page) so that dirty air can't circulate through the inside of the motor. Since heat can be a problem for any motor, this type is cooled by both internal and external fans driven by the motor itself. The totally enclosed motor carries a slight price premium, but is an excellent choice for virtually all woodworking machines exposed to sawdust. Some debris will collect on the back of the fan cover, but routine housekeeping will keep this from causing trouble.

The third type of motor enclosure is the so-called hazardous location or explosion-proof. It looks like the TEFC type, but has tightly fitting seams and a rupture-proof casing to prevent internal explosions from igniting vapors or gases from combustible solvents or dusts outside the motor. Explosion-proof motors—UL-rated for Class 1, Group D applications—are the definitive choice for

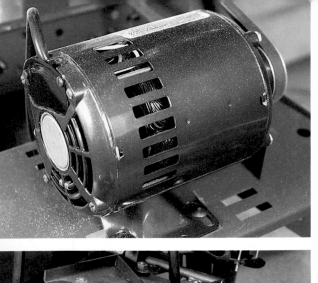

You can see the wire windings in the open drip-proof motor frame on top, while the totally enclosed, fan-cooled (TEFC) motor above is sealed tight to prevent the invasion of dust and grime. The TEFC motor uses both an internal and an external fan to circulate cooling air and dissipate harmful heat buildup.

Fig. 3: Motor identification plate

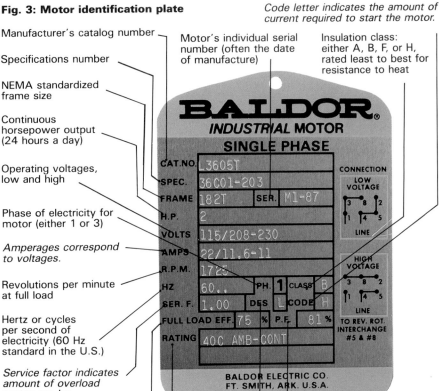

Code letter indicates the amount of current required to start the motor.

Manufacturer's catalog number

Specifications number

NEMA standardized frame size

Continuous horsepower output (24 hours a day)

Operating voltages, low and high

Phase of electricity for motor (either 1 or 3)

Amperages correspond to voltages.

Revolutions per minute at full load

Hertz or cycles per second of electricity (60 Hz standard in the U.S.)

Service factor indicates amount of overload motor can be expected to handle. For example, a motor with a service factor of 1.15 would have a 15% overload capacity.

Full-load efficiency— measures percentage of input power actually converted to work output.

Motor's individual serial number (often the date of manufacture)

Insulation class: either A, B, F, or H, rated least to best for resistance to heat

Design specification

Ambient temperature rating—maximum safe room temperature surrounding motor operating continuously at full load (40° Celsius/ 104° Fahrenheit in this case).

Power factor is percent measure of motor's requirements for magnetizing amperage.

spray-booth exhaust fans, where volatile fumes from woodworking finishes are encountered.

Frame size and mounting—When choosing a motor for a particular application, it's important that the physical characteristics of the motor fit the mounting situation. Fortunately, the frame sizes of modern electric motors have been standardized by the National Electrical Manufacturers Association (NEMA), so motors with the same size and power specifications made by different manufacturers are interchangeable. The frame number stamped on the information plate (see figure 3) is indexed to an extensive NEMA-compiled chart listing all motor dimensions and statistics, such as shaft diameter and housing size. Although the chart lists dozens of different frame sizes, most motors in the ⅓- to 5-HP range are either size number 56, 143, 145, 182 or 184.

The motor should be solidly attached to the stationary power tool's mounting plate to reduce any vibration a running motor and belt drive may produce. Better-quality machines have a cast iron, rather than pressed-steel, motor mount. A flimsy mounting plate can be reinforced with flat iron bars if necessary.

In addition to firm mounting, a motor needs well-aligned pulleys and the correct belts to deliver power effectively. Pulleys are made from either cast iron or zinc alloy, the former being more durable, the latter less expensive. These are almost always keyed to the motor shaft or arbor with a Woodruff or square key, then fixed with a setscrew. V-belts come in standard cross-sectional sizes. The most common are A-size and fractional horsepower

(FHP) belts, which are narrow, and wider B-size belts. Belts must be selected to match pulley width. The general rule is this: for low-torque, high-speed applications (such as jointers), smaller-section belts can be used; in high-torque applications—tablesaws, for instance—larger-section or multiple belts are required. If you're not sure about the length of the belt you need, an approximate length can be determined by adding twice the distance between the center of the motor and arbor shafts to half the sum of the circumference of the drive and driven pulleys (measured around the rims). Belt tensioning should strike a balance between too much, which places strain on the bearings, and too little, which allows belt slippage. Ideally, a belt should flex about ¹⁄₃₂ in. for every inch of span between pulleys when slight pressure is applied.

Motor controls—In addition to installing the motor correctly, single- and 3-phase motors 2 HP and larger should be protected with magnetic motor starters. Beside providing a regular on/off switch, this starter has a small heating element selected to match the amperage rating of the motor with which it's used. When heat generated from the current draw of the motor exceeds a certain threshold (lower than a temperature which would damage the motor), the element trips a thermal switch and shuts off the power. A magnetic starter has one additional safety advantage: if power in the shop suddenly quits, an electromagnet disconnects the starter in the switch; the motor stays off, even after the power is restored. To start the motor again, you have to deliberately switch it on.

Many single-phase motors are equipped with a built-in manual overload device that can be used with a separate on/off switch. The device adds a small amount to the cost of the motor, but provides substantial burnout protection. The device is normally mounted on the side or end of the motor housing and is designed to sense the motor's current load and internal temperature, as well as ambient air temperature. After excess heat or an overload trips the device, the operator must wait for the motor to cool off before resetting the button and putting the motor back to work.

I *strongly* urge woodworkers to avoid, at all costs, motors with built-in thermal protectors that automatically reset after an overload shutdown. These motors, often found on pumps and air conditioners, can be bought used at tempting prices. They look and work just like any induction motor, but the automatic resetting feature can have potentially disastrous consequences.

For motors under one HP, a fractional-horsepower manual motor starter (simply an on/off switch with a heating element) can provide thermal protection for a fraction of the cost of the magnetic type. These must, however, be manually turned off in the event of a power failure. Other small, low-amperage motors may be started with regular toggle switches as long as the voltage and amperage rating on the switch match the voltage and maximum current draw of the motor. Regardless of which type of motor or control you use, always make sure that the switch is connected to break continuity with the *hot* lead(s), not the neutral (see figure 2). Also, make sure the motor and switchbox are properly grounded.

Once you have your motor ready to plug in, consider what you're going to plug it into. An inadequate power supply will cause the voltage to drop and the wiring to heat up during heavy use. Sagging voltage dims the lights; more important, it causes motors to draw excessive current. Since voltage (the measure of electrical force or pressure) and amperage (the measure of electrical flow) are inversely related, a 10% voltage drop results in a 10% amperage increase. This diminishes motor performance, leading to overheating and a subsequent shortening of motor life. Even worse, overheated wires could ignite workshop sawdust and start a fire. It's fairly normal to see a slight flickering or momentary dimming of the lights when one of your larger machines is switched on. But if you notice this effect during routine operations, you probably need to consider upgrading

Understanding horsepower

Few shops these days employ the power of the hoof, but for the sake of evaluating electric motors, we've inherited the measure of horsepower established during the 1800s to compare the output of the steam engine to that of the horse. "Power" is defined as work per unit of time, and since the average workhorse can lift 33,000 pounds one foot in one minute, 33,000 foot-pounds per minute is the force equivalent to one horsepower.

Since induction motors run on electricity, it seems logical to determine their power output by figuring the amount of electricity they consume. If we calculate a motor's power consumption in terms of wattage—a measure of electrical power equal to voltage times amperage—the following formula should give us its horsepower:

$$\frac{\text{Amperage} \times \text{Voltage}}{746 \text{ (No. of watts in 1 HP)}} = \text{HP}$$

But, in practice, it doesn't work this way: a motor can't convert all of the electrical energy it uses into mechanical power. Some energy goes toward magnetizing the rotor and the windings. Power factor is a measure of this. Generally, the more powerful a motor, the higher its power factor. Also, a motor's full-load efficiency is the percentage of electrical input that's successfully converted into mechanical power. The rest is lost to friction, windage and electrical resistance. On new motors, efficiency and power factor are printed on the motor's nameplate (see figure 3).

As with motor design and construction, the National Electrical Manufacturers Association (NEMA) has standards for measuring and labeling motor output. These standards consider a motor's work capacity (stated as horsepower) and the allowable amount of temperature rise while peforming at that capacity. A motor's output must be tested by connecting it to a dynamometer, a mechanical device that measures torque. The horsepower is then determined with the formula:

$$\text{Horsepower} = \frac{\text{Torque (in ft. lb.)} \times \text{RPM}}{5,252 \text{ (constant)}}$$

As the motor is forced to run under full load at its rated horsepower capacity, the rise in its internal temperature is carefully measured. The amount of allowable temperature rise depends on the type of insulation used in the motor's windings. A motor with Class B insulation, for instance, is allowed to heat to 80°C or less above the specified 40°C standard ambient temperature of the air surrounding the running motor. If it gets any hotter, its full-load nameplate horsepower rating must be lowered, or the motor must be redesigned for better cooling.

NEMA's standards for induction motor horsepower are based on a motor's ability to deliver its nameplate rated power continuously, 24 hours a day, under full load. But these standards can also be qualified by time-duty ratings of 15 minutes, 30 minutes and 1 hour, each representing the period of time the motor can deliver its rated horsepower without overheating. A duty-limited motor will always be marked accordingly on its nameplate. Continuous-duty motors are commonly used on stationary woodworking machinery.

This capability, however, is rarely needed for machines, such as saws, jointers, or planers, which are seldom operated at continuous full load.

Machinery manufacturers aren't compelled to comply with NEMA's rating standards; they may devise their own methods for measuring the output of their motors. It's not unheard of for a tool manufacturer to take liberties with claimed horsepower ratings: the *same* motor design could be rated at its *continuous-duty horsepower* by one manufacturer and *peak power output* by another.

Any electric motor is capable of producing far greater than its continuous-rated power, if temperature rise is ignored. A 3-HP motor, for example, can generate up to 7 HP for short time periods. Beyond that, it reaches its pullout or breakdown point and stalls, just like an airplane attempting an overly steep climb. If you don't cut the power or reduce the load, the motor will overheat and burn up.

On inexpensive tools that have induction motors of questionable pedigree, watch out for the words "maximum developed horsepower," which is advertising talk for a motor whose claimed output is right up near its pullout point. You can't operate the motor for very long at its maximum output without thermally damaging the motor. Some small induction motors rated at $2\frac{7}{8}$ maximum developed horsepower perform more like 1-HP continuous-duty motors. Furthermore, never mix apples with oranges and attempt to compare a machine rated in continuous-duty horsepower to a machine rated in maximum developed horsepower. *E.H.C.*

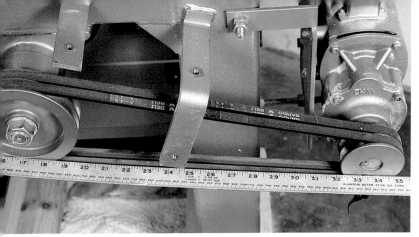

Proper alignment of pulleys, essential to good machine performance, can be checked with a straightedge. Multiple belts are used on this resaw bandsaw to handle high torque.

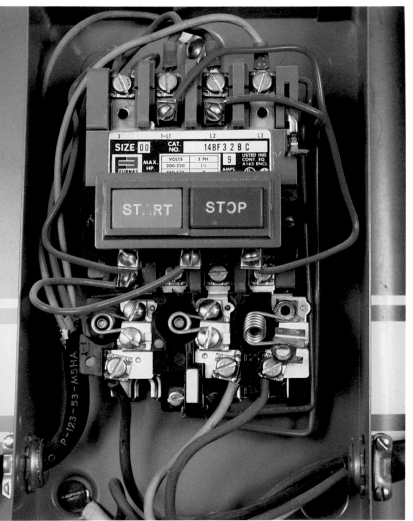

With the power off and cover plate removed, you can see the three coil-like heating elements inside this three-phase magnetic motor starter, located below the start and stop buttons. The element on the right has been partially removed to afford a better view.

Fig. 4: Table of wire gauges

		Length of circuit wiring or extension cord			
		25 ft.	50 ft.	100 ft.	150 ft.
Amperage rating of single-phase motor, 110v or 220v	5	14 ga.	14 ga.	12 ga.	10 ga.
	8	14 ga.	14 ga.	12 ga.	10 ga.
	10	14 ga.	14 ga.	12 ga.	10 ga.
	15	14 ga.	12 ga.	12 ga.	10 ga.
	20	12 ga.	10 ga.	8 ga.	8 ga.
	30	8 ga.	8 ga.	8 ga.	6 ga.

your shop power system. If the machine is a considerable distance from the power panel or plug, use heavier-gauge wire (see figure 4) to avoid voltage drop. This applies to extension cords for portable power tools as well.

Maintenance—Thanks to modern ball bearings, most electric motors require little maintenance. In fact, sealed bearings usually need to be replaced by the time they need lubrication. Too much well-intended maintenance can be damaging; motor bearings are more likely to fail from too much (or incompatible) lubrication than they are from lack of lubrication. If you're in doubt about whether or not to lubricate, *don't.* However, this advice doesn't apply to older motors with bronze sleeve bearings. The oil cups on these motors should be filled with high-grade SAE 10 to 20 non-detergent machine oil (don't substitute plain motor oil), always with the motor shut off. Over-lubrication won't hurt these bearings.

One regular maintenance habit will extend a motor's life: vacuuming the sawdust out of cooling passageways in the motor housing. To reduce the hazard of fire, clean out electrical junction boxes and switchboxes occasionally, cutting off the power first.

Troubleshooting—Unfortunately, there are no simple tests to determine the internal condition of a motor. In capacitor-start motors, centrifugal switch or capacitor failures are common faults. Switches wear out, burn or stick in one position. Capacitors can open, short out or change value. Whether a starter switch or capacitor fails, the result is the same: the motor hums but won't start. You can sometimes temporarily get the motor going with a quick hand turn of the pulley. But use extreme caution in doing so, and keep your hands clear of blades or cutters. When the starter switch fails to open, the motor will come up to speed but will draw excessive current (amperes) and overheat quickly. If the starting capacitor changes value as it becomes weak, the motor will be slow in starting and won't come up to speed as quickly as it should. Low line voltage caused by wire that's too small can produce the same symptoms.

Failure to react to any of these indications can lead to a complete motor meltdown, where the heat that builds up from an overload or component failure causes windings to overheat, burn off their insulation and short out. Do *not* continue to operate any motor on a machine or power tool when erratic performance or unusual noise is evident. Things will only get worse—and repairs more expensive—if problems are ignored, since capacitor or centrifugal switches can be replaced at a fraction of the cost of rebuilding or replacing the motor.

If you do burn out a standard-size single-phase or three-phase induction motor, it's usually quicker—and cheaper—to replace rather than rebuild it. But if the motor has a special mounting or isn't of a frame size or type carried by your local distributor, you may have no choice but to pay for a rebuild by a local motor repair shop. □

Ed Cowern is an electrical engineer and president of a company that distributes electric motors. For information on how electric motors are rated, contact the National Electrical Manufacturers Association, 2121 L St. N.W., Washington, D.C. 20037.

Further reading

How Electric Motors Start and Run by Harold Parady and Howard Turner and *Electric Motors* by James Allison are available from the American Association for Vocational Instructional Materials, 120 Engineering Center, Athens, GA 30602.

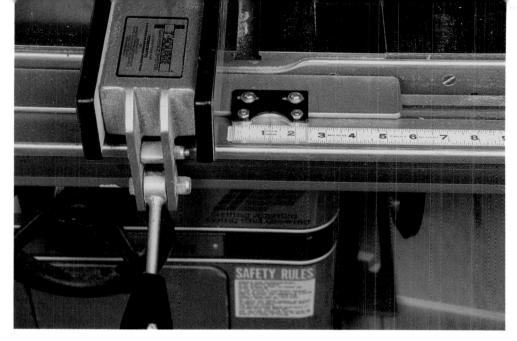

Features that are built into most aftermarket rip fences, like the cam-action lever, hairline cursor and built-in tape measure on this Biesemeyer T-Square saw fence, provide fast, accurate means of one-handed setting and locking.

Replacement Rip Fences
Bolting new precision to your old tablesaw

by Sandor Nagyszalanczy

What are the hallmarks of a good tablesaw? Things like a true-running arbor and well-machined castings come to mind, but it's very easy to overlook the rip fence. Even relatively expensive tablesaws come with stock fences that aren't up to the same standards of design and quality built into the rest of the saw. Most stock fences have limited rip capacity, are cumbersome to set, are inaccurate and tend to drift out of parallel with the sawblade. Ripping on an otherwise great tablesaw equipped with a second-rate fence is like driving a Ferrari with bicycle tires—you can never realize the full potential of the machine.

Having recognized this, at least five manufacturers have developed high-quality, large-capacity replacement rip fences that they claim will cure the ills of a stock fence. For prices ranging from $242 to $425, you can bolt one of these aftermarket fences directly to your stock tablesaw just as you might install high-performance parts to soup up a stock automobile. But do these fences live up to the ad-copy claims and are they worth the money? I answered that question for myself two years ago, at least partially, when I bought a Paralok fence for my old Boice-Crane tablesaw. It worked beautifully and made ripping on the saw a real pleasure. But I wondered how well the other brands worked, so last summer I borrowed and installed fences made by Vega Enterprises and Excalibur and spent some time using saws equipped with the Biesemeyer T-Square saw fence system and the Delta Unifence. To back up my research, I interviewed owners of some of these fences.

Before I discuss my impressions of these replacement fences, however, it's worth explaining the problems each is intended to solve. Probably the chief shortcoming of most stock fences—even

the better ones—is that they don't maintain parallel with the sawblade when locked down, either because the rip rails are misaligned or because of slop in the locking mechanism. This can sometimes cause the fence to toe in toward the back of the blade, binding the cut and burning the wood, or worse, causing a violent kickback. For the same reason, an out-of-parallel cut aggravates splinter and tearout when ripping plywood. All of the aftermarket fences go a long way toward correcting this, in fact, it's a major selling point, along with improved locking mechanisms that *keep* the fence parallel once it's set.

If you work much with 4x8 sheets of plywood, you know that a stock tablesaw's ripping ability is sharply limited by both its short rails and the lack of a large, stable surface to safely support a heavy panel. Replacement fences offer vast improvement: All of them have rails long enough to allow crosscutting to the center of a 4x8 sheet and can be fitted with extension tables on the right side of the blade. In addition, aftermarket fences have various other features, the nicest being built-in tape measures that allow setting rip width without tedious measuring. Between the five of them, there's a replacement fence to fit most common tablesaws, not to mention some worthy antiques like my 45-year-old Boice-Crane. Before buying, however, check your application with the manufacturer or dealer, just to be sure.

The Biesemeyer fence—Woodworkers, professional and amateur, owe a debt of gratitude to Bill Biesemeyer, who introduced the first affordable, accurate rip fence nearly a decade ago. Biesemeyer, a cabinetmaker and boatbuilder for 35 years, became thoroughly disgusted with stock tablesaw fences and decided to manufacture his

From *Fine Woodworking* magazine (January 1988) 68:41-45

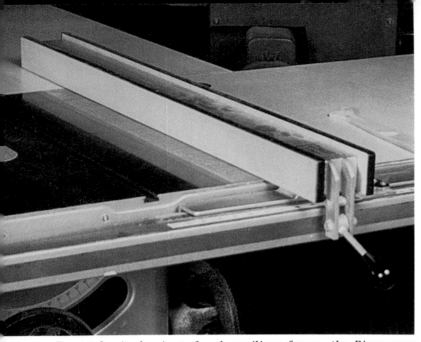

Except for its laminate-faced auxiliary fences, the Biesemeyer fence is built entirely of steel and is an available option on the Powermatic model 66, shown here.

The Vega fence has two locking levers: The smaller on the right sets the micro-adjusting mechanism, while the larger lever locks the fence to the rail. Vega's Finger Saver combines a push stick and a cut-off stop in a carriage that slides atop the fence bar.

own. His fence has been much imitated and serves as a point of departure for other manufacturers, but it was the pioneer in the field. And, at $299 for the model 50, it's the second cheapest.

As its name implies, the Biesemeyer fence works much like a draftsman's T-square: with the fence as the square's blade and a chunk of steel angle iron as the head. This angle-iron head rides on a beefy rail made of square steel tubing, which bolts solidly into the front of the saw table. The fence bar itself, also made of tubular steel, is faced on both sides with laminate-covered plywood, a good safety feature. Unlike most stock fences, the Biesemeyer fence locks *only on the front rail*. Because of this, you'd think that the end of the fence, way out there on a 42-in.-long lever arm, would deflect. But from what I can tell, it's more than able to sustain a good whack from a mishandled sheet of plywood. This is so, I suspect, because of the Biesemeyer fence's robust construction: It's the only one made almost entirely of steel, which gives it a solid, albeit heavy feeling compared to the others.

The Biesemeyer fence's locking mechanism—a handle welded to an eccentric cam—presses hard against the guide rail, locking the fence firmly where it's set. Unlocked, the fence can be slid along the rail for adjustment or lifted off entirely. The fence doesn't stay parallel with the blade during adjustment, but it snaps into line when the lever is locked. The fence bar is adjusted for parallel by a pair of setscrews on the crossbar. This requires a little trial and error, since the fence must be removed to get at the screws. But once set, it seems to stay in alignment, according to Frank Klausz, a cabinetmaker in New Jersey who let me try out one of the two Biesemeyer fences he owns.

Klausz is very pleased with the Biesemeyer fences he uses in his shop, but reports two minor frustrations. The holes bored in the rails of his Biesemeyer fence, sold as a special edition to match the Powermatic model 66 saw he'd bought, didn't align with those in the saw table. Biesemeyer says this has since been remedied. Klausz's other gripe is that his Ripstrate, a wheeled, hold-down device that holds the wood against the fence, doesn't work because the downward pressure it exerts on the stock lifts the back end of the fence bar. Although I didn't install the model 50 myself, the instruction manual is clear and well illustrated.

The Biesemeyer fence's rip width is set by aligning a hairline cursor scribed on a clear plastic window over a tape glued to the guide rail. The window is adjustable so it's possible to zero the fence against the blade. It's very accurate, too. I found the ripped piece was within ⅟₆₄ in. of where I set the cursor.

The long guide rail allows rips 50 in. to the right of the blade and 6 in. to the left, and must be used with an extension table to support long crosscuts. To strengthen the connection between the saw and table, there's an angle-iron rear rail included. Biesemeyer offers a full line of ready-made extension tables, other fence models with longer rails, as well as a less-expensive version of the Biesemeyer fence that's for home-shop use. Also, Biesemeyer will adapt to fit an old or odd saw at no extra charge. If such personalized service seems unusual, it stems from Biesemeyer's almost evangelical belief in his product: It's his goal to get his fence into every shop in America.

The Vega model 50—Although not as well known as Delta or Powermatic, Vega Enterprises of Decatur, Ill., makes a full line of stationary power tools, including a replacement fence that retails for $242.50. The Vega is designed to fit 10-in. saws made by Delta, Powermatic, Jet and Sears, although some saw-table drilling may be necessary on older saws. The model 50 comes with rails long enough for cutting 50 in. to the right and

9 in. to the left of the blade. Like the Biesemeyer fence, the Vega has a 42-in.-long fence bar, though a 50-in. fence and longer rails are available.

It took me less than an hour to install the Vega on a Delta Unisaw. Like the Biesemeyer, the Vega stays parallel and resists deflection by relying on a beefy front rail and a cam-actuated locking mechanism. The rip rail is round instead of square, and there's a back rail too, but the fence only rides on it, without locking. The front rip rail mounts to the saw through two very heavy cast brackets whose holes are slotted to allow the rail side-to-side adjustment. Each bracket also has a jacking-plate screw mechanism, which allows fine adjustment of the clearance between the fence bar and saw table. I was impressed that the Vega came with all the hardware I needed—even two fine-thread, ⅜-in. bolts to attach the rear rail directly to the tapped holes on the back of the Unisaw.

Since the fence can ride on the full-length back rail, you don't have to make an extension table, but I'd recommend one anyway. Otherwise, thin plywood or plastic laminate would slip under the fence when it was extended beyond the saw table. The fence bar attaches to the solid cast-alloy head with four Allen-head bolts that must be torqued down with some force, because they're all that keeps the fence bar aligned. To aid the tightening, Vega includes a cheater bar that fits an Allen wrench, also provided.

Despite similarities between the Vega and the Biesemeyer fences, they feel distinctly different to use. I liked the Vega's lightweight aluminum fence bar, which requires less force to move than the heavier Biesemeyer fence. Still, the bar feels stiff enough to take a good sideward jolt, and seems to stay put once it's locked down.

Although similar to the Biesemeyer fence, the thing I least liked about the Vega is locking it. When the lever is pressed down, the fence pivots around the round rip rail, causing the back of the fence to rise only to clunk down again when the lever is released. Fortunately, Vega is now including a rear hold-down as standard equipment with the model 50. It slides on the rear rail, keeping the far end of the bar down and allowing the use of spring-loaded hold-downs on the bar.

Besides the usual cursor and tape arrangement, the Vega has a micro-adjustment device for fine-tuning the rip width. This works via a second locking lever that holds part of the carriage in place while you fine-tune the fence position with an adjustment wheel on a threaded shaft. This feature isn't necessary for setting rip width, but it is an excellent aid in fine-tuning the fence position if you're using the fence as a cut-off stop for sawing tenon shoulders. The Vega's cursor window magnifies the tape, which I found hard to use—it overmagnified and I couldn't clearly distinguish the scale marks on the measuring tape. Fortunately, Vega now provides an extra non-magnifying cursor.

An optional accessory for the Vega is a safety device called a Finger Saver. It's a wheeled push stick that rides up and down the fence bar on rollers held captive by rails that are part of the extruded aluminum bar. You grip the Finger Saver's plastic handle on top and a little replaceable wooden stick pivots down to push any thin stock you're ripping past the blade. I find this a welcome innovation—a push stick attached to the saw means you're more likely to use it and not your fingers. The Finger Saver also has a flip-down stop intended for cut-off work with the tablesaw's miter gauge. It's optional and costs $22.50. If you don't want the fence, Vega will still sell you a Finger Saver and a rail kit that will mount to other brands of fences.

The fence bar on Delta's Unifence slides forward and back, and can be dropped all the way down to the saw's table so thin laminates won't sneak underneath during cutting.

The Unifence—It's nice to see that at least one tablesaw manufacturer, Delta International, makes a high-quality rip fence for its own saw. The Unifence is a vast improvement over the age-old Jet Lock design that's still standard equipment on most Delta saws. The Unifence is designed to be a companion to the Unisaw or any of Delta's 10-in. saws, but it's also sold separately and, with a little drilling, will fit just about any other tablesaw. At $425, the Unifence is the most expensive fence I tested. Its rail allows a 51-in. ripping capacity right and 8¾ in. left of the blade.

Like the Biesemeyer fence, the Unifence is a front-rail-only fence, which, incidentally, allows you to use a flush-fitting out-feed table, so thin stock can't slip under the out-feed table as it comes off the saw table. But its unique fence bar, body, and rail distinguish it from the other front-locking fences.

The nicest feature of the Unifence, in my opinion, is the fence bar itself. It's a complex aluminum extrusion that, in addition to being entirely removable, is shaped so it can be mounted in the fence body in either of two positions. A high fence position (3½ in. high) is for general ripping, while a low position presents a ½-in. surface to the work, allowing you to cut laminated or veneered panels to size without having to pre-trim one edge. The overhanging-surplus laminate on both sides of the panel runs wild above and below the thin fence bar, which contacts only the center core material. This feature is bound to be handy for a shop that does a lot of commercial cabinetwork. There are two cursor hairlines, one for each fence bar position.

Two plastic thumb screws lock the aluminum bar to the fence body and adjust the bar's up-and-down motion. You can drop it dead to the table for cutting very thin stock or laminate, which might otherwise slide under. The Unifence's standard bar is 43-in. long, but for crosscutting, Delta makes a special 10½-in.-long cut-off fence (part no. 34-878). This bar acts as a stop for repetitive cuts, providing clearance behind the blade to keep cut-off scraps from binding and being hurled away.

As much as I liked the versatility of the Delta's fence-bar design, I found a couple of shortcomings. To rip to the left of the blade, the entire fence bar and locking mechanism must be removed and flipped around, quite a hassle if you need to do it often. Also, the Unifence's extruded bar has an odd shape that doesn't seem thick enough to drill and tap threads into. It also would be awkward to bolt through it to attach an auxiliary face to the bar—not to mention hold-down devices or other fixtures.

I didn't install the Unifence, but I learned from Paul Levine, a Connecticut cabinetmaker, that it takes about 45 minutes, including installation of the extension table. Delta, by the way, is the only manufacturer who provides a steel frame, legs, and mounting hardware for an extension table. You can buy their plywood tabletop (part no. 34-998), or make your own. After making do with a second-rate fence for years, Levine was so eager to get a Unifence that he forgot to check if the longer rails would fit inside his small shop. They didn't. He had to wait until larger quarters were available to set up the new fence. Keep this in mind if your floor space is limited, regardless of which fence interests you.

I found the Unifence quick to set and lock, although the locking bar, which is captured in a channel in the front rail, would bind occasionally and I'd have to push in on the fence to free it. Levine says he keeps the saw running when setting the fence, using its vibration to keep the bar from binding as he moves it. The measuring tape is glued to a part of the rip rail that slopes toward the operator, making it easier to see and less likely to accumulate sawdust. Adjusting the Unifence for parallel is the simplest of all the front-locking fences. The two adjusting screws are on the front of the fence body, where they're easy to get at.

From my own trials and Levine's two years of experience with the Unifence, I'd say it's a well-built, accurate piece of equipment. You really can keep your tape measure in your pocket and rely on the fence's built-in measuring system.

The Excalibur—The newest replacement fence to come on the market is the Excalibur T-Slot. It's manufactured in Canada and distributed by J. Philip Humfrey, who also sells the General line of woodworking machines. At the outset, the Excalibur's slick appearance contrasted sharply with the utilitarian looks of the Biesemeyer fence and Vega fence. But the difference is more than cosmetic. The Excalibur's design is quite different from the others, in that it locks to both the front and back rails.

At $325 (including delivery from Canada), the Excalibur's capacities are similar to the other fences: Its 78-in. rails allow 50-in. ripping to the right of the blade and 12 in. to the left. The fence bar itself, a complex aluminum extrusion with two open slots on top, is 45 in. long, which carried it well out past the back edge of the Unisaw I had installed it on. The extra length would be handy if you wanted to add an out-feed table behind the saw. The Excalibur's front rip rail is made of steel channel iron that's been slightly overbent, resulting in a downwardly sloping top surface that sheds sawdust and chips that might hinder the movement of the fence or obscure the measuring tape.

For smoothness of travel along the rails, the Excalibur is a walk-away winner. This is because it doesn't just sit atop the rails, as the other fences do, but rides on three aluminum rollers, one at the rear and two at the front. These rollers, which are on spring-loaded axles, track along the edge of the rip rails, allowing the fence to glide along like a runaway roller skate. In fact, it's almost too smooth. I kept wanting to push against a little resistance as I brought the cursor to the mark and locked the handle down. Locking is accomplished by a cam-action handle that pulls against the rear roller, collapsing the front roller's springs and seating the fence crossbar against the rip rail. Lifting the handle to the horizontal position frees the fence to roll, and moving it to the vertical position allows it to be removed. An adjustment nut at the back end of the fence can be turned to position the rear roller, adapting the fence bar to tablesaws up to 33 in. deep. An optional bar goes to 45 in. deep.

Because the Excalibur locks by pulling in against the rip rails, the rails must be *firmly* seated and parallel within 1/16 in. along their entire length. It may take some shimming of the rails and fussing with the fence adjustment before the fence will travel smoothly and lock reliably.

A lot of thought has gone into accessories for this fence. The fence bar has two T-slots along its top designed to accept an entire line of accessories, including a push stick device similar to the Vega, a wheeled hold-down, anti-kickback attachments, and even an adjustable auxiliary fence for use with a router mounted in the extension table. Excalibur also has a router table mounting kit with a pivoting baseplate that fits most routers. Humfrey says more jigs and accessories will be available in the future.

The Paralok—Manufactured by Quintec Mfg. in Portland, Ore., the Paralok is the replacement rip fence that's most different in design from the others. It's also the one I've had the most experience with. It sells for $350 retail, plus shipping. By way of another drafting analogy, the Paralok fence works like a parallel straightedge on a drafting table: Cables guided by small pulleys maintain the fence's parallelism with the blade while allowing it to move back and forth freely along a pair of angle-iron rip rails bolted to the front and back of the saw (see photo facing page).

Installing a Paralok involves much more than the other fences. So

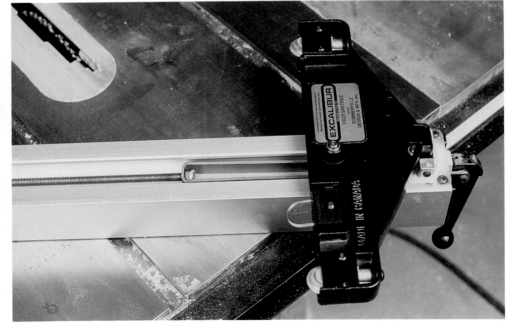

Above: The sloping top surfaces on the guide rails of the Excalibur fence prevent the accumulation of sawdust. Right: A view of the underside of the Excalibur fence shows the two front guide rollers, each held in its clevis and spring-loaded.

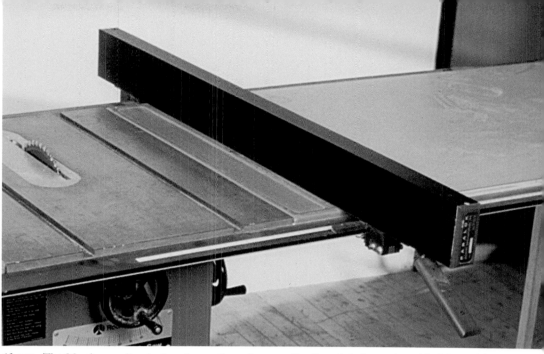

Above: The black-anodized aluminum fence bar on the Paralok fence is guided by cables that run through pulleys underneath the guide bars. It's one of two fences (the other is the Excalibur) that locks both in front and back. Left: Aircraft-type cables cross under the saw table at the far right instead of in the middle, as on a drafting table.

the fence will fit any saw, the rails come sans mounting holes. Thus, you have to position them, bore the holes and mount them with your own fasteners. The standard 72-in. rails give a rip capacity of 53 in. to the right of the blade and 13 in. to the left, but stock rails from 48 in. to 104 in. are available. Threading the cable through all the pulleys was a challenge and I'd recommend commandeering a helper to aid in this task. The cable meets at a splice block and tightens with a sliding nut at the front-end pulley. You'd think that the steel cable would stretch or break and become the fence's weak link, but it's very strong and I haven't had to tighten or adjust it since I installed it 2½ years ago.

The fence bar requires some assembly, including bolting on two rail-like feet the fence rides on. These can be shimmed to adjust the fence at a right angle to the saw table if necessary. The fence attaches to the cable with two cable blocks that slip into U-shaped cleats on the underside of the fence bar, front and rear. While this isn't difficult, if you need to take the fence off the saw often, the Paralok is harder to remove than any of the other fences. It can, however, be reversed on the rails—a neat trick that also works with the Excalibur. Use it with a router in the extension table and another measuring tape on the back rail. The parallelism of the fence is adjusted by moving one of the cable blocks until the bar is parallel, then locking it with a setscrew. Fine cable adjustments are made with sliding pulleys at the ends of the rails.

The cables seem to keep the fence constantly parallel so it glides along smoothly rather than bumping and skewing, as the Biesemeyer fence and Unifence seemed to do. Like the Excalibur, the Paralok locks at both ends, but instead of pulling in against the rails, it clamps down on them individually, so it's not important that the rails be perfectly parallel. A vernier scale on the Paralok's cursor allows setting it to extremely fine settings—Quintec claims the fence is accurate to within a 0.002-in. tolerance, but I've never needed the vernier scale to set the fence to the ¹⁄₆₄-in. tolerances I typically work to.

One minor complaint I have about the Paralok, other than the skimpy installation guide (Quintec says they're preparing an improved version), is that the wide rails accumulate sawdust that obscures the measuring scale. But a whisk broom keeps this from being a problem.

Which fence to choose?—All five fences are thoughtfully designed and well-made products that promise a huge improvement over stock rip fences, so the question may be not so much *which* fence, but whether to buy one or not. If you use your tablesaw constantly or saw sheet stock regularly, a replacement fence will make the job much more pleasurable. The time you save in measuring alone will make it worthwhile. If price is most important, the Vega is a solid, full-featured fence with useful accessories at the lowest price. If you do production laminate work and panel trimming, the Unifence's unique two-position fence bar might be worth its high price. The Biesemeyer fence, on the other hand, is an all-purpose, heavy-duty workhorse with nearly a decade of field trial, and it's often available at a discount price when purchased with a new saw.

If I add up points for overall features, though, the Excalibur comes out first for its smooth-as-silk roller suspension system, ease of operation, assortment of accessories, and quality for the money. I'd still be concerned about the rails requiring a lot of shimming to get them accurately mated to the edges of the saw—especially mounting it to a cheap saw with a rickety extension table. The Paralok is a close second and my personal favorite, perhaps because I've used it for so long. Despite the involved setup, I like the Paralok's solid front and back locking mechanisms and the positive parallelism of its cable system. And for my tastes, it has the best locking action and most easily read cursor. □

Sandor Nagyszalanczy is an assistant editor of Fine Woodworking. *Wayne Wilkerson of Houston, Tex., contributed to the report on the Vega fence.*

Sources of supply

Biesemeyer T-Square saw fence system: Biesemeyer, the T-Square saw fence co., 216 S. Alma School Road. Suite 3, Mesa, AZ 85202.
Vega Saw Fence: Vega Enterprises Inc., Route 3, Box 193, Decatur, IL 62526.
Unifence: Delta International, 246 Alpha Drive, Pittsburgh, PA 15238.
Excalibur T-Slot: J. Philip Humfrey International Inc., 3241 Kennedy Rd., Unit #7, Scarborough, Ont. M1V 2J9.
Paralok: Quintec Mfg. 5128 N.E. 42 Ave., Portland, OR 97218.

A Shop-Built Rip Fence

Aluminum construction requires no welding

by Marshall R. Young

I've had 50 years of experience with both home-shop and industrial-quality tablesaws equipped with fences that lock to both the front and the back rails. I've found that these fences generally did not achieve the accuracy and setting consistency that is possible with a fence that references and locks to the front rail only. I decided to design a saw fence for my Canadian-made Beaver tablesaw that's simple to make and costs less than $100 to build. Although my fence was inspired by the well-known Biesemeyer T-Square saw fence system, there are significant design and construction differences.

The fence consists of an aluminum fence bar bolted to a crossmember that aligns and locks the fence to a single guide rail. The crossbar has a measurement cursor that aligns with a tape stuck to the rail below it, allowing the fence to be set to precise rip widths. The fence locks to the rail when a locking bolt pulls a locking bar tight against the inside of the steel channel rail.

The fence is bolted together, so no welding is required. The only metalworking tools you'll need are a set of high-speed drills, a set of taps, a hacksaw and a file. Aside from a few steel parts, most of the fence is made of aluminum, which cuts and machines nicely with regular woodworking tools. A 60- to 80-tooth carbide tablesaw blade is best for cutting the aluminum—which should be cut slowly, to avoid kickback—but a bandsaw with a fine-tooth blade, lubricated with a silicone stick, is fine. In either case, wear eye protection.

The steel front channel is available from electrical or mechanical contractor supply houses. Be sure to get the heavy duty channel, such as 1⅝-in. Unistrut, P-1000 (for local source, call Unistrut Building Systems, 35660 Clinton, Wayne, Mich. 48184; 313-721-4040). Drill holes in the channel to match those in the front edge of your tablesaw and extension table. Bolt the rail ½ in. below the table's surface so it'll clear the miter slots and allow room for the cursor assembly. I made the guide rail on my saw 51 in. long, but it can be made any length to fit other tablesaws and applications. For the rest of the fence's part sizes, refer to the dimensions given in the drawing.

I cut the aluminum-channel fence bar slightly longer than the saw table's depth. If you're planning on cutting plywood, you'll want the bar to extend beyond the front and back edges of the saw table. Drill two holes through the channel for the cursor bar to be bolted on later. I bolted auxiliary fences made from Baltic-birch plywood to each side of the fence bar by drilling and tapping ¼-20 holes in the bar and countersinking the screw heads into the ½-in. plywood. Avoid putting the screws near the blade area. Seal the plywood with Watco oil, then several coats of wax. With epoxy, glue a piece of plastic laminate to act as a glide where the

underside of the fence bar will ride near the saw top's back edge.

Cut a piece of aluminum angle for the crossbar so it's about one-third the length of your fence bar. Using ³⁄₁₆-in. pop rivets, attach a ¼-in.-thick flat aluminum bar to the face of the angle to act as a spacer between the crossbar and locking bar. Cut the steel locking bar that will ride inside the guide rail and drill a ½-in. hole threaded with a ½-13 tap in the center of it. Next, drill a ½-in. hole through the center of the angle and spacer for the locking screw. Construct the locking screw assembly as shown in the side view. Finally, square up the crossbar to the fence bar with a framing square and clamp them together. Drill and tap a ²³⁄₆₄-in. hole for a ⅜-16 pivot bolt and two ⁷⁄₁₆-in. holes for the locking bolts. The oversized holes for the locking bolts allow the bar's angle to be adjusted. Use self-locking nuts and washers to keep the locking bolts from coming loose and ruining the accuracy of the fence.

Cut a notch in the aluminum cursor bar, and drill and tap two holes for 10-32 machine screws that match the position of the holes you drilled in the fence bar earlier. Screw the cursor bar in place. Cut a Plexiglas window and mount it to the cursor bar with machine screws through slotted holes in the bar to allow adjustment. Make sure the slot closest to the bar clears the auxiliary fence. Scribe a hairline in the center of the plastic and fill it with colored wax or ink. An adhesive-backed steel measuring tape (available from Garrett Wade Co. Inc.) is stuck down to the top of the rail below the cursor. Peel off a few inches of the backing paper and stick it down so the cursor will read zero when the fence is up against the blade. Then peel and stick a few inches at a time until you've gone the length of the rail.

Slide the fence on the guide rail from one end to see that it operates smoothly. The bar should lock without too much tightening of the locking knob. Set the fence parallel with the saw table, which should be parallel to the blade, by measuring to the miter slot at the front and back edges of the bar. Adjust the angle of the bar and lock it in place by torquing the two locking bolts. To ease the friction of the fence sliding on the rail, rub a coating of paraffin on all bearing surfaces.

The dimensions I've given here are fine for a small saw like the 8-in. Beaver, but you might wish to increase the size of the fence and dimensions of components on larger saws. You can count on it taking about 20 hours to build your custom fence, but consider your construction time an investment in improving the precision and enjoyment of your tablesaw. □

Marshall R. Young is a retired electrical contractor and part-time woodworker and machinist. He also teaches woodworking at Sunrise Shop in Victoria, B.C. Photo by author.

From *Fine Woodworking* magazine (January 1988) 68:46-47

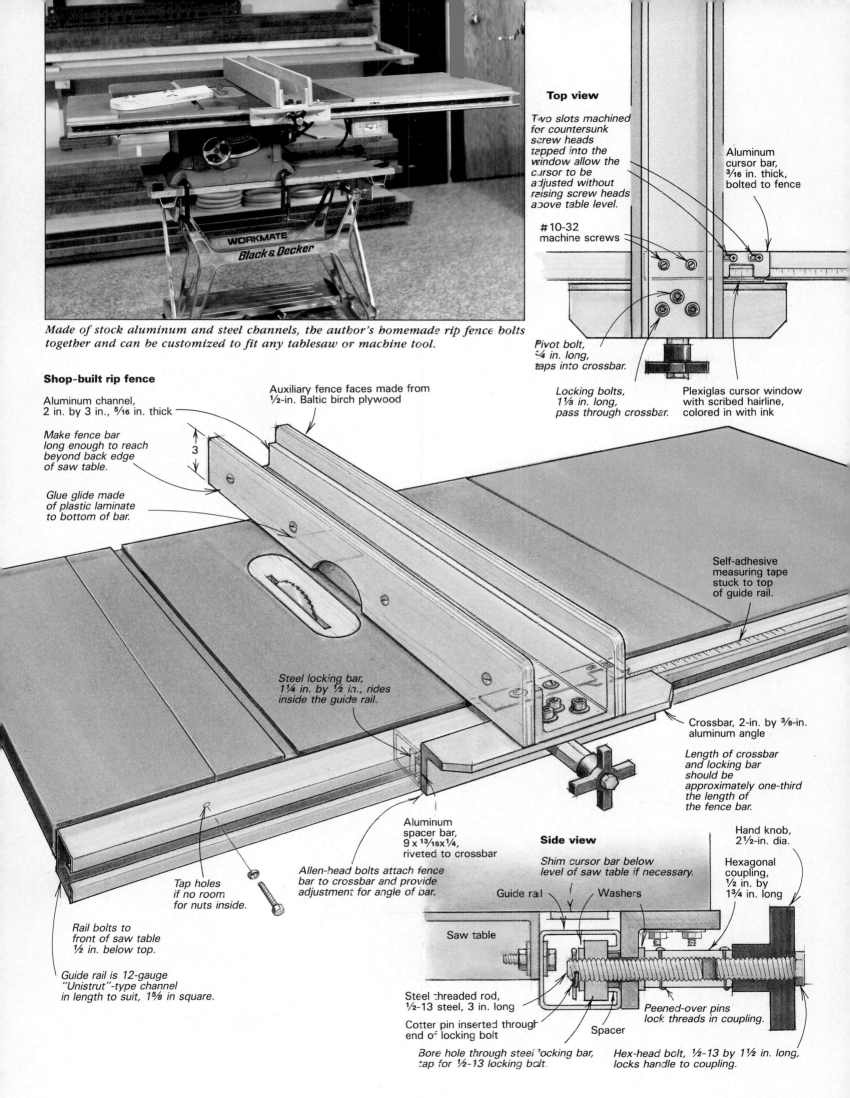

Made of stock aluminum and steel channels, the author's homemade rip fence bolts together and can be customized to fit any tablesaw or machine tool.

Top view

Two slots machined for countersunk screw heads tapped into the window allow the cursor to be adjusted without raising screw heads above table level.

#10-32 machine screws

Aluminum cursor bar, 3/16 in. thick, bolted to fence

Pivot bolt, 3/4 in. long, taps into crossbar.

Locking bolts, 1 1/8 in. long, pass through crossbar.

Plexiglas cursor window with scribed hairline, colored in with ink

Shop-built rip fence

Aluminum channel, 2 in. by 3 in., 5/16 in. thick

Make fence bar long enough to reach beyond back edge of saw table.

Glue glide made of plastic laminate to bottom of bar.

Auxiliary fence faces made from 1/2-in. Baltic birch plywood

3

Self-adhesive measuring tape stuck to top of guide rail.

Steel locking bar, 1 1/4 in. by 1/2 in., rides inside the guide rail.

Crossbar, 2-in. by 3/8-in. aluminum angle

Length of crossbar and locking bar should be approximately one-third the length of the fence bar.

Tap holes if no room for nuts inside.

Aluminum spacer bar, 9 x 13/16 x 1/4, riveted to crossbar

Allen-head bolts attach fence bar to crossbar and provide adjustment for angle of bar.

Rail bolts to front of saw table 1/2 in. below top.

Guide rail is 12-gauge "Unistrut"-type channel in length to suit, 1 5/8 in square.

Side view

Shim cursor bar below level of saw table if necessary.

Guide rail   Washers

Saw table

Hand knob, 2 1/2-in. dia.

Hexagonal coupling, 1/2 in. by 1 3/4 in. long

Steel threaded rod, 1/2-13 steel, 3 in. long

Cotter pin inserted through end of locking bolt

Spacer

Peened-over pins lock threads in coupling.

Bore hole through steel locking bar, tap for 1/2-13 locking bolt.

Hex-head bolt, 1/2-13 by 1 1/2 in. long, locks handle to coupling.

Making a Panel Saw

Sears saw serves as the basic machine

by Larry Kellam

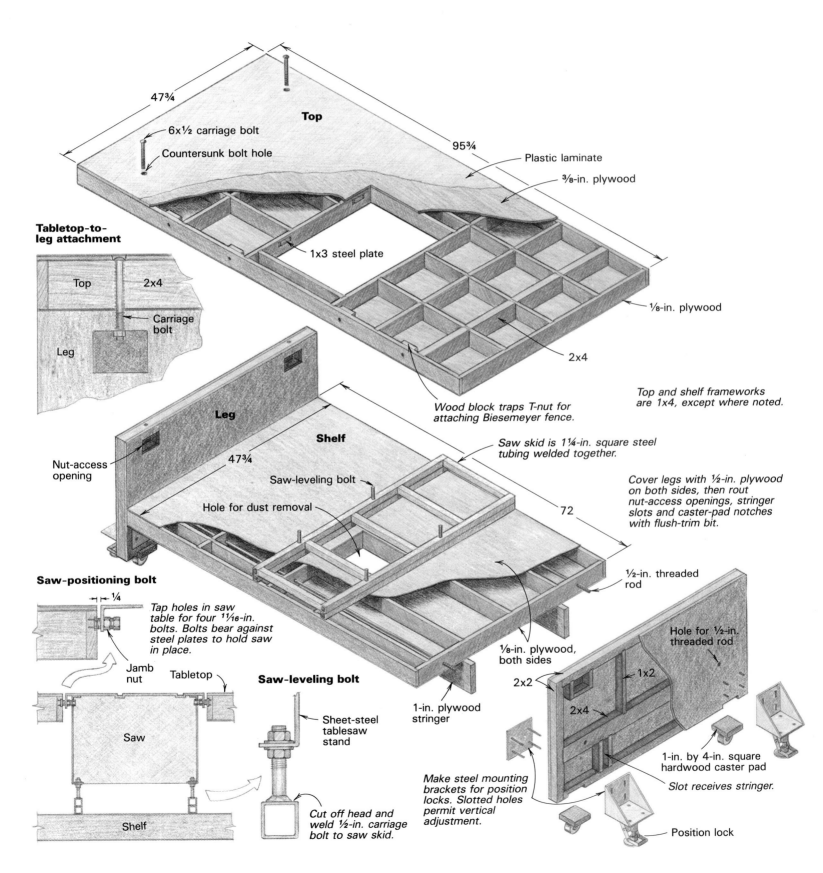

Top

47¾

6x½ carriage bolt

Countersunk bolt hole

95¾

Plastic laminate

⅜-in. plywood

1x3 steel plate

⅛-in. plywood

2x4

Tabletop-to-leg attachment

Top

2x4

Carriage bolt

Leg

Wood block traps T-nut for attaching Biesemeyer fence.

Top and shelf frameworks are 1x4, except where noted.

Leg

Shelf

Nut-access opening

47¾

Saw-leveling bolt

Hole for dust removal

Saw skid is 1¼-in. square steel tubing welded together.

Cover legs with ½-in. plywood on both sides, then rout nut-access openings, stringer slots and caster-pad notches with flush-trim bit.

72

½-in. threaded rod

Saw-positioning bolt

¼

Tap holes in saw table for four ¹¹⁄₁₆-in. bolts. Bolts bear against steel plates to hold saw in place.

Jamb nut

Tabletop

Saw

Shelf

⅛-in. plywood, both sides

1-in. plywood stringer

Saw-leveling bolt

Sheet-steel tablesaw stand

Cut off head and weld ½-in. carriage bolt to saw skid.

Hole for ½-in. threaded rod

2x2

1x2

2x4

Make steel mounting brackets for position locks. Slotted holes permit vertical adjustment.

1-in. by 4-in. square hardwood caster pad

Slot receives stringer.

Position lock

From *Fine Woodworking* magazine (March 1985) 51:68-70

In the ten years I've been building furniture, kitchen cabinets and store fixtures, my two biggest problems have always been lack of space and the absence of an additional pair of hands. To deal with the space problem, I've mounted each of my major power tools on casters so I can roll the machine I need to the center of the shop and go right to work.

Finding an extra pair of hands hasn't been as easy. I've always worked alone, which is fine until it comes to tossing around heavy 4x8 sheets of particleboard. You wouldn't believe the pain I used to put up with just to cut that stuff on my little 27-in. by 40-in. tablesaw. I tried some alternative solutions: roughing sheets with a circular saw and straightedge; ripping them on my radial-arm saw with cobbled-up extension tables. Then I got the idea of housing my tablesaw in a big, roll-around worktable. As the photo shows, my saw table is little more than a Sears 12-in. tablesaw, a Biesemeyer T-Square saw fence and a large table. Should the need arise, the saw can be completely dismantled.

While the Sears saw is by no means industrial-quality, I've never had any problems with it, so I couldn't see spending a small fortune on a better one. For about $60, I had the surface of the cast table ground to take out a nasty $\frac{1}{16}$-in. warp. The Biesemeyer T-square saw fence is the backbone of my design. The joy of being able to set a fence up to 48 in. from the blade in about two seconds borders on the euphoric. I'm consistently getting truly straight and square carcases, and the reason for this is that I'm getting truly straight and square cuts. Thank you, Mr. Biesemeyer.

Basic construction—The table consists of four large panels: the top, the shelf that supports the saw, and the two legs. Each panel is a torsion box—a light wooden gridwork skinned over with plywood (see drawing on facing page). I positioned the saw to the right of center because, unlike most people, I rip with the fence on the left side of the blade. But you can suit yourself. Right or left,

what's important is that there's enough room to set the fence 48 in. away from the blade. This allows you to cut to the center of a 4-ft. by 8-ft. sheet. I use this saw only for cutting panels and ripping, so I didn't extend the miter-gauge grooves into the table. If you want to extend the grooves, use thicker plywood for the top.

I made the torsion-box frames from clear fir. If I were to do it again, I'd probably use 3½-in. wide pieces of ¾-in. ply, simply because it's straighter. So the grid parts would stay put during glue-up, I assembled them with ⅛-in. deep dadoes.

Before gluing on the plywood skin, I positioned the Biesemeyer fence's angle-iron mount on the front edge of the top. I drilled holes for the mounting bolts and inserted a T-nut on the inside of each hole. I glued a small block of wood over each T-nut to make sure the nut could never come off. Once the plywood is glued down, the T-nuts are inaccessible.

I glued plywood across the entire top and bottom of each grid, and cut the openings later with a router fitted with a flush-trim bit. The top is ¾ in. smaller than a plywood sheet, so I could neatly trim the edges with the router. Contact cement works fine for gluing the ⅛-in. plywood to the grid, and the plastic laminate to the top. You can fasten the thicker plywood with white or yellow glue and screws.

Assembly—The legs are held together by two 76-in. long, ½-in. dia. threaded rods that pass through the shelf. I had these made at a machine shop for about $30, but you could also couple shorter lengths of threaded rod. The two plywood stringers slip into their mortises (don't glue them) and the shelf simply rests on the stringers. The saw goes in place on the shelf, and rests on a frame made from 1¼-in. square steel tube, which a blacksmith made for $100. Oak or maple would also do, and cost less. Four carriage bolts welded to the frame are used to level the saw.

To position the top, I used the bolt holes through the top panel

Four torsion-box panels and a Biesemeyer fence convert a Sears tablesaw to an accurate, versatile panel saw. Outrigger-like position locks extend to hold the rolling table in place. Auxiliary infeed and outfeed tables can be positioned for more panel support.

Photo this page: Larry Kellam; drawings: Lee Hov

Shopbuilt sliding table

by Rick Williams

I made a sliding table for my Sears saw from scrap plywood, and produced the ugliest saw in the world. It rolls on six ball-bearing nylon roller-skate wheels—four ride on top of the track, the other two on the vertical plywood track support. I made the track from a steel clothesline pole, but any sturdy, straight pole about 7 ft. long would do.

Everyone who sees my sliding table pushes down on the outside corner of the table, and when it moves up and down they ask, "Doesn't this cause any problems?" No. Since the workpiece itself must be on both the saw table and the sliding table at the same time, the workpiece actually holds the table in place.

I've made several other modifications to the 10-in. saw, such as replacing the metal legs with a plywood box. The box has a large drawer that wheels in from the end to catch the dust that used to fall on the floor and then rolls out for emptying. I've also made a safety guard that suspends from the ceiling. It combines an anti-kickback device and a dust-collection system.

I replaced the 1-HP motor with a 1.5-HP, 220-volt motor on a 24-volt relay. I've hooked up a three-way switch setup with one switch at the front of the sliding table so I don't have to climb under a 4x8 panel to turn on the saw, and one switch on the front of the saw for when I'm working on smaller pieces.

I'd estimate the total cost of the project (including saw, new motor, and sliding table) at $500. Every time I lay a piece of ¾-in. ply on the thing and slide it through a cut, I'm amazed that anything that looks so strange could cut so well. □

Rick Williams is a cabinetmaker in Stanley, Kans. Photos by the author.

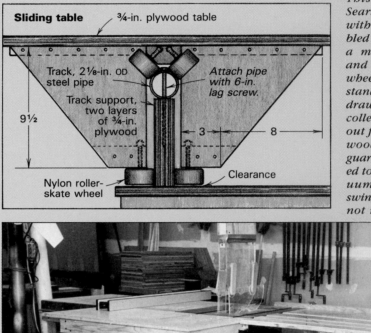

Sliding table — ¾-in. plywood table

Track, 2⅛-in. OD steel pipe

Attach pipe with 6-in. lag screw.

9½

Track support, two layers of ¾-in. plywood

3   8

Nylon roller-skate wheel

Clearance

This homely setup is a Sears tablesaw outfitted with a sliding table cobbled from scrap plywood, a metal clothesline pole and six nylon roller-skate wheels. The plywood saw stand contains a wheeled drawer that slides in to collect sawdust and rolls out for emptying. The plywood and acrylic blade guard (below) is connected to a dust-collection vacuum system. The guard swings up and away when not needed.

as a guide and drilled through the top 2x2s in the legs. Then I secured the top to the legs with four ½-in. dia. carriage bolts. Lastly, I fastened the Biesemeyer fence to the top.

The height of the saw is adjusted with the leveling bolts. When the saw is flush with the top, tighten the bolts in the table casting against the steel plates mortised into the saw opening.

To keep the table from rolling around in use, I attached four position locks (made by Bassick Div., Stewart-Warner Corp., 960 Atlantic St., Bridgeport, Conn. 06602) to the legs with steel brackets. The bolt holes in these brackets are slotted, so it's easy to level the table on an irregular floor.

Frankly, I'm a little embarrassed about the amount of money I've channeled into this project. All told, I've invested about $1,000. That includes the $300 I paid 10 years ago for my saw—today the same saw costs more than $600. Was it worth it? Yes. Every nickel. Besides, anything I build for the shop, I build to last a lifetime. I look upon my shop as a reflection of me and my work—a showroom, so to speak—and therefore I feel that everything that goes into it should be efficient, neat and well thought out. It's good for business. □

_____

Larry Kellam is a professional cabinetmaker in Miami, Fla.

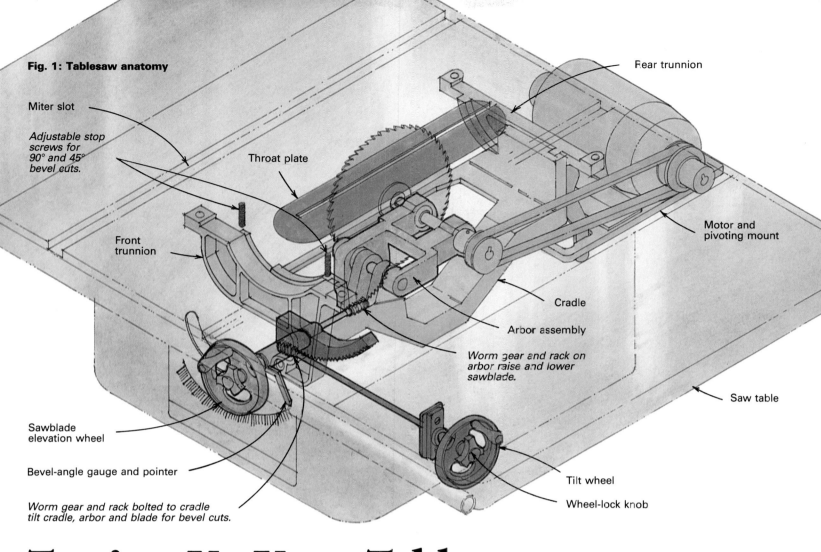

Fig. 1: Tablesaw anatomy

Miter slot

Adjustable stop screws for 90° and 45° bevel cuts.

Throat plate

Rear trunnion

Front trunnion

Motor and pivoting mount

Cradle

Arbor assembly

Worm gear and rack on arbor raise and lower sawblade.

Saw table

Sawblade elevation wheel

Bevel-angle gauge and pointer

Worm gear and rack bolted to cradle tilt cradle, arbor and blade for bevel cuts.

Tilt wheel

Wheel-lock knob

Tuning-Up Your Tablesaw
Basic adjustments for accuracy and safety

by Mark Duginske

Of all the machine tools in a woodworking shop, the table-saw is the workhorse. But whether you own an 8-in. hobbyist's saw or a 12-in. production model, you won't get maximum accuracy and efficiency from your saw unless it's tuned up. This means that its working parts, including the trunnions, bevel stops, miter gauge and rip fence, must be properly adjusted and aligned. Safety is also a major concern; many woodworking accidents, especially those caused by kickback, can often be traced directly to poor saw setup.

Fortunately, tuning up your saw is fairly simple. It doesn't take any special tools or require either esoteric knowledge or brute strength. Even a cheap saw can be tuned to perform admirably. And the small amount of time that must be invested in a tune-up is more than repaid in workpieces that are cut accurately the *first* time. In this article, I'll show you a simple step-by-step procedure for testing and tuning up your tablesaw, including how to adjust

the tilt mechanism, the miter gauge and rip fence; how to square the blade to the table; and how to align the blade parallel to the miter slots. But before we delve into the tune-up, let's get better acquainted with the different internal parts of a tablesaw.

Tablesaw anatomy—Figure 1 above illustrates the internal components of a typical tablesaw; this example is similar to saws made by Delta, Powermatic, Sears and Taiwanese manufacturers. Bolted to the underside of the saw table is the saw cradle (or carriage) and trunnion assembly. The cradle supports the saw arbor, which is basically a shaft held by either sleeve or ball bearings. The arbor has a sheave on one end for the V-belt, and the sawblade is secured by a flange and nut on the other end. There are two trunnions, one at each end of the assembly, that support and align the cradle, as well as the motor on most saws. Because the trunnions are semicircular, they make it possible for the cradle to be tilted

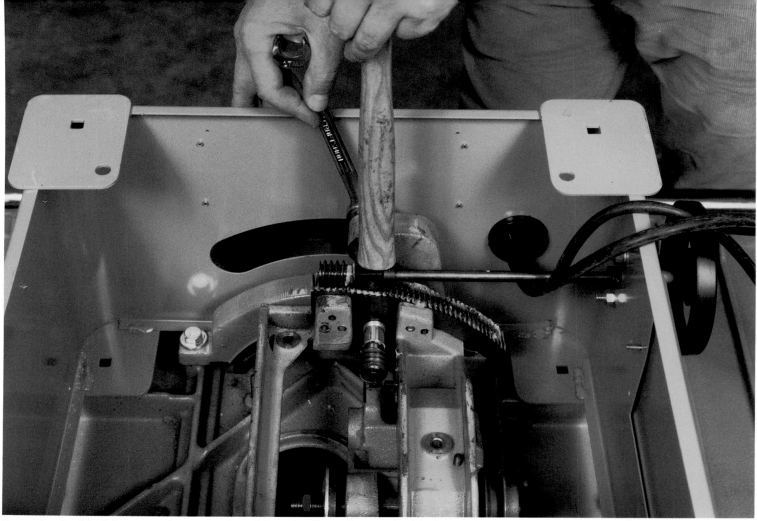

Removing backlash between the gears of a tablesaw's tilt mechanism is crucial to eliminating the play in the cradle that supports and aligns the arbor and sawblade for accurate cuts. Here, the backlash between the worm gear and rack on a Delta 10-in. Tilting Arbor Bench Saw is taken up by using the handle of a hammer to press down on the block that supports the worm gear.

for bevel cuts. The tilt mechanism itself generally has a worm gear that engages a semicircular rack on the front trunnion; when the saw's tilt wheel is rotated, the angle of the cradle, and in turn the angle of the blade, changes. Two adjustable screw stops set the limits of trunnion travel, usually at 90°- and 45°-blade positions. Another wheel-driven system similar to the tilt mechanism pivots the arbor to raise and lower the blade.

While many of the tune-up steps I'll describe involve adjustments atop the saw table, the first step in the tune-up procedure takes place inside the saw: adjusting the trunnions and tilt mechanism. It's important that you follow the tune-up procedure in the same order as the steps are presented here because the accuracy of subsequent adjustments is often dependent on previous steps.

Adjusting the tilt mechanism—As we have seen, the trunnions and cradle are ultimately responsible for keeping the sawblade running straight and true during both square and bevel cutting. But excess play in the tilt mechanism can make the whole cradle shift, causing the blade's angle to shift during the cut. This not only decreases the accuracy of the cut, but it increases the tendency for the blade to bind or pinch, which can cause a dangerous kickback. You can detect excessive tilt-mechanism play by making trial crosscuts with the miter gauge. You have a problem if the cut is square at the beginning of each cut, but not at the end. This problem shows up even more with beveled cuts in thick stock.

There are several ways to adjust the tilt mechanism depending on the particular design of your saw. Unless your tablesaw is an industrial behemoth, you'll want to flip it upside down to make the adjustment. First, remove the motor assembly to reduce the weight of the saw, then flip it over on a low table or blocks. If you leave

the motor in place, be sure to unplug the saw; you'll want to leave it unplugged for most of the tune-up. Now, grab the cradle by the motor-mounting plate and wiggle it back and forth to determine the amount of play.

The most common tilt mechanism on many Taiwanese saws and Delta and Powermatic models relies on the worm gear and rack mechanism illustrated in figure 1 on the previous page. With this design, the solidity of the cradle depends on having a close fit between the worm gear on the tilt mechanism and the rack on the front trunnion. Tightening the lock knob at the center of the tilt wheel only locks the position of the tilt mechanism—it doesn't tighten anything inside the saw. While the basic design of the tilt mechanism is shared by many saws, manufacturers provide several ways to snug up the fit between the worm and rack gear, and get rid of any play, known as backlash. On the Delta 10-in. Tilting Arbor Bench Saw, a locknut secures the position of the block that houses the worm gear shaft. By loosening the locknut and pressing down on the block, as shown in the photo above, backlash is reduced. On Powermatic's Artisan saw and on some Sears models, reducing backlash is a matter of pivoting the tilt-adjustment wheel's shaft. Loosen the two screws that hold the tilt wheel's mounting plate to the outside of the saw housing, and shift the wheel opposite the direction the worm gear moves. Once you make the adjustment, tilt the blade a couple of times to make sure the tilt mechanism operates smoothly. If it doesn't, the gears may fit too snugly, which can cause premature wear. In this case, loosen the backlash adjustment a bit.

In addition to the tilt mechanism, some tablesaws, such as the Boice-Crane and some Sears models, employ a separate tilt lock that clamps the front trunnion and the cradle together. Once the angle of the blade has been set with the tilt wheel, a spring-loaded handle on the front of the saw locks the setting. On these saws, gear mesh isn't crucial and requires no adjustment because the handle secures the cradle. But remember to use the lock whenever you change the blade angle. Also, tightening the lock can change the blade angle slightly, so recheck the blade angle after the lock is tightened. On Shopsmith saws, some Inca saws and most older saws, the table tilts instead of the blade for angle cuts. If your saw isn't based on one of the tilt systems described here, consult your saw's manual or contact the manufacturer for instructions.

You can reduce wear on the trunnions and tilt mechanism parts by lubricating the trunnions, cradle and gears. First, blow sawdust out of the gears with compressed air, and then lubricate the gears with a dry spray lubricant, which is usually based on Teflon or silicone. Be sure to lubricate the gears' hard-to-reach areas using the long applicator nozzle included with the spray can. You should avoid using machine oil or grease because they will attract sawdust, which will gum up the gears.

The saw cradle may still have play after the gear mesh has been set and/or the tilt lock has been tightened. In this case, a small clamp can be used as a homemade trunnion lock to secure the cradle to the rear trunnion, as in the top photo on p. 75. A word of caution: *Because vibration may loosen the clamp, make sure it's impossible for the clamp to fall into the running sawblade.* After adding the clamp, you should recheck the blade angle to ensure that the locking action didn't change it.

After you've made these adjustments and are satisfied with the firmness of the cradle, you're ready to flip the saw back over and perform the remaining adjustments from atop the saw.

Squaring the blade – The next steps are to adjust the level of the saw's throat plate, square the blade and set the stops for 90° and 45°. You've probably made these adjustments on your saw in the past, but even so, do them again now because they are important prerequisites for the steps that follow.

The saw's throat plate, or table insert, should be adjusted so that it's a couple of thousandths of an inch lower than the saw table in front, and about the same amount higher than the saw table in back. This prevents the workpiece from hitting the plate before the cut or binding on the table after the cut. Throat plates on some Delta and Powermatic saws provide Allen screws for adjusting throat-plate height. On saws without screws, you may have to do some filing or use tape or cardboard shims to change the level of the plate.

The next step is to square the blade. Release the saw's tilt lock and remove the rear trunnion clamp, if you're using one, and raise the blade as high as it will go. Optionally, you can remove the throat plate so that the body of a try square will sit flat on the saw table. To check blade squareness, use a high-quality try square that's dead on 90°. My favorite is an all-steel Starrett square, available from the L.S. Starret Co., 121 Crescent St., Athol, Mass. 01331; (508) 249-3551. Place the blade of the square against the sawblade, making sure you're not on a tooth, and look for a gap between the square and blade. Fiddle with the saw's tilt adjustment until the gap of light disappears. If the blade won't tilt far enough, you may have to loosen the stop screw (see figure 1 on p. 71). Next, secure the cradle with the trunnion lock or clamp, as previously described, and recheck the blade for squareness.

Now that the blade is square, adjust the stop for 90°. On the Delta 10-in. Tilting Arbor Bench Saw, the tilt stops are screws that are accessible through the saw top. But on most saws, you'll have to reach up under the saw to loosen the locknut and screw the

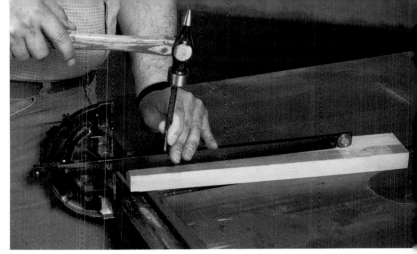

A snug fit between the miter gauge bar and the table slot is key to making accurate crosscuts on the tablesaw. Here, the author peens the bar, which causes the metal around each indentation to expand, and increases the width of the bar for a tighter fit in the slot.

stop in or out. Once again, make sure the saw is unplugged and consult your saw's manual. Ideally, the blade should reach 90° just as you start to feel resistance at the tilt wheel, which is a sign that the trunnion is hitting the stop. Never apply excess pressure to square the blade; if the blade goes past 90°, the stop should be reset. Also, don't depend on the stop to square the blade perfectly every time: For critical cuts recheck using a try square. You can follow the same procedure for setting the 45° stop, but use a plastic drafting triangle for checking the angle. Finally, realign the bevel gauge by zeroing the pointer on the front of the saw. This will make the gauge a rough yet fairly accurate indicator for quickly setting odd-angle bevel cuts.

Adjusting the miter gauge – The miter gauge bar usually fits too loosely in the slot in the saw table to yield accurate crosscuts. Since it's easier to rework the bar rather than remachine the slot, the first step is to adjust the bar to fit more snugly. The best way to do this is to peen the side of the bar, as shown in the photo above, using a pin punch to make small, dimple-like indentations. The peening expands the metal around each indentation, effectively making the bar wider. Peen only on the side of the bar nearest the blade and dimple every inch or so. Stagger the dimples width wise on the bar so they won't wear a groove in the side of the slot. When you're finished, the bar should slide smoothly along the length of the slot without hanging up, and there should be a minimal amount of side-to-side play. Check the fit in the table slot you use most often; most right-handed people use the left slot for crosscutting. Unless the slots on your saw are identical, the bar probably won't fit as well in both slots. If the dimples in any one area cause the bar to stick in the slot, smooth them with a flat mill file. Use a non-silicone wax to lubricate the table slot and the bar; silicone wax may transfer to the workpiece and later cause finishing problems.

Next, use your square to set the head of the miter gauge perpendicular to its bar. Although you may be tempted to square the head to the sawblade, don't do it; that won't produce good crosscuts unless the miter slot and the blade are parallel to one another. This isn't always the case though, and we'll be checking and adjusting this alignment later in the article. After squaring the head and tightening the gauge's lock screw/handle, set the adjustment screw on the 90° stop if your miter gauge has one. Don't trust these stops for fine work though. Like the tilt stops, they're not perfectly accurate.

Aligning the blade to the miter slots – For the miter gauge to crosscut accurately, the blade has to be perfectly parallel to the

Parallelism of the sawblade with the saw table's miter slot is essential for smooth, accurate crosscuts. To test for parallelism, the author rotates the blade by pulling on the motor's V-belt, and he listens to the sound of the sawblade rubbing against a test piece, which is clamped to the miter gauge, to determine whether the slot is parallel to, closer to or farther from the slot at the back of the blade.

path the workpiece travels during the cut. This means the miter slot has to be parallel to the blade. When the blade and slot aren't parallel, the sawblade is heeling and has a tendency to recut the workpiece at the back of the blade. This double cut is not only inaccurate, but also dangerous because the back of the blade can lift the binding workpiece and kick it back.

The first step is to test the saw's alignment. Raise the blade as high as it will go and clamp a piece of wood to the miter gauge; a ¾x2x12 piece is big enough. Crosscut the test piece and unplug the saw. Now, slide the miter gauge with the test piece still clamped to it next to the front of the sawblade, and rotate the blade by hand-turning the belt or using a motor pulley. Don't grab the blade because your hand may deflect it. As you rotate, one or two teeth will rub against the wood the hardest, making the loudest sound. Mark those teeth and slide the test piece to the back of the blade (see the photo above). The same teeth that rubbed against the workpiece at the front should rub against it at the back, making the same sound. You may have to move the piece to the front and the back several times to test the sound. If the sound is the same, the table slot and the blade are in alignment and you will not have to make any adjustments. If you get a louder or softer sound at the front than at the back, the distance between the blade and the slot will have to be increased or decreased accordingly.

Realigning the blade parallel to the miter slot is fairly straightforward and involves rotating the trunnion relative to the table. Most contractors' saws have four bolts, two in front and two in back, that secure the trunnions to the underside of the table. On cabinetmakers' saws, such as the Delta Unisaw, the saw table is usually secured directly to the saw's shell or frame rather than the trunnions. In either case, the bolts must be loosened, with one of the front bolts left a bit snug to act as a pivot point for the top—the

right front bolt if the top must be rotated clockwise and the left front bolt for counterclockwise. Also, the trunnion lock (if your saw has one) should be tightened and the back trunnion should be clamped, as described earlier, to keep the two trunnions in alignment during the operation.

To rotate the trunnion assembly, a wooden wedge is driven between the trunnion and the table casting at the back of the saw, as shown in the top photo on the facing page. This is the most civilized method, but if there isn't room for a wedge, you can use a pry bar or a rubber mallet to move the trunnion. If the mallet isn't effective, use a hammer. Put a piece of wood on the trunnion and pound the wood; don't hammer directly on the saw or you could crack the castings. Make a slight adjustment and slide the test piece by the blade as you did earlier. Keep rotating the trunnions until the sawblade bears against the test piece and sounds the same at the front and back. When you're satisfied, tighten the bolts, plug in the saw and make another test cut to make sure the saw isn't double cutting. It may take several attempts, but stay calm and take your time. Once the slot in the top is aligned with the blade, you should, theoretically, be able to crosscut with the miter gauge in either slot. Unfortunately, it's my experience that the slots in many saws aren't perfectly parallel to each other. For this reason, you should employ the slot you use most often to make the final test cut.

Rip fence alignment—In theory, the rip fence should be aligned so that it's perfectly parallel to the blade. But in practice, it works best if the fence is slightly farther from the back of the blade than from the front. This prevents the wood from binding between the blade and the fence if the workpiece warps as it's being ripped.

By lowering the sawblade below the table, you can use the same test piece used for crosscut alignment to set the rip fence. After loosening the bolts that lock your fence's angle relative to the guide rail, set the miter gauge with the test piece at the front of the saw and lock the rip fence against it. Then, slide the test piece until it's over the back of the saw's throat plate. There should be about 0.015 in. (about ¹⁄₆₄ in.) clearance between the test piece and the fence. To gauge the amount of clearance, use a feeler gauge, as shown in the middle photo on the facing page, or a dollar bill folded over twice. Finally, tighten the fence's bolts and make a test cut.

Feedback from the workpiece—Once you've tuned up your tablesaw, it's worthwhile to get into the habit of checking its accuracy often, especially if you have an important job that requires great precision or if the saw has been moved. This accuracy check takes only a few minutes and a single cut on a scrap of wood. Just clamp a test piece, like the one used to check blade-to-slot alignment earlier, to the miter gauge and cut it in half. Unclamp the piece, put the two halves back together the way they were before the cut and mark both with an X through the saw cut. Now, flip one piece so that the X faces the opposite direction and match the two pieces back together, as shown in the bottom photo on the facing page. With the pieces either on edge or lying flat, the saw cut should match as well as it did before one piece was reversed. Any error that is present will be doubled and a glance at the test piece will show you which adjustments are still good and which must be redone. For instance, if the test cut is off with the pieces lying flat, only the squareness of the blade to the table is off and needs adjustment. The test piece also shows the direction in which you'll need to make corrections, as well as how much of an adjustment is needed. □

Mark Duginske is a woodworker and author in Wausau, Wis. His new book, Bandsaw Handbook, *is available from Sterling Publishing Co. Inc., 2 Park Ave., New York, N.Y. 10016; (212) 532-7160.*

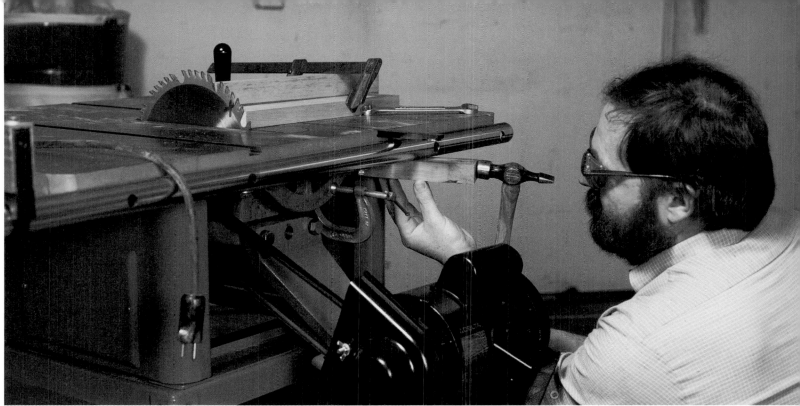

To realign the table's miter slot with the blade, Duginske hammers on a wooden wedge set between the rear trunnion and the flanges cast in the underside of the saw table. The wedging gently rotates the trunnion. A small C-clamp is applied to the saw's rear trunnion, which keeps the trunnion and cradle in the same relationship as the assembly is rotated.

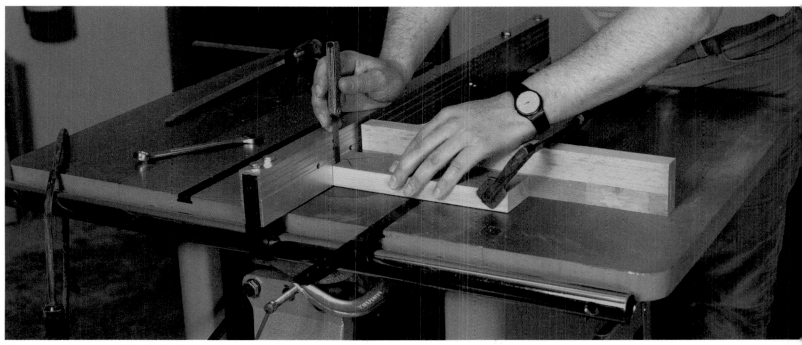

The author uses a 0.015-in. feeler gauge to set the rip fence at the back of the throat plate slightly farther from the blade than it is at the front of the throat plate. This prevents the workpiece from binding and kicking back if it warps as it's being ripped.

Cutting and examining a test piece is an easy way to check the squareness of your saw cuts, both miter and bevel, and to tell when it's time to do another saw tune-up. By reversing the halves of the test piece set on edge and seeing how well the cuts match, the author confirms that his saw is crosscutting exactly at 90°.

A Shop-Made Crosscut Saw
Table slides smoothly on linear-motion bearings

by T.H. Ralph

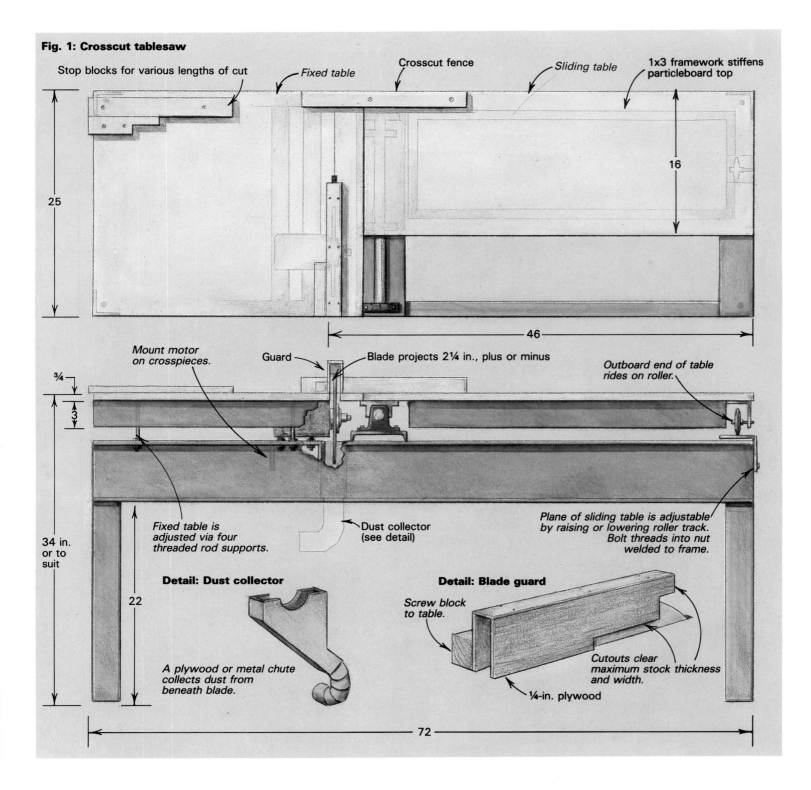

Fig. 1: Crosscut tablesaw

Stop blocks for various lengths of cut

Fixed table

Crosscut fence

Sliding table

1x3 framework stiffens particleboard top

16

25

46

¾

3

Mount motor on crosspieces.

Guard

Blade projects 2¼ in., plus or minus

Outboard end of table rides on roller.

34 in. or to suit

22

Fixed table is adjusted via four threaded rod supports.

Dust collector (see detail)

Plane of sliding table is adjustable by raising or lowering roller track. Bolt threads into nut welded to frame.

Detail: Dust collector

A plywood or metal chute collects dust from beneath blade.

Detail: Blade guard

Screw block to table.

Cutouts clear maximum stock thickness and width.

¼-in. plywood

72

During the five years I've been manufacturing a wooden needlework frame holder in my shop, I've learned that the key to successful production work is accurate tooling. My frame holder has 14 wooden parts, each of which must be precisely crosscut to length to fit boring, shaping and sanding jigs, and so they'll go together correctly at assembly. Industrial tablesaws will do the job, but it seems a shame to invest in a machine best at ripping when what you really want is a crosscut tool. The sliding-table crosscut saw shown here is my solution to this dilemma. I built two—one is permanently set up to crosscut parts of five different lengths, the other to cut four lengths.

My saw design is based on two pieces of specialized hardware: linear-motion bearings and a compact direct-drive electric motor. Linear-motion bearings have been used in industry for years in applications where a cutter or tool of some kind must slide back and forth. The bearings themselves are sleeves or pillow blocks with rows of tiny ball bearings set into grooves inside the bearing's bore. The pillow blocks are fastened to the sliding member and they, in turn, ride on a precision-ground shaft. The bearings I used for my sliding table are made by Thomson Industries Inc., Channel Dr., Port Washington, N.Y. 11050, (516) 883-8000. Thomson doesn't sell direct, so you'll need to write or phone and ask for your local distributor. For my saw, which has a 9-in. travel, I used SPB 20 pillow blocks, 1¼-in. shaft and SB 20 shaft supports. The total cost was about $200. For greater travel, just buy a longer shaft.

The motor is a 2-HP, 3-phase induction motor made by a Ger-

man firm, Himmel. It's ideal for this application because it is only 4¾ in. high so it fits snugly under the saw's fixed table, allowing 2¼ in. of a 12-in. blade to protrude above the table. The motor output shaft is a 1-in. threaded arbor. I bought mine from American Contex Corp., 964 Third Ave., New York, N.Y. 10155, for $290. A less expensive solution would be to mount an arbor on pillow blocks beneath the fixed table and then belt it to a standard single-phase motor mounted on a frame under the saw.

I welded my saw frame out of heavy channel and angle iron because I happened to have it. Straight framing lumber, glued-up plywood, or lighter steel members bolted instead of welded will work just as well, as long as the frame is rigid. The fixed and sliding tables are made of ¾-in. particleboard, stiffened by 1-in. by 3-in. frames glued and screwed to their undersides. In assembling the saw, there are two critical relationships: the motor arbor must be precisely perpendicular to the linear-motion shaft and parallel to the horizontal plane of the sliding and fixed tables. To square the motor to the bearing shaft, I mounted a blade, assembled the sliding table, then used a dial indicator to position the motor relative to the table travel. Once it was perfectly square, I bolted it down. Use an accurate trysquare to adjust the tables in the horizontal plane, then, with a long straightedge, make sure they're aligned.

Once the saw is set up and aligned, it should produce reliably accurate crosscuts with only occasional adjustments. □

T.H. Ralph operates Roadrunner Woodworks in Albuquerque, New Mexico.

T.H. Ralph's sliding-table crosscut saw has 9-in. travel and will saw stock up to 2¼ in. thick. The Thomson linear-motion bearings, visible in the photo at near right, ride on a 1¼-in. precision-ground shaft mounted in a pair of steel supports. The sliding table's outboard end rolls on a wheel cannibalized from garage-door hardware. Its bearing surface (photo at far right) is a piece of heavy angle iron that can be raised or lowered to square the table to the blade in the horizontal plane.

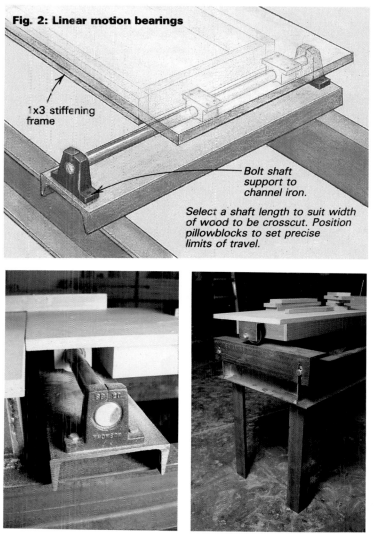

Fig. 2: Linear motion bearings

1x3 stiffening frame

Bolt shaft support to channel iron.

Select a shaft length to suit width of wood to be crosscut. Position pillowblocks to set precise limits of travel.

Fig. 1: Jointer

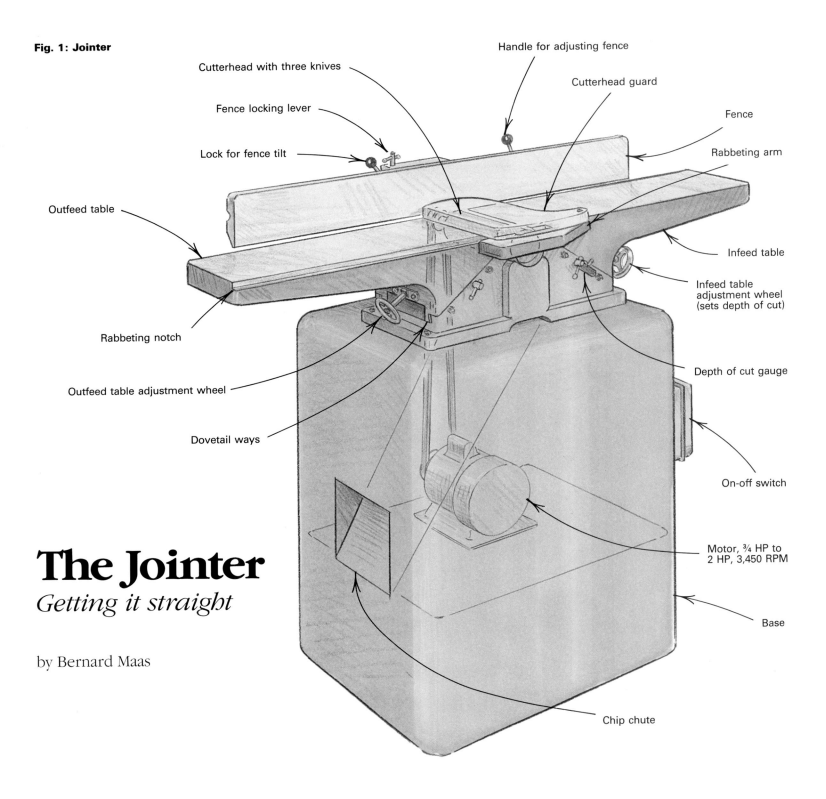

Handle for adjusting fence

Cutterhead with three knives

Cutterhead guard

Fence locking lever

Fence

Lock for fence tilt

Rabbeting arm

Outfeed table

Infeed table

Infeed table adjustment wheel (sets depth of cut)

Rabbeting notch

Depth of cut gauge

Outfeed table adjustment wheel

Dovetail ways

On-off switch

Motor, ¾ HP to 2 HP, 3,450 RPM

Base

Chip chute

The Jointer
Getting it straight

by Bernard Maas

A properly tuned up jointer is essential for precision wood-working. Without the jointer to machine a straight, true and square edge or flatten a rough, irregular surface, the other tools in the shop can't fulfill their potential for precision work. If you want to pull straight, flat boards out of the planer, you must start with a jointer-trued surface facedown on the planer table. If the stock is bowed or twisted going into a planer, the feed rolls will clamp it flat during the cut, but the wood will pop back to its old shape on the outfeed. A tablesaw is even more dependent on a jointer; without a straight edge to run against its fence, a tablesaw cannot be safely used. And, of course, when edge gluing boards, that last pass on the jointer guarantees a perfect joint. Even after the panels are glued up, the jointer can be of service, cutting rabbets for joinery and chamfering edges for a finishing touch.

A jointer is a simple machine. It consists of a two-, three- or four-blade cylindrical cutterhead, infeed and outfeed tables and a fence, as shown in figure 1 above. However, this simplicity belies the machine's complex geometry. The infeed and outfeed tables must be perfectly flat and parallel with each other and, across their width, parallel with the axis of the cutterhead, as shown in figure 3 on the facing page. The knives must be installed in the cutterhead so that they all protrude the same distance and the highest point of their arc is tangent to the plane of the outfeed table. If the various components are not properly aligned, the jointer cannot machine a straight and true surface and it therefore becomes practically useless. So, before I get into the specifics of its operation, I'll discuss the jointer itself—its parts, maintenance and adjustment.

Jointer anatomy—Jointers range in size from 4-in.-wide hobbiest models up to 24-in.-wide cast-iron monsters used in mills. The size

Drawings: Roland Wolf

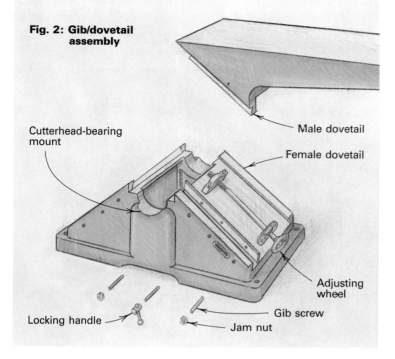

Fig. 2: Gib/dovetail assembly

Cutterhead-bearing mount

Male dovetail

Female dovetail

Adjusting wheel

Locking handle

Gib screw

Jam nut

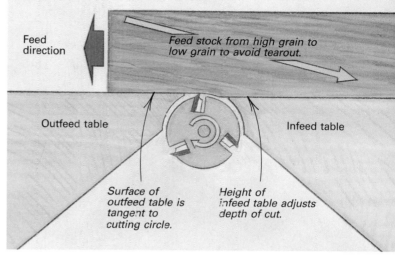

Fig. 3: Table alignment and direction of feed

Infeed and outfeed tables must be parallel with each other and with the cutterhead across their width.

Downward pressure is transferred from infeed table to outfeed table as stock passes over cutterhead.

Feed direction

Feed stock from high grain to low grain to avoid tearout.

Outfeed table

Infeed table

Surface of outfeed table is tangent to cutting circle.

Height of infeed table adjusts depth of cut.

designates the maximum width of the cut the machine can make, based on the length of the knives and the cutterhead cylinder, which in turn dictates the width of the tables. If you walked into a small- to medium-size cabinet shop, you'd most likely find a 6-in.- or 8-in.-wide jointer with a total table length of 4 ft. to 6 ft. Narrower models aren't wide enough to be much good for flattening surfaces of boards and their correspondingly shorter tables don't provide enough support for accurately edge jointing long pieces. The 6-in.- and 8-in.-wide machines strike a balance between performance and cost, their tables are long enough for accurately edge jointing long boards, wide enough to allow some surfacing of boards, and they range in price from $400 to $1,200. As the table width increases, so does the size of the motor and the weight and price of the tool. Most 12-in. jointers qualify in all respects as heavy-duty industrial machinery.

Mid-size jointers generally have a ¾-HP to 2-HP, 3,450-RPM motor that drives the cutterhead between 4,000 RPM and 5,000 RPM with pulleys and a V-belt. To keep your jointer running smoothly, you should periodically check the cutterhead for bearing wear, the V-belt for wear and the pulleys for alignment. The cutterhead bearings should have a solid feel and turn silently. Wobbles, vibrations and grating noises are obvious signals that the bearings should be replaced. As with an automobile fan belt, it's important that the jointer belt is not frayed or nicked. Check the pulley alignment by placing a straight edge flat against the outer rim of one of the pulleys. If they're in line, the straight edge will just contact the rim of the other pulley. Adjust, if necessary, as indicated in your owner's manual. Out-of-line pulleys will not only lead to premature belt failure, but the continuous uneven pressure could eventually erode the arbor hole in the pulley until it won't stay on its shaft.

Depth of cut is regulated with either a lever or handwheel that raises or lowers the infeed table. The distance between the top of the infeed table and the highest point of the cutting arc determines the depth of cut. On some jointers the outfeed table adjusts up and down like the infeed table, which can be handy when replacing knives and aligning the tables.

For edge jointing, the fence is usually set 90° to the table. This ensures that the edge being machined will be square with the surface that's run against the fence. The top photo at right shows the type of fence most commonly found on high-quality jointers. This

The Rockwell fence, above, is typical of the center-mount fences found on most 6-in. and larger jointers. The fence is attached to a casting that covers the cutterhead pulley and the exposed knives behind the fence. The lever on the casting unlocks the fence's movement across the tables and the smaller lever unlocks the fence to set its tilt. A plunge pin is a positive stop for 90° and 45°. The knob attached to the fence itself is a handhold for adjusting the fence.

Another common type of fence slides in a channel in the front end of the infeed table. The knob operates a socket wrench that can be slipped over one nut to adjust the tilting mechanism or over another nut to control the side-to-side movement of the fence.

Fig. 4: Cutterhead geometry and the effects of dull knives

Locking bar

Knife

Set screw

Depth of cut

Outfeed table

Infeed table

Cutterhead

Cutting circle

When knives are dull or secondary bevel is too great, the trailing edge of the bevel will rub on the work, burnishing and compressing the wood fibers. In addition, as the bevel increases, the cutting arc drops below the level of the outfeed table.

Rake angle, 60°

Knife bevel, 35°

Dull knife or secondary bevel

With sharp knives, trailing edge of bevel will clear work.

With dull knives, trailing edge of secondary bevel will rub on work.

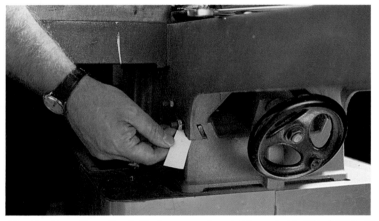

If adjusting the gibs fails to correct a table sag or tilt, brass or paper shims can be inserted as shown to lift the table.

fence usually has a positive stop for both 90° and 45°, and the casting supporting the fence doubles as a guard to cover the cutterhead behind the fence. The most common fence on smaller and/or less expensive jointers slides along a bar or track at the front of the infeed table (see the bottom photo on the previous page). Before buying a jointer with this fence, make sure the tilting lock and the side-to-side lock are separate from one another or you will have to reset the fence to 90° each time you move it. It's a good idea to move the fence from time to time to ensure even wear along the entire width of the knives. I like to save 1 in. or 2 in. at the rear of the knives so I have a pristine edge for those final clean-up cuts.

The blade guard is a cast-metal fixture that rotates on a spring-loaded pivot in the infeed table and covers the exposed portion of the cutterhead. Make sure the tension on the spring is great enough to swing the guard up against the fence after the trailing end of the work passes over the cutterhead. Woodworkers can argue all day about the pros and cons of tablesaw guards, but there's no good reason not to use a jointer guard. It's simple and it works.

Aligning the tables—New jointers should come from the factory with their tables parallel to each other and the cutterhead. However, because this alignment is so crucial to a jointer's performance, it's prudent to recheck it anytime the tool is moved or knives are replaced. In the university shop where I teach, I occasionally catch a student cusing the outfeed table as a seat. After my blood pressure has gone back down, I check the table for sagging (drooping front to rear) and tilting (angling side to side).

To check table alignment, raise the infeed table to the same

height as the outfeed table and hold a reliable straightedge, at least 3 ft. long, near one side of the infeed table. If all is well, the straightedge will contact both tables along its full length and no light will show beneath it. Repeat this on the forward side of the tables. If light shows on one side and not the other, there's tilt. If light shows at the rear of the outfeed table and not at the front, it indicates sag. A gap of even a few thousandths of an inch is a problem.

If adjustments are needed, check your owner's manual for the recommended procedure. Don't panic if that doesn't work. The instructions for the 8-in. Rockwell in our shop call for a detailed readjustment of the gibs, which are the keys that fit in the dovetail ways that the table moves along (see figure 2 on the previous page). This has never worked for me. What does work is loosening the gibs, lifting the end of the table and inserting a few shims until everything is back where it should be, as shown in the photo at left. Brass shim stock is ideal, but matchbook covers and index cards are okay and they'll last for years.

Changing the knives—Because of the precision required, some woodworkers dread their first knife change so much that they put it off indefinitely. The knives continue to cut, but they develop a secondary bevel as they dull, as shown in figure 4 above. When this secondary bevel gets to be larger than about 1/64 in., it no longer provides adequate clearance and begins to rub against the wood fibers behind the cut, burnishing and compressing them so they will not glue or finish reliably. You can avoid this by changing the knives when you see a heel forming behind the cutting edge. By the way, honing dull knives with a sharpening stone while the knives are still in the machine will only enlarge the secondary bevel and increase the burnishing problem; it is not a substitute for changing knives. Some books and instruction manuals recommend honing a minute secondary bevel, *as the last step when installing sharp knives,* in order to extend cutting edge life. However, it should be noted that if the honed bevel is too large, you will have the same burnishing problem as with dull knives (see figure 4).

Unless you're experienced at precision-grinding, send your knives out to be professionally sharpened, and keep a spare set of sharp knives on hand to avoid downtime. The knives should come back to you ground with a single bevel of about 35°. Repeated sharpening will reduce the height of the knives. Be careful: Eventually the lock bar may not be able to grip the knife solidly. To avoid a dangerous situation, check your manual or contact the manufacturer for minimum knife height. One more thing to be aware of: Most manufacturers warn that removing all the knives at once and then replacing them one at a time can dangerously stress the cutterhead. Instead, remove a single knife, replace it with a freshly sharpened one and tighten it down completely before removing the next knife.

The basic strategy of installing knives is simple. The knife is inserted into the cutterhead slot and held firmly, but not too tightly in place, with two or three set screws. At this time, the knife should be parallel with and slightly higher than the outfeed table when the cutterhead is rotated so the cutting edge is at top-dead center. Then, with the cutterhead set at top-dead center, push the knife down until it just brushes a straightedge extending off the outfeed table, as shown in the photo below. When the knife is in line with the outfeed table along its entire length, secure it by tightening down all the set screws.

Simple enough, right? Well, yes, except for the tendency of the knife to devilishly squirm a hair's breadth out of alignment as the set screws are tightened. This tendency can be reduced by tightening the middle set screw first and then alternately tightening the other screws as you work out to the ends. One improvement on the basic system for aligning the knives is to use a piece of ¼-in. or thicker Plexiglas, which spans the width of the cutterhead, instead of a straightedge. This lets you set the height of the knife all along its length in one step. Somewhat more effective is the "Magna-Set," available from Uniquest Corp., 585 W. 3900 South, Suite 6, Murray, Utah 84123; (800) 331-1748. This device has magnets that grip the knife and hold it in alignment while the set screws are tightened. I've found this to be the best solution so far, but even it can be humbled by the proclivity of the knife to squirm as the lock bar is tightened.

Using the jointer—A jointer demands respect! Read your instruction manual and heed its safety warnings. Never run anything shorter than 10 in. through a jointer. Short pieces can tip into the jointer's throat and be kicked back by the cutterhead, potentially exposing hands to serious injury. Likewise, be wary of face jointing thin stock. It chatters, is difficult to feed and may creep uncontrollably under the guard and fence. When edge jointing narrow stock, anything that doesn't stand as tall as the fence, take special care to keep your fingers clear of the cutterhead; nipped fingertips from inadvertently dragging them over the cutterhead are one of the most common injuries in the woodshop. Use push sticks whenever possible, and maintain your balance when feeding stock. You should never be pushing so hard or leaning on the work so much that your hands would be in danger should the piece kick back.

Even standing idle, a jointer cutterhead, with its razor-sharp knives, smacks of potential danger, so keep the guard in place.

Work is always fed from the right at a moderate rate. Rate of feed is important. If it's too fast, scallops appear; too slow and burn spots show. Feed pressure is in three directions: sideways against the fence to ensure a square cut, downward to eliminate vibration and chatter and forward to advance the lumber. At the outset, both hands bear against the work on the infeed table. As the work passes over the cutterhead, you must transfer your downward pressure to the outfeed table with your left hand and continue the pressure on the outfeed table as you finish the cut to ensure that the flat plane being created on the underside of the work is parallel with the plane of the outfeed table. As you transfer the pressure, you should maintain a constant feed rate because abrupt slowdowns or complete stops will show on the finished surface.

Whenever possible, feed the lumber into the jointer so the cutterhead will be cutting with the grain, as shown in figure 3 on p. 79. Of course, this is the ideal grain picture. Quite often, the grain direction will reverse somewhere along the board. If so, take your best guess and run the piece slowly at a moderate depth of cut. If there's too much grain tearout, reverse the board and make another pass to see if there's any improvement. Tearout can be minimized, and often eliminated, by reducing the depth of cut and drastically slowing the feed rate to a creep over the problem area.

Finally, keep in mind that jointing opposite faces or edges doesn't ensure that they are parallel. For parallelism, true up one face with the jointer, and then run the board through a thickness planer with the flattened face on the table. The same principle holds true for edges. Straighten one edge on the jointer and run this edge against the tablesaw fence as you rip the board to width. If you rip the board 1/32 in. to 1/16 in. wide, you can clean off the saw marks with a single pass on the jointer.

Surfacing—To true up a face, line up the fence with the far end of the knives to allow maximum width of cut. This means full knife exposure because a wide workpiece forces the guard completely aside; so before you begin, see that the blade guard functions properly and you have a solid, reliable hold-down. Figure 5 below shows a hold-down I designed for this purpose. I keep several sizes for different lengths of stock in the university's shop and they've given reliable and safe service for more than 10 years.

If the board is bowed or cupped, it's best to flatten the concave

To set the knife height, hold a straightedge on the outfeed table and rotate the cutterhead back and forth. Adjust the knife height until it just brushes the straightedge. Set the height at both ends of the cutterhead and then tighten the set screws, beginning with the center one and moving out to both ends. This reduces the chance of the knife squirming out of alignment as the set screws are tightened.

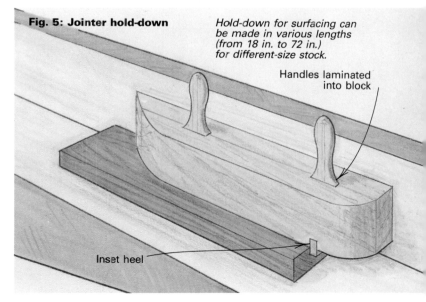

Fig. 5: Jointer hold-down

Hold-down for surfacing can be made in various lengths (from 18 in. to 72 in.) for different-size stock.

Handles laminated into block

Inset heel

side, which allows the workpiece to rest on its "ears" or corners. If you must joint the convex side, flatten the center or high point first. Don't rock the piece over the cutterhead or you'll end up either tapering the work or planing the curve.

Set the infeed table for a cut of 1/32 in. to 1/16 in. and no more! You'll be cutting maximum width and you don't want to lug down the motor. In addition, if you have to use excessive feed force, you increase your chances of slipping. With the heel of the hold-down firmly against the butt end of the stock and with a firm grip on the handles, feed the lumber at a slow to moderate rate over the knives. If the board is twisted, tip it so you're planing down the high corner. Don't let the work tip or rock, but keep it steady and on line. As a flat area is created, press it snug to the outfeed table. Check the surface after each cut to make sure you're removing the high spots. The planed area should increase with successive passes. With bowed boards be careful not to force the bow down as the board passes over the cutterhead or you'll be planing the curve instead of eliminating the high spots.

Experienced woodworkers sometimes surface boards that are wider than the jointer knives by working alternately from both edges of the boards. It's kind of a hit-and-miss process, but with a little practice you can flatten a board up to twice the width of the jointer. Don't worry about perfectly matching the opposing cuts; as long as the board will lie flat, the planer will clean up the job.

Edge jointing—When your properly flattened boards emerge from the thickness planer, they'll have straight, parallel faces. Next, you'll want to establish an edge that is square with the freshly planed faces and straight along the length of the board. For most edge jointing, set the fence exactly 90° to the tables with a square. The exceptions to this would be intentionally beveling an entire edge to a specific angle or chamfering an edge (planing a small bevel along the edge). In these cases, set the angle of the fence with an adjustable bevel square that's been set with a protractor.

If the edges of the boards are nowhere near straight, work the concave edge whenever possible, just as when surfacing. If the convex edge must be worked, go after the high point of the curve first. On extremely arched edges, it might save time to snap a chalkline lengthwise on the face of the board so you can bandsaw it as close to straight as possible before jointing.

The most common error when edge jointing is not holding the trued face tightly against the fence all the way through the cut. Attention to this is even more critical when making beveled or chamfered cuts because the face has a tendency to slide off the angled fence. If your fence tilts in both directions, you can reduce the sliding by tilting the fence so that it creates an acute angle with the table instead of an obtuse angle.

There is one other exception to the rule of setting the fence to 90° for edge jointing. In production shops, it's fairly common to set the fence a couple of degrees out of square when jointing boards to be glued up for doors and panels. As the boards are glued up, the face that was run against the fence is alternated from the front to the back of the panel on each adjacent board. This method results in a flat panel because combining the two angles will always add up to 180°. This technique works fine in a production situation in which panels are glued up from 2-in.- to 3-in.-wide boards without concern for grain match. In this instance, the panels all tend to match because they're all random. However, if grain match is important, jointing from alternating faces might force you to joint an edge against the grain, which could result in tearout. That's why most specialty and one-of-a-kind shops set the fence at precisely 90°; the boards can then be arranged for the optimum grain match and their edges jointed from whichever face will allow the least chance of tearout. □

Bernard Maas is a woodworking teacher at Edinboro University in Edinboro, Pa.

Sources of supply

The following companies manufacture mid-size jointers.
Busy Bee Machine Tools Ltd., 475 N. Rivermede Rd., Concord, Ont., Canada L4K 3R2
Delta International, 246 Alpha Dr., Pittsburgh, PA 15238
Farris Machinery, 2315 Keystone Dr., Blue Springs, MO 64015
Grizzly Imports Inc., Box 2069, Bellingham, WA 98227
Hitachi Power Tools, 4478-E Park Dr., Norcross, GA 30093
Jet Equipment and Tools, Box 1477, Tacoma, WA 98401
Lobo Power Tools, 9034 Bermudez St., Pico Rivera, CA 90660
Makita USA, 14930 Northam St., La Mirada, CA 90638-5753
Mini Max, 5933-A Peachtree Industrial Blvd., Norcross, GA 30092
Powermatic, Morrison Road., McMinnville, TN 37110
Ryobi America Corp., 1433 Hamilton Parkway, Itasca, IL 60143
Sears Power Tools, Sears Tower, Chicago, IL 60684
Shopsmith Inc., 3931 Image Dr., Dayton, OH 45414
Sunhill-Nic Inc., 1000 Andover Park E., Seattle, WA 98188
TCM Industries Inc., 322 Paseo Sonrisa, Walnut, CA 91789
Wilke Machinery Co., 120 Derry Court, York, PA 17402

Jointing beyond the basics

Rabbeting: There are a number of tools to cut a rabbet, including handplanes, routers, dado sets on the tablesaw and high-speed shapers, but when the rabbet runs with the grain, my choice of tools is the jointer. It's easy to set up and it gives crisp and clean results.

Sadly, not all jointers are equipped for rabbeting. In order for a jointer to have this capability, an arm is either bolted to or cast as part of the infeed table to support the work as it's passed over the near end of the knives. A notch (or rabbet) milled into the outfeed table allows the unrabbeted portion of the work to clear the outfeed table, as shown in the photo on the facing page. In addition, the knives should be installed so their ends all extend the same distance beyond the end of the cutterhead.

To set the width of the rabbet, measure from the near end of the knives to the fence. Set the infeed table for a 1/16-in.-deep cut and feed the workpiece into the knives. For each succeeding pass, increase the depth of cut by 1/16 in. or less until you reach the desired depth. The rabbet's maximum depth is limited by the notch in the outfeed table; its maximum width is limited only by the length of the knives. Because the guard must be removed for rabbeting, extra care should be taken with this operation. To ensure adequate hand clearance, the stock should be at least 6 in. wide. If the rabbeted piece must be narrower than 6 in., rabbet a wider piece and then rip it to the narrower width.

End-grain jointing: Many experts advise against jointing endgrain because the hardness of endgrain dulls knives and also increases the danger of the piece tipping into the jointer's throat and being kicked back by the cutterhead. While there's no doubt that endgrain is harder on knives than side grain, a tight knot is also rough on knives. The likelihood of kickback is not really due to grain orientation; the chances of kickback would increase if the end-grain section wasn't long enough so the panel could be held tightly to the infeed table to prevent the leading edge from tipping into the throat.

I believe that end-grain jointing can be a reasonably safe alternative to the hours of tedious sanding required to remove every last burn and saw mark from the stubborn endgrain on wide, glued up panels. But end-grain jointing is only safe if the following criteria are met: the panels are at least 18 in. wide across the grain and tall enough to generously clear the height of the fence; very light cuts are taken ($\frac{1}{32}$ in. or less); and the endgrain of the panel is held firmly to the infeed table until the leading edge has passed over the cutterhead and is supported by the outfeed table.

If these precautions are taken, the end-grain will come through the jointer clean and crisp. However, when the trailing edge hits the knives, the unsupported grain at the back side of the panel will split out. Figure 6 above shows three methods to avoid this. Keep in mind that end-grain cuts are only for cleanup. If you take more than one or two passes, you risk trimming the end out of square with the edges.

Cheap tricks: Following are some quick fixes that add a touch of detailing to a job and give it that million-dollar look of meticulous hand-crafting. For instance, if you're putting up a set of shelves, a simple $\frac{1}{8}$-in. chamfer on the edges turns square-nose carpentry into cabinetry. Set the jointer fence to 45° and run both edges through—total time is 45 seconds! Use the same approach to create quickie moldings, cabinet door stops and so on. It's an easy way of softening a corner and the effect is both visual and tactile.

Drawer problems? Perhaps you built them last winter when household moisture was low. When summer brought heat and humidity, your once carefully fit drawers wouldn't budge. The jointer can remedy this in a few minutes.

If the width of your jointer matches or exceeds the height of your too-tight drawers, the fix is easy. Treat the side of the drawer as though you are surfacing lumber. Protect your corner joints by following the rules for preventing split-out when end-grain jointing. Set the jointer for an absolute minimal cut and pass the drawer through. Let the rear of the drawer be the trailing edge, just

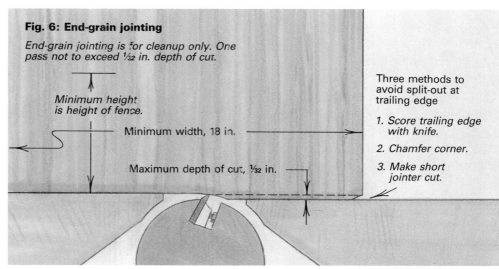

Fig. 6: End-grain jointing

End-grain jointing is for cleanup only. One pass not to exceed $\frac{1}{32}$ in. depth of cut.

Minimum height is height of fence.

Minimum width, 18 in.

Maximum depth of cut, $\frac{1}{32}$ in.

Three methods to avoid split-out at trailing edge

1. Score trailing edge with knife.
2. Chamfer corner.
3. Make short jointer cut.

The rabbeting arm supports the board, and the notch in the outfeed table lets the un-rabbeted portion of the board go by. Here the author is on his third pass; when rabbeting, the infeed table is lowered an additional $\frac{1}{16}$ in. for each successive pass.

to be on the safe side. Check for fit and repeat the process if needed.

Are the drawers too high? Use the rabbet setup procedure. Slide your fence forward until the distance between it and the near end of the knives is equal to the thickness of the drawer sides. In turn, pass all four edges (tops or bottoms) of the drawer sides through the jointer. Feather away any cross-grain ragging with sandpaper.

If you're building a cabinet with a door, rabbet the forward faces of the top and bottom boards with the jointer before you assemble the carcase. A $\frac{1}{4}$-in.-deep rabbet slightly wider than the thickness of the door should do. The upper and lower rabbets will not only serve as door stops, but also prevent dust intrusion.

While you're working on that cabinet, consider using a continuous piano hinge to hang the door. You can't beat it for strength or the jewel-like detailing of the long, polished barrel. The problem with a piano hinge is mounting it perfectly straight, but if you've got a jointer that can cut rabbets, you've got the solution. Before the carcase is assembled, rabbet both the hinged side of the cabinet and the door edge to just fit the hinge leaf. Be sure to let the entire barrel protrude beyond the door and frame. Now, here's the trick: When you're locating the screw holes with the awl, punch them off center, toward the rear of the rabbet. Then, as the hinge is screwed down, it will be drawn tightly to the wall of the rabbet and be dead on line. —*B.M.*

Weighing in at only 30 lbs., the 6 1/8-in. Ryobi JP-155 jointer at right, can be tucked under the arm and carried to a job site, or stowed out of the way to save space in a cramped workshop.

The Delta DJ-15, far right, is a full-size, 300-lb., 6-in. jointer. Its parallelogram table supports replace the usual inclined dovetail ways.

Two New Jointers

Innovative approaches to a standard shop machine

by Bernie Maas

Jointers are pretty generic. There are green ones and gray ones and they all have infeed and outfeed tables, a cutterhead and a fence. But two new 6-in. jointers that recently came into our university woodshop made me do a double take: Ryobi's JP-155, a companion to the popular AP-10 planer, and Delta's DJ-15, the 6-in. member of the new Invicta series. However, these two tools are on opposite ends of the pricing spectrum: The Ryobi retails for $618 and the Delta for $1,288; but this price difference doesn't so much reflect a difference in quality as it does a difference in market orientation. The Ryobi is lightweight and meant to be portable, while the Delta is a full-size jointer designed to be a permanent fixture in the shop.

Ryobi JP-155—Compact and under 30 pounds, the JP-155 (see the photo above) is perfect for amateurs' home workshops and pros who haul equipment to various job sites. Although we found the 28-in. table adequate for most work, accessory extensions that increase the capacity to handle large jobs, such as doors, are available. The most impressive part of this machine is the electronic, variable-speed, 10.5 amp motor that tops out the two-knife cutterhead at 16,000 RPM. Because of this high speed, we've been able to feed virtually every grain configuration (knots, reversals, you name it) into this jointer—from pine to cocobolo—and *never a tearout*! In addition, the JP-155 sports a 2½-in. chip exhaust. When it's connected to an everyday shop-vac, operation is fairly dust free.

To evaluate the JP-155 for durability, I turned it over to my students for two semesters. No problems—only normal blade wear. The students became so comfortable with it that they went to the trouble of hauling it out of its storage cupboard and setting it up instead of using the 8-in. Rockwell workhorse that's been a familiar fixture in the shop for years.

Changing knives usually puts knots in my stomach. Ryobi's thoughtful engineering takes most of the teeth-gnashing out of this job. In the first place, two knives are easier to set than three. Secondly, a cutterhead lock holds the knives firmly at top dead center. And thirdly, the lock bars, which are shaped so they wrap themselves under the knives, are slotted to receive the heads of lifter screws. As these screws are turned in and out, they raise and lower the lock bars that in turn force the knives up and down. Working a screwdriver in tandem with Ryobi's plastic feeler block makes knife setting a 10-minute breeze.

On the downside, the Ryobi isn't equipped for rabbeting and its outfeed table isn't adjustable. Positioning the fence is sometimes a bit sticky—a minor annoyance that the company says it has improved on newer models. Finally, with its router-style motor, the JP-155 is loud. Close your eyes and you can imagine yourself on a runway at O'Hare, so you'll want to wear earmuffs.

Delta Invicta DJ-15—In contrast to the lightweight Ryobi, the Delta Invicta (see the photo on the facing page) weighs in at close to 300 lbs. This industrial-grade machine is powered by a ¾-HP motor and is quiet and smooth when running.

If you're familiar with Delta jointers, the first thing you'll notice that sets the Invictas apart from their predecessors are lever-controlled infeed and outfeed tables. Gone are the "crouch-down"

From *Fine Woodworking* magazine (January 1990) 80:80-81

handwheels and "squint-to-read-'em" depth scales. When I first saw these levers in a showroom, I was skeptical about whether they would provide enough control, but using the tool made me a believer. Raising and lowering the tables is smooth and precise thanks to springs that counterbalance the tables' weight. And since you can adjust the infeed table without crouching down, the depth-of-cut scale is placed so it can be read from a standing position. The dual centimeter/inch depth scale is a nice touch, but the depth indicator itself blocks the scale so it's hard to read and additional numbered graduations would help. When I questioned the wisdom of using plastic for the tables' locking-clamp handles, Delta's product manager, Steve Holley, told me that the fiber-reinforced polycarbonate handles had a field failure rate of zero.

Delta's engineers are doing quite a bit of chest-thumping when describing their novel "parallelogram-action" table support system (see figure 1 below). Infeed and outfeed tables don't slide up and down along the usual inclined planes, but raise and lower in an arc that keeps them close to the cutterhead. The result is improved chip breaking and chip capture. The parallelogram system is "set for life" at the factory. However, things happen in a shop that'll knock permanent settings out of whack, so I was a little concerned to find that fine-tuning the table supports is not covered in the owner's man-

ual. But Delta's Holley says this adjustment is user-serviceable. Although he couldn't explain why it wasn't discussed in the manual, he assured me that someone at the company's Tech Support department at the Memphis, Tenn., headquarters would be glad to walk or talk a DJ-15 owner through the process. (The Tech Support department can be reached at 800-223-PART; in Tenn., 901-238-PART.)

A minimum/maximum positive lock allows preset finish cuts and pre-fixed rabbet depths. The mechanism is simple; knurled screws, threaded through the jointer's cast base, act as stops when they bear against small cast-iron blocks fastened to the underside of each table. By adjusting these screws, the upper limit of the infeed table can be set so you can quickly return to a fine finish cut of $\frac{1}{32}$ in. and for coarse cuts, the table's lower limit can be fixed to never exceed $\frac{1}{8}$ in.—an excellent safety feature for a school shop!

I have my doubts about the DJ-15's extra-long infeed table. Apparently, Delta's design engineers felt that most woodworkers prefer to have an extra 6 in. of support at the infeed end for dealing with bulky stock. But there are two schools of thought here. I'd prefer the extra length on the outfeed because the greater the contact between the stock and rear table, the straighter the edge, or flatter the face, is going to be.

The DJ-15 has a pair of replaceable aluminum lips bolted to the ends of the tables on either side of the cutterhead. The product literature claims that the lips compensate for wear, which seems strange to me because jointers don't exhibit any particular wear at these two points. According to Holley, these lips might protect the knives if they are set too high or happen to come loose, but I suspect that it's an easy way to bring the table ends close to the cutting arc without casting the tables to this arc.

Standard equipment includes jack screws to take some of the sweat out of knife setting, a rabbeting ledge and a double-jointed, tilt-in/tilt-out, three-stop fence. Options include dust control ports and a 24v magnetic switch. An additional cutterhead assembly, including bearings, housing and a set of three knives, can be purchased as an accessory and installed in place of the original cutterhead to avoid downtime during sharpening. Lastly, whoever packed this machine really piled on the protective grease. It only took 20 minutes to put the machine together; it took a heck of a lot longer to soak off the gunk. □

Bernie Maas teaches woodworking at Edinboro University in Edinboro, Pa.

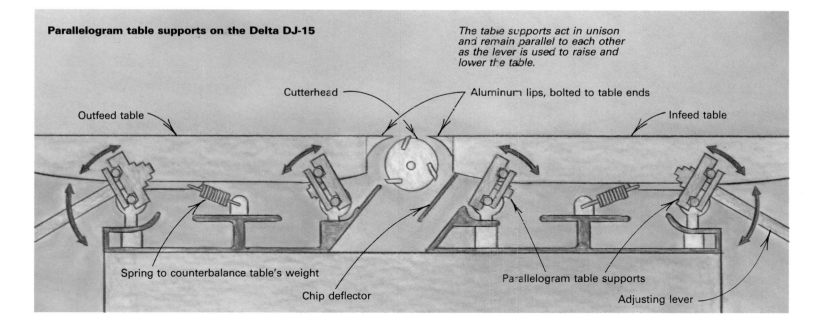

Parallelogram table supports on the Delta DJ-15

The table supports act in unison and remain parallel to each other as the lever is used to raise and lower the table.

Outfeed table

Cutterhead

Aluminum lips, bolted to table ends

Infeed table

Spring to counterbalance table's weight

Chip deflector

Parallelogram table supports

Adjusting lever

Jointer Talk
Getting along with home-shop machines

by Jim Cummins

There are two jointers in my shop, a fairly new 6-in. Rockwell and an old 4-in. Sears. Neither one has an adjustable outfeed table, so setting the knives has been a trial-and-error chore that I used to put off as long as I could. Three years ago, I decided to set up the Sears for finishing work, particularly to get some good surfaces on a series of small boxes I was making in my spare time.

Following directions I'd read somewhere, I set each knife a hair higher than the outfeed table, then turned the jointer on. I put a fine, flat India stone on the outfeed table and slowly passed one end of it over the whirling cutterhead. This process, called jointing, removed a tiny bit of metal to lower each knife edge exactly even with the outfeed table. Of course, it blunted the knives at the same time, leaving a little hairline flat instead of a cutting edge. To resharpen each knife, I lowered the infeed table and laid an 8-in. hard Arkansas stone on it so that the stone rested on the knife bevel. Then I clamped the cutterhead so that the stone, moved by hand in a series of tight circles along the length of each knife, was at the proper angle to hone the flat away, as shown in the photo at the bottom of the page. The infeed table was protected by a sheet of paper under the stone.

This procedure forms a small secondary bevel. The cutting edge has a little more steel behind it than a single-bevel knife, and is, therefore, a little more durable. It took almost an hour to set, joint and hone the knives, but it proved worth it—the edges lasted much longer than they ever had before (partly, I'm sure, because I had more respect for the machine and took some care about what I was feeding it). One benefit came as an unforeseen bonus. The machine was set up so well that I began to sense how my own work habits subtly influenced its performance.

After a while I could walk up to that venerable, rackety old jointer with absolute confidence. On my good days I can surface bird's-eye maple box lids without tear out—I double-tape the lid to a heavier piece of wood that damps out vibration and acts as a push stick. Then I feed ever so slowly, imagining each knife taking a separate delicate slice, getting maybe three hundred cuts per inch. The waste box under the jointer slowly fills with slivers of wood as fine as featherdown.

With anything but super-sharp blades, such a method would be all wrong. In general work, if the feed rate is too slow the blades will rub the work and cause friction that burnishes the wood, as shown in figure 1. Such a surface may look all right, but it won't finish well or glue reliably—the surface fibers will have been pounded flat, overcompressed and overheated. A really dull set of knives can leave burn marks, but the wood can be damaged and chemically altered long before that point.

Usually, the first sign of dulling comes when I'm trying a slow feed on a hard wood, and the work rides up, resulting in a tapered cut. This is the point where I have to decide what's most important: a flawless surface or a straight joint. The blades are probably still sharp enough for general work, but I'll have to feed the work harder and faster. This usually cures the problem for a while. The surface will show some washboard marks, but at least glue joints will be straight and chemically unaltered.

The other choice is to change the blades. Nowadays, since I discovered the gadget described in the box on the facing page,

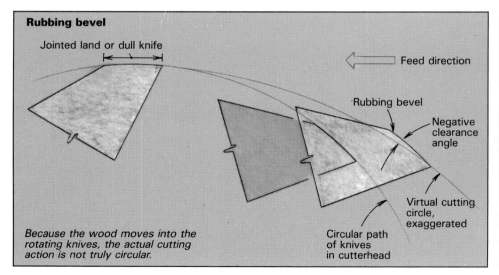

Rubbing bevel

Jointed land or dull knife

Feed direction

Rubbing bevel

Negative clearance angle

Virtual cutting circle, exaggerated

Because the wood moves into the rotating knives, the actual cutting action is not truly circular.

Circular path of knives in cutterhead

To double-bevel knives, first level the cutting edges with a stone placed flat on the outfeed table and the jointer running, then hone them sharp as shown, with the cutterhead clamped steady. This gives a lasting edge.

From *Fine Woodworking* magazine (November 1985) 55:72-74

this is no great chore. But it wasn't always that way. I went through the stone-and-hone routine once with my 6-in. jointer, but within half an hour one of my helpers put a nick in the knives and I swore: "Never again." Instead, I devised a method that uses a pane of glass to set the knives. Coincidentally, Joe Robson of Trumansburg, N.Y., showed the same idea in a Methods of Work column in *Fine Woodworking* magazine.

First you set the infeed table level with the outfeed table, checking alignment with a straightedge. Then you put a new knife in position, tightening the locking screws just enough to allow the knife to slide if pushed. You pull the knife up a little higher than the table and span the cutterhead opening with a pane of glass, holding the glass flat against both tables. Rotating the cutterhead backwards by hand brings the knife in contact with the bottom surface of the glass and pushes it down exactly the right amount. Then you remove the glass and tighten the screws, snugging each one down a little at a time, working from the center out, until all are evenly tight (otherwise you can bow the knife). Talking about distortion, don't take all the old knives out at once, but change one at a time so the tensions in the cutterhead stay balanced.

As a final check when all knives are set, you can press the glass down directly over the cutterhead as you turn the machine by hand. The glass will flex enough to let you feel each knife "drag" on it. If one knife drags more than the others, you should reset it. The accuracy of this method depends on how carefully you set up the sliding fit of the knives. Too loose, and they'll be pushed down too far. Too tight, and they'll be too high. The screws must be set evenly across the width of each knife, too, or one corner will end up higher than the other. The drag test will show you where adjustments are needed, and they usually are.

If your jointer has an adjustable outfeed table, you can set knives entirely by drag. Take a straight, light piece of scrap about 1 ft. long and lay it over the cutterhead. Rotate the cutterhead so the knife grabs the stick and moves it forward onto the infeed table. Mark the distance on the stick. When all knives move the stick the same distance, tested at various places across their width, their height is the same. You then adjust the height of the outfeed table to get a straight cut. The method is accurate, though tedious, and it won't work very well on jointers with fixed outfeed tables—unless you want the knives set high.

High knives do have one application, they produce what's known as a sprung joint, one slightly open in the middle. A tabletop joint with the right amount of spring would let you slip a cigarette paper between the boards at the middle. At glueup, the clamps easily pull this tight. The advantage is that the joint at each end of the tabletop is slightly overcompressed and therefore less liable to crack open in a dry spell. You can get a sprung joint either by setting the knives a few thousandths high in the first place or, on some jointers, by loosening the outfeed-table clamp screws, which causes the table to sag a bit.

Never having had an adjustable outfeed table myself, I have never been able to take advantage of the feature—when I want a sprung joint I take a pass or two with a block plane. Yet I know people who subscribe to arcane and magical outfeed table settings. Me, I like the machine to be level and parallel, with the knives exactly flush with the outfeed table. As long as the machine is at the same setting all the time it will be predictable.

The first step in jointing is to check the stock. The edge of the wood has to be roughly straight before a jointer can do its job. If the edge is severely convex, I take a pass or two just in the middle. Then it will ride right. The same goes for a badly concave edge, or a board with too much taper—I nip away the offending

This new magnetic jig sets knives accurately, holding each in alignment as the gibs are tightened. A set of knives can be changed and set perfectly in less than ten minutes.

Magna-Set makes it easy

In a book once, I saw a photo of a man adjusting jointer knives with a large horseshoe magnet. He laid the magnet on the outfeed table, with the poles above the cutterhead. Next he rotated the cutterhead so that the cutting edge of a knife was at top dead center, and the magnet held the knife up in position while he locked the gibs. "Bingo!" I said, and started looking all over for a large horseshoe magnet. But such magnets are obsolete, and I eventually gave up the search, falling back on my old methods and putting off changing knives as long as I could.

Yet an ingenious inventor, George Hessenthaler of Quest Industries (Box 7768, Murray, Utah 84107), has come up with a $40 gadget that, instead of one large magnet, uses six small ones to imitate a giant, adjustable horseshoe. I tested the device, called Magna-Set, on my 6-in. Rockwell the other day, using it to move two of the knives sideways a little in opposite directions (this trick misaligns the little nicks in the knives and gives a smooth surface again). The job took just five minutes, and the jointer works great.

Here's the procedure: First, you figure out where top dead center is. The easiest way to determine top dead center is to look straight down at the cutterhead, and rotate it until the cutting edge is centered over the cutterhead shaft where it enters the bearings.

With top dead center as a reference, you scribe permanent lines on your jointer to index the jig. The jig is held flat to the outfeed table by four of its six little magnets, and the other two hold the blade in alignment while you tighten up. It's dead easy. Without affecting accuracy, you can even slide the two arms of the jig sideways if you need more room for your tools. The standard jig will slide open to span a 6-in.-wide jointer table, and there are optional rods that extend the reach as far as 12 in.

Can you use Magna-Set to set the knives a little high to make a sprung joint? Sure, there are two ways: either raise the jig with a sheet or two of plastic wrap, or experiment with different jig positions until you find one that works, then scribe a second reference line (any position other than with the knives at top dead center will leave them high).

This invention is so simple, straightforward and accurate that I may start changing jointer knives for the sheer fun of it. George Hessenthaler deserves as much credit as the guy who invented the self-piloting router bit. —*J.C.*

ends before taking a full-length cut. I check the quality of these roughing cuts to see if I've guessed right about grain direction.

When jointing faces, except when feeding very thick or very thin pieces, I use the push blocks that came with the Rockwell. They have comfortable hand grips and a flat, non-slip bearing area. I begin a full cut with controlled pressure on the infeed table, trying to guide the work level over the cutterhead onto the outfeed table. As soon as enough of the work is over the outfeed table I apply downward pressure directly over the cutterhead with one push block (to help prevent vibrations), and with the other block I press down just beyond the cutterhead. The idea is to register the cut against the outfeed table as soon as the jointed surface is long enough to bear properly. As the work moves along, I simply keep exchanging hand positions, taking care to keep the feed rate even and not to let the work ever stop.

If you are routinely getting edges that are concave or convex even though your knives are sharp, first check that your tables are parallel, and correct them according to your owners' manual if they're not. Then think about knife height—if knives are too high, you'll get a concave cut, and vice versa. But if your knives are level with the outfeed table, try adjusting the way you feed the work before you experiment with different settings.

Be conscious of the back pressure from the knives as they cut; if it diminishes, it means the stock is riding up and you'll have to take another pass at a faster feed rate. Listen for telltale "snick" or "pop" noises caused by thick chips tearing out ahead of the cut; if you slow the rate of feed your final surface may still be all right. Take note of everything: When a jointer is working right it sings a harmony of knives whacking away, motor shouldering the load, feathery chips flying against the chute and bearings humming under pressure. It pays to listen for such music—I've found that sharp senses are as important as sharp blades. □

Jim Cummins is an associate editor of Fine Woodworking.

Face bevels

by Galen J. Winchip

If you experience tear out and chipping on your jointer (or planer), even though the blades are sharp, here's an idea borrowed from industry that may eliminate the problem.

Most jointers are designed to handle both hardwoods and softwoods and have a rake angle of about 30°, as shown in the sketch. For softwoods, such an angle works fine, but it's too acute for many hardwoods—when you cut against the grain, the wood splits ahead of the cut, chipping and tearing the surface. Hardwoods are best worked with a steeper rake angle, in the range of 10° to 20°. This more scraping cut leaves a smooth surface.

Rake angles in this range can be achieved by a process called back-beveling or face-beveling, and there's no major surgery

required on the machine. All you need is a thin bevel on the flat face of each knife. It doesn't have to be any deeper than the thickness of the chip you're taking—realize that this is not the depth of cut, but the thickness of the individual chips that go into making a full cut. A bevel of 1/64 in. will certainly do the job, and a bevel half that wide would probably work fine.

To determine the proper bevel angle, you will need an accurate drawing of the cutterhead and knives in your machine. After you have worked out the necessary angles, you can ask your sharpening shop to grind both the sharpness bevel and the face bevel. I do not recommend that anyone grind jointer knives without special wet-grinding equipment. Dry-grinding

in the home shop produces microscopic heat fractures at the cutting edge. Even home-shop honing can be done wrong. It is best to work the stones perpendicular to the edge, not parallel to it, otherwise the cutting edge is weakened by the scratch lines.

Cutting speed, surprisingly, has no effect on the cutting process in wood—think what a good job a hand plane can do. High speed tools such as routers make smooth cuts not because the cutter is moving faster, but because the faster speed means that the chips are thinner. The same applies to a jointer. Chip thickness depends on cutterhead speed, the number of knives, the depth of cut and the rate of feed. The thinner the chips, the less tear out.

Face beveling your

jointer knives is the same idea as choosing a cabinet scraper instead of a hand plane. Some woods are more prone to chipping and tearing than others, but for most work, you'd probably want the plane. Consequently, face bevel your knives only if you have chipping and tearing problems. There is no optimal rake angle for all work, unless it's the 30° angle that manufacturers already use. While you can modify this for special cases, don't over-do. For example, a rake angle of 5° will let you surface bird's-eye maple with no tearout, but the tradeoff is that it will take a lot of force to feed the machine, you'll have to take a shallow cut and reduce the feed rate, and the process will be noisy as well as a large load on your jointer. These drawbacks will apply to any other woods you may run over the machine, but there won't be any corresponding gain in surface quality.

Lastly, for good jointer performance, learn to feel your jointer work. The human being is the most variable and important part of the cutting process. □

Galen Winchip teaches computer-aided design and manufacture at Illinois State University, Normal, Ill.

Face beveling

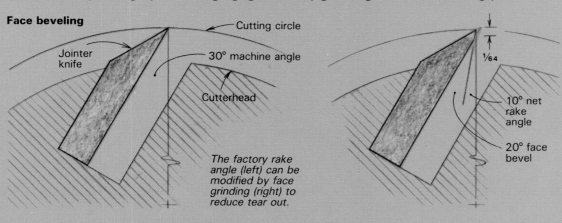

Jointer knife

Cutting circle

30° machine angle

Cutterhead

The factory rake angle (left) can be modified by face grinding (right) to reduce tear out.

1/64

10° net rake angle

20° face bevel

Vintage Machines
Searching for the cast-iron classics

by Tom Howell

Inspecting a roomful of vintage, cast-iron woodworking machines gives a fascinating glimpse into American industrial history. Engraved with colorful phrases like "hand-built on the banks of the Wabash," these behemoths exhibit the proud, hands-on craftsmanship and attention to detail rarely found today. To me, the finest general-purpose woodworking machines ever made were those produced between 1930 and 1960.

I have equipped my factory, where we build woodworkers' benches, with more than 40 of these machines. Most people who see them in operation—from hobbyists to full-time professionals—seem overwhelmed by their size and power, and by nostalgia for a bygone era when me-

Large cast-iron woodworking machines like this 1930s planer may be obsolete by today's industrial standards, but they can give a small shop top-notch performance at scrap-iron prices.

fair price and have room for it, there's no reason why it can't be used for lighter work. Just restoring a machine can be rewarding, particularly for the tinkerer who has the same affection for old tools that some people have for vintage cars. But if you're not mechanically inclined, you'd be better off sticking to consumer- or trade-quality tools, which also represent some excellent used bargains. The Sears tablesaws of the '40s and '50s are, in my opinion, among the best light-duty machines ever made.

Thousands of vintage machines are lying dormant in factories, warehouses, salvage yards and other crannies of industrial America, especially near wood-manufacturing centers. Tracking them down may take a little time, though. For

ticulous labor, cheap materials and over-engineering were the rule. Romanticism aside, cost is what matters most: my vintage machines deliver about 95% of the performance of new industrial tools at about 20% of the cost. For example, one new industrial-quality tablesaw model sells for $8,000 to $9,000. I bought an equivalent, used, cast-iron model for $1,000, spent about $500 restoring it, and ended up with a high-quality saw for about the cost of a trade-tool-quality saw. And my saw won't wear out every couple of years, or depreciate in value. While such bargains can be hard to find, similar comparisons can be made for other tools most needed by woodworkers, especially jointers, bandsaws and planers. If you want something special, like a 30-in. planer, but don't have bundles of cash, old machines are the only way to go.

The cast-iron classics aren't for everyone, of course. Economically, they make the most sense for professionals who continually do the kind of heavy sawing, planing and shaping for which these machines were designed. For the commercial shop just starting out, buying used industrial machines is an economical road to top-notch equipment. I wouldn't rule these beauties out for the hobbyist, though. If you find decent old equipment at a

a start, find out which school systems, utilities, prisons, government installations or construction companies in your area regularly hold sales. Of late, electric utilities have become an excellent source—some are unloading tons of woodworking equipment bought to make concrete forms for nuclear plant projects since canceled. Many good bargains come through large, poorly advertised government disposal sales. The best way to get on the mailing list for these sales is to buy something, even something small, at an auction or sale—you'll soon be on everyone's list. A trip to the junkyard may turn up serviceable old machines bought as scrap from people unwilling or unable to repair them. Also check publications. The *Classified Exchange,* a monthly national newsletter (available for $20/yr. from Box 34908, Memphis, Tenn. 38184), lists hundreds of older machines. Visit nearby woodworking shops and plants for equipment that has been taken out of service. Auctions are great fun, but set limits on what you will bid, or else you might suffer bidding fever.

Finally, if you prefer a dependable sellers' warranty, search out a reputable dealer in used production-woodworking machines. Most have on-site restoration facilities and will give a one-year warranty or a one-year buy-back or trade-in, although the best bargains are machines that are not in peak condition.

If you go shopping for old machinery, you should allow enough time to check each machine carefully, and be willing to spend a little money to get the quality, production capacity and investment value offered by good vintage equipment. Throughout this evaluation, your primary concern should be how much time and money it will take to get the machine into your shop in accurate, running condition. Try to anticipate all costs—everything from paint and transportation (which usually is at least 2% to 5% of the machine's price) to new blades and cutterheads. Even if you enjoy fiddling with machinery, you should realize that restoration work will cut down on your woodworking time. You probably won't be able to find parts either, and will have to pay a machine shop to make them. You may have to replace motors, rewire your shop, install three-phase power or upgrade your dust-collection system. And remember that some of these tools may be too big for your shop (I have one tablesaw with a table as big as a queen-size bed).

Before doing a detailed evaluation, make a quick survey of the machine's general condition to see if it is even worth serious study. Be critical. For every ten machines you look at, figure on rejecting nine, due to price, condition or other factors.

One quick way to sort prospects is to consider weight—buy machinery the way you buy potatoes, by the pound. These machines are about 95% cast iron, and that's what you're buying. The remaining 5% includes bearings, shafts and motors, which have to be periodically replaced anyway. In general, don't pay more than $.30 per pound for defunct machine frames requiring a great deal of restoration, or more than $1 per pound for a completely rebuilt machine with a sellers' warranty. New machines usually are more than $3 per pound. If you can't get the old machine for less than half the cost of a new one, forget it.

If the machine looks promising, make a detailed analysis of its condition. First of all, the machine body should be 100% cast iron, not steel or sheet metal. Cast iron is very heavy (a woodworking machine can't be too heavy) and will absorb vibration,

thereby increasing safety and accuracy. It does have one fault, however: it cracks easily, and such cracks are difficult to repair. I'd reject any machine with a crack that goes through the metal or that is wide enough to stick a piece of paper in. A crack that's at least an inch long and wider at one end than at the other is liable to grow if the machine is subjected to much vibration. Rust less than $1/16$ in. deep usually isn't a problem.

Identifying specific brands is easy. The makers cast their name, the city of manufacture and the serial number into the base of each unit—an iron-clad guarantee of a machine's authenticity. The first two digits of the serial number usually indicate year of manufacture; for example, "49-103" would indicate the hundred and third machine built in 1949. If the manufacturer is still in business (many of them aren't anymore), the serial number may help you obtain blueprints and other information, such as the name of the original owner. You're likely to find about 50 brands in your search for vintage machines (see box, below left, for several). The one I've encountered the most is one of the best, Yates-American. Still operating in Beloit, Wis., today the company manufactures only custom molders and surfacers averaging about $80,000 apiece, but it does have some parts for its old bandsaws, lathes, tablesaws and planers.

Once you're satisfied that the cast-iron base is in good shape, check the electrical system, which may include one or more motors, a starter, wiring and controls. Each motor should have a nameplate, stating its type, RPM and voltage. A majority of industrial machines are three-phase, 440-volt, though some may be 220-volt. Most homes are wired for single-phase, 110-volt current. Converting equipment from three-phase to single-phase is expensive and in many cases it may not be worth it. Besides, three-phase motors are much more efficient, so you're better off installing three-phase power in your shop, if possible. If you can't get three-phase or can't afford the conversion, consider buying a phase converter, basically a large, 3-phase motor used like a generator; when you drive the converter with 220-volt, single-phase current, you get 220-volt, 3-phase current out of it.

Next check the starter. If your shop is large enough to be regulated by the federal Occupational Safety and Health Administration (OSHA), you must replace any manual starters with more expensive magnetic starters—not a bad idea even in a small shop. In the event of a power failure, a tool with a magnetic starter won't restart until it's reset; with a manual starter, a stalled machine will restart as soon as power is restored, and could send pieces of wood flying all over the shop. Make sure that the controls work. Also figure out how much wire you'll need to install the machine. With some big machines, you may have to add a larger electrical service and more breakers and panels. Brace yourself for higher electric bills—big machines built in the days of cheap energy really consume the kilowatts.

After checking the electrical components, give the machine a good old-fashioned going-over. Think about where the stress points on a machine are—shafts, gears, fences and adjusting devices—and inspect these areas for warp, wear and cracks. Use your hands as well as your eyes; often you can feel play and wear in something like a shaft better than you can see it. If you can fit the edge of a business card between gear teeth or if teeth are missing, it's a sure bet the machine has been used heavily and will need work. Have a straightedge handy to check all tables and beds for flatness; grinding a table down can be expensive. If you find a machine that runs, insist on operating it yourself. Bring wide, warped boards to test planers, or tough hardwoods to test saws. Run the machine for as long as the owner will let you. As you operate it, think about safety. A dangerous machine is an asset to no one. Plan on installing proper guards on every moving part, belt or chain. Also, old blades and cutters may be cracked and dangerous, so inspect them carefully or count on buying new ones.

Check the bearings, which usually will be worn and often are hard to replace. Most machines built before World War II have babbitt bearings, which is fine but lowers resale value. If the bearings are damaged or leak grease or oil, you may be able to repair them by melting and pouring the babbitt into the mold formed by the bearing shell and shaft. If the machine has ball bearings, bring them up to speed to see if they chatter or get hot. Some machines have six large bearings—at $50 apiece for replacements, you're talking about a quick way to spend $300. Some bearing sizes are no longer made, so you might have to enlarge the machine fittings to accept standard-size bearings. Look at the machine's grease fittings (there could be two dozen)—if they're plugged, dry or corroded, you can bet the machine hasn't been serviced regularly.

Some dealers or manufacturers may stock parts for the machine, but don't get your hopes up. Fortunately, old machines are unabashedly low-tech and don't have all that many moving parts, so almost any custom machine shop can make the parts that you need, but you'd be wise to get at least three bids on each job.

Regardless of how good a machine looks, though, if it won't meet your specialized needs, don't buy it. If you're in business, a good used machine should be able to pay for itself in three years or less. But whether you're an amateur or a professional, I think you'll find that these machines are a joy to work with. □

Tom Howell, president of Tennessee Hardwood Company, gives tours daily at his plant, 800 W. Main St., Woodbury, Tenn. 37190. Three-phase power converters are available from Ronk Electrical Industries, 106 E. State St., Nokomis, Ill. 62075; Arco Electric Corp., PO Box 278, Shelbyville, Ind. 46176; and Cedarberg Industries, 5408 Chicago Ave. S, Minneapolis, Minn. 55413.

Used machines and abused buyers

by Chuck Seidel

As one who couldn't make a living as a woodworker, I went to work selling industrial woodworking machinery. Since I've had the benefit of being both buyer and seller, I'd like to offer a few tips for those shopping for used equipment.

First and foremost, let the buyer beware! Every day I visit furniture plants, cabinet shops and other woodworking operations, and it is astonishing how much junk is offered for sale. Less than 10% of what I see is suitable for purchase; the rest is either broken down or worn out, obsolete, or too specialized for most shops.

Although it's unreasonable to expect the average buyer to know as much about machinery as a dealer does, there are some rules of thumb that may save you grief. **Beware of auctions.** Auctions may seem like great places for bargains, but they often bring premium prices for equipment (why do you think sellers love to hold them?). Also, unless you can buy large quantities of equipment (without caring too much what kind it is), the time and expense involved in attending the auction—not to mention the cost of transporting the machinery back to your shop—may turn an apparent bargain into an expensive item.

Also remember that many people who attend auctions are canny and experienced buyers who will bid up to a reasonable price and then drop out, leaving novices to bid up to stratospheric levels. Unless you know what you're doing, you can get burned.

Beware of machinery over 15 years old. Though it may be romantic to think "they made 'em better in the old days" and "a good machine is a heavy machine," in reality many old machines are a pain in the neck. The 24-in. vintage planer you "stole" for $1500, and which "needs a little work," may not be such a bargain when you discover that the company went out of business in 1920 and parts haven't been made for years. You may be even more chagrined when you get a $350 bill for transporting that 4,000 lb. of antique cast iron five blocks.

It's wrong to dismiss today's machines as inferior to products of the past. Ask any old hand to compare changing belts on his new Timesavers wide-belt sander with changing the drums on his old Solem. The former is a two-minute job; the latter can mean hours of wrestling chunks of steel and crawling around inside the machine.

By and large, today's industrial machines have superior bearings and motors, are more efficiently designed, and are quieter and safer. They may not be as heavy as their predecessors, but they're heavy enough. A lot of old machines are dinosaurs, and about as efficient.

Ask yourself whether you are in the woodworking business or the machinery-restoration business. You should also question if you can afford to spend a week of production time trying to get a machine going, keeping in mind that the time and money required increase in proportion to the age of the machine.

Know what you are buying. There are thousands of machinery manufacturers, many with product lines decades old. If you're unsure of what you're buying, get the model and serial numbers of the machine and its motor. A call to a local dealer may help you avoid an expensive pitfall.

A case in point is a buyer I heard of who was congratulating himself on finding a wonderfully preserved, vintage 12-in. tablesaw. It looked almost new and sounded great. But when he got it home, he discovered that it had a tilting table and couldn't be adjusted to make a square cut.

Never buy a machine you can't see under power and under load. Look for signs of abuse—if a machine doesn't look good, it probably isn't. Examine the motors and wiring. Few people do this, but this precaution makes sense when you consider, for example, that a new motor for a Unisaw costs more than $600. Older machinery most likely has had its motors replaced, often with motors unsuited to the equipment. Old wiring tends to become brittle and may break or short out, leaving you with an expensive rewiring bill.

The best rule, however, is that no matter what you do, proceed carefully and with circumspection. Believe it or not, the most common machines—tablesaws, jointers and shapers—are the hardest to find, especially if economic conditions are good. When products are selling well, shops want to hang on to every bit of production capacity they have, running these useful tools until they're just about shot. I guarantee that if you walk into the largest, most mechanized furniture factory in the world, you'll find an old tablesaw or two stuck off in a corner somewhere.

If you can't afford to buy new equipment, be prepared to spend some time finding good used machinery. There are bargains out there, but if they were easy to find, they wouldn't be bargains. □

Chuck Seidel is a woodworker and sales representative for a Dallas, Tex., machinery dealer.

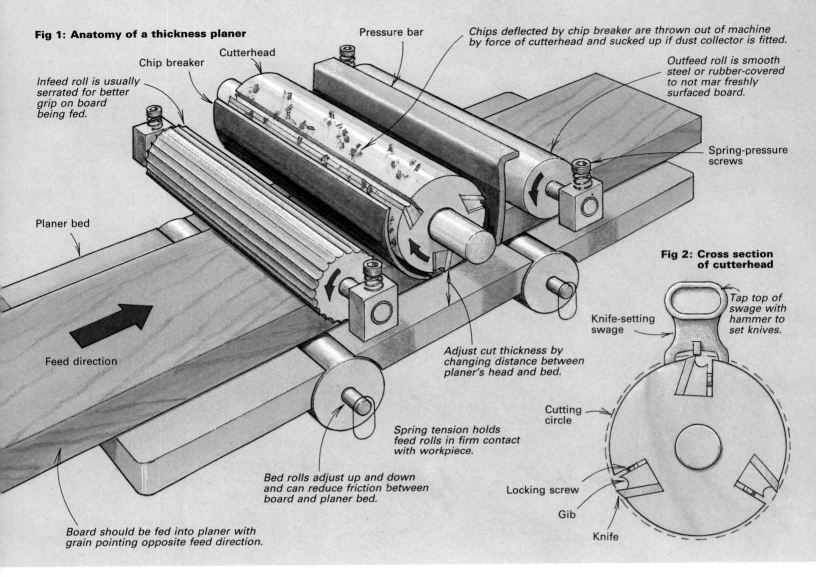

Fig 1: Anatomy of a thickness planer

Pressure bar

Chips deflected by chip breaker are thrown out of machine by force of cutterhead and sucked up if dust collector is fitted.

Chip breaker

Cutterhead

Outfeed roll is smooth steel or rubber-covered to not mar freshly surfaced board.

Infeed roll is usually serrated for better grip on board being fed.

Spring-pressure screws

Planer bed

Fig 2: Cross section of cutterhead

Feed direction

Adjust cut thickness by changing distance between planer's head and bed.

Knife-setting swage

Tap top of swage with hammer to set knives.

Cutting circle

Spring tension holds feed rolls in firm contact with workpiece.

Locking screw

Bed rolls adjust up and down and can reduce friction between board and planer bed.

Gib

Knife

Board should be fed into planer with grain pointing opposite feed direction.

Thickness-Planer Primer

Fine-tuning is the key to smooth planing

by Alfred E. Holland, Jr. and David Kinter

There are many types of planers on the market, ranging from small hand-fed 4-in. to 6-in. models to large production machines with multiple cutterheads capable of surfacing a million feet a week. Despite differences in size and features, all planers operate on the same principles. If you understand these principles, you can adjust your planer properly to obtain consistently flat lumber that's smooth as silk. The planers we'll discuss in this article are those most commonly found in the home shop or small woodworking business—the single-cutterhead surface planer with a maximum width of 12 in. to 18 in., often called a "cabinet" or "pony" planer.

A typical planer consists of a flat bed supported by a frame, usually cast iron. The frame supports a 1½-HP to 3-HP motor that drives a multi-knife cutterhead suspended above the bed. The motor also powers a series of rolls above the bed that push wood through the machine. A board placed on the bed is grabbed by the infeed roll, which presses it flat and drives it into the spinning cutterhead. Just ahead of the cutterhead, a metal bar called the chip breaker helps break off chips raised by the cutterhead and clear shavings out of the planer. Behind the cutterhead is another bar, called the pressure bar, which also holds the wood flat against the bed. An outfeed roll behind the pressure bar pulls the wood out of the planer. Depth of cut is determined by the distance between the bed and the cutterhead arc and is controlled

From *Fine Woodworking* magazine (May 1988) 70:58-63

by turning a crank wheel that either moves the head (containing the cutterhead and feed-roll assembly) or the bed up and down.

Unlike a handplane blade, which slices a single shaving at a pass, the multiple knives in a planer's cutterhead each take many small shavings as the board is fed past. The cylindrical cutterhead has slots in it that hold two, three or four knives. The knives are held in place by locking screws, which let the knives be adjusted or removed. These screws don't bear directly against the knives, but contact knife-length bars called gibs, which distribute the pressure of the screws evenly and help curl over the wood chips sliced off by the knife.

The infeed and outfeed rolls on small planers are driven by chains or belts connected via a gear-reduction box to the cutterhead. The rotational speed of these rolls determines how fast the lumber passes through the planer. The infeed roll is typically a serrated steel cylinder that grips the top surface of the rough stock fed into the planer. The outfeed roll is usually either smooth or rubber-covered steel, so it won't mar the freshly milled surface of the wood. Both feed rolls must press the stock flat against the bed to ensure a straight cut, but must also accommodate the irregular thickness of rough lumber. To achieve this, the rolls are spring-loaded and travel vertically to allow for thickness variations. Bed rolls are not usually powered and are positioned in openings in the bed directly below the feed rolls. They reduce feed friction by lifting the board off the bed slightly.

For a smooth cut, the wood must remain flat on the bed during the cut, so the chip breaker and pressure bar are very important. Besides holding the work down, the chip breaker also directs the chips out of the machine (and into the dust collector, if one is fitted) and minimizes tearout by breaking off chips lifted by the cutterhead's cutting action. The pressure bar is a rigid steel plate adjusted to align with the lowest swing of the rotating knives, and therefore, to the thickness of the just-planed lumber. Some of the smaller machines get along without a pressure bar, but these planers usually have slower feed rates and can't remove as much material in a single pass as those with pressure bars.

More sophisticated planers employ a segmented infeed roll that can accommodate greater surface irregularities than a single serrated roll. This prevents slipping when boards of varying thicknesses are run simultaneously through the planer. The feed speed on some planers can be adjusted either by flipping a lever or changing a belt. This is a critical feature if you surface both hardwoods and softwoods, because hardwoods usually require a slower feed speed than softwoods.

Some planers are also equipped with anti-kickback fingers or pawls to prevent the cutterhead from throwing a board back at the operator. Knife-setting devices that can knock the drudgery out of changing knives are also common on more elaborate planers. These devices include jacking screws built into the cutterhead to raise or lower knife height or separate jigs that clamp the knives in the proper position while they're being locked into the cutterhead. Production-model planers usually offer a knife-grinding attachment that allows the knives to be jointed, ground and honed while they're still in the cutterhead. Most small shops, however, send their knives out for professional sharpening.

Tuning up a planer—Start by leveling the planer—both side to side and front to back. A spinning cutterhead works like a gyroscope and runs smoothest when level. When out of level, it strains against its bearings and causes excessive wear. If the floor you place the planer on is fairly level, it should be heavy enough to stay put, but we've always bolted our planers down to ensure they don't move and that each foot assumes its share of the load.

If you remove the head and turn it upside down, you can see (from left to right) the anti-kickback pawls, serrated infeed roll, chip breaker and smooth-steel outfeed roll on this Delta 13-in. planer. A pressure bar, normally located between the cutterhead and the outfeed roll, has been omitted on the Delta.

The cylindrical steel cutterhead has three slots milled in it to hold the knives. The knife-locking screws don't bear directly on knives, but distribute their pressure on wedge-shaped gibs. Each gib has a flute along its upper edge to help deflect chips.

For most adjustments, the cutterhead is the main reference surface. Its position in the frame can't be altered, so the other components must be aligned to it. First, check to see that the planer's bed is parallel to the cutterhead along its length. You can measure the distance between the bed and each end of the cutterhead with an inside caliper or pass a trued-up block of wood between the two components. Place the block under the cutterhead and reduce the thickness adjustment until the block just passes through the opening. If you feel an equal amount of drag as you pass the block through the opening at several points along the cutterhead, the head and bed are parallel. If the block sticks at one end and flies through at the other, you'll have to adjust the bed. When the bed and cutterhead are out of alignment, you might also find that the thickness adjustment is difficult to crank up or down or that you can wiggle the bed up and down or side to side. Realigning the table will likely cure these problems, too.

If the thickness adjustment is based on the synchronized rotation of two or more threaded rods, raising the bed's lower edge by repositioning the drive gear(s) on the end of the rod will level the table. If you have a planer bed with gibs and ways (slotted

With this Delta planer's head partially disassembled and on its side, you can see the infeed-roll pressure spring, which bears on a sliding bearing block supporting the roll's shaft. A screw on top of the head adjusts the spring's tension and how hard the roll presses down on the work. Screws at either end of the roll must be set to give equal pressure.

When the pressure of the infeed roll is set too high, the roll's steel serrations will often emboss a pattern into the planed board. If a light cut is taken, marks will usually remain.

Though it doesn't often need to be reset, the chip breaker's height is set on many planers by turning two adjusting screws that raise or lower the chip breaker relative to the cutting arc.

tracks), you may have to readjust the gibs in the ways by adding metal shim stock between them or by judiciously filing or scraping. If the thickness adjustment is based on two wedges that slide against each other, check for dirt between the mating surfaces. Also, file or scrape away any high spots on the surfaces. If you still can't align the bed and cutterhead, a last resort is to set the knives parallel to the bed by locking them in the cutterhead at a slight angle, but we don't recommend this as a final solution. Get a machinist to take a look at the machine first.

Feed roll adjustment—On most planers, feed rolls are set by tightening or loosening the spring-pressure screws found on top of the planer (see figure 1). The infeed setting must strike a balance—the pressure should be sufficient to move the board but not so great that the serrated roll leaves an imprint deeper than the thickness the cutterhead will plane off. Start with the springs at their lowest compression, then try a paper-thin pass. If the infeed roll slips, increase the spring pressure. Embossing can sometimes be a real problem with thin, soft stock. In this case, it's okay to raise the infeed rolls until they barely contact the wood, as long as you take thin cuts that require less feed pressure. CAUTION: Don't forget to lower the rolls before taking any heavy cuts or else a dangerous kickback could occur. The outfeed-roll pressure isn't as great as on the infeed, but it shouldn't slip on the wood or allow the wood to lift from the bed. The outfeed roll is adjusted the same way as the infeed.

Chip breaker and pressure bar—The chip breaker should be set so its bottom edge is far enough below the cutterhead arc to keep the stock from lifting off the bed. The chip breaker rarely needs adjustment. While the chip breaker's setting isn't critical, the pressure bar is another matter. If it's set too low, the workpiece will jam in the planer. If it's too high, the wood will bounce under the cutterhead, resulting in chatter or tearout. Because the adjustment is so important, we never do it until after we're sure the feed rolls are right and the bed leveled. After thicknessing a scrap, shut the planer off, unplug it and wait for the cutterhead to come to rest. Now slip the surfaced scrap into the planer and check to see if it just slips under the pressure bar with a friction fit. This is largely a matter of feel, but with some practice you'll be able to tell if the piece is sticking or if there's too much play. If necessary, loosen the retaining bolts and adjust. After years of use, the pressure bar will wear more in the center than at the ends, so a board might jam along the edges of the bed but chatter when passed through the center. If this happens, remove the bar and file it straight or have a machinist grind it true.

Bed rolls—How you set the bed rolls depends on the kind of surfacing you do. The rougher the lumber, the higher the bed rolls must be set to reduce friction between the lumber and the bed. If the bed rolls are set too high, the workpiece passing over them may begin to vibrate, creating a rippled surface. While this won't be a problem with 8/4 maple, even a well-adjusted machine will devour thin wood with gusto. Smaller machines generally plane thin stock more successfully, because the smaller-diameter heads and closer positioning of feed rolls shortens the length of a board that can vibrate. For finishing cuts on relatively smooth surfaces, the bed rolls should be set just about dead even with the bed's surface. Measure the setting by laying a straightedge across both rolls on one side of the machine and inserting a feeler gauge between the straightedge and the bed. Settings will vary from 0 in. to 0.002 in. for finish planing and up to 0.008 in. for surfacing rough stock. The bed rolls can be quickly adjusted by

With a straightedge spanning the bed rolls, insert a feeler gauge between the straightedge and table to measure bed-roll length. Eccentric bolts at the ends of the bed-roll shafts can be turned to raise or lower each end of the roll independently. For planing thin lumber, the bed rolls can be lowered flush with the table. The planer's head has been removed for clarity.

built-in levers on some planers; on others, locking bolts must be loosened before any adjustment can be made.

The belts that drive the cutterhead and feed rolls should be checked occasionally for wear and tightened if necessary, but don't overdo it. Overtightening a belt strains bearings and shortens their lives. A good rule of thumb is that when slight pressure is applied, the belts should flex about $\frac{1}{32}$ in. for every inch of belt between pulleys. Apply belt dressing, available in spray cans or solid sticks at auto-supply stores, a couple of times a year to reduce slipping. Chains and sprockets exposed to dust and shavings should be lubricated with graphite or other dry lubricants. If they're enclosed in a tight case, a light greasing will do.

Sharpening and installing knives—No amount of adjustment will make up for dull, improperly installed knives. Knife replacement can be tedious, but the more accurately you work, the smoother the surface your planer will produce. Unless your planer is equipped with a special knife-grinding attachment, dull knives must be removed from the head before they can be sharpened. To shorten downtime, keep an extra set of sharp knives handy to swap with the dull ones. After removing the dull knives, clean the slots in the cutterhead, removing any debris that might prevent the knives from seating properly. Use oven cleaner or a Scotch-Brite pad moistened with diesel oil to remove the accumulations of pitch and resins, then wipe the head with a damp rag and let it dry thoroughly.

If you're ambitious or own a knife-grinding setup, you can joint and sharpen your own knives. But it's difficult to get them perfectly straight, so most woodworkers we know send them out to a sharpening shop. When you get your knives back, make sure each edge has been jointed straight and hasn't been burned blue. Properly sharpened knives will have a burr on the edge that must be honed away on a water or oil stone prior to installation. Keeping the bevel flat on the stone, lightly hone each knife until its edge is smooth and shiny. It's likely the bevel will be hollow ground, so the stone will contact only the tip and heel of the bevel, thus reducing the amount of metal that must be removed to eliminate the burr. If you often surface difficult woods, like curly maple, a small bevel can be honed on the back of each knife, blunting the cutting angle slightly and giving it more of a scraping action that's less apt to lift wild grain. (For more on back beveling, see "Face bevels," p. 88.) These dubbed-over edges are more likely to burn the stock, however, and put additional stress on the cutterhead bearings. When the honing is completed, clean the knives with mineral spirits or naptha.

Install each knife in the cutterhead with its gib and tighten the locking screws enough to hold the knife in the slot, yet leave it loose enough to be moved later on. The trick is to get all the knives to protrude the same amount from the head so each shares the cutting load equally. Otherwise, the knives will wear unevenly and the cut will be rippled. Setting the knives to exact height is best done with a dial indicator on a crow's foot base (see accompanying sidebar on p. 96) or a knife-setting gauge, which sits astride the cutterhead and references the precise knife height.

Tap each knife down into the head (or raise it up if the cutterhead is equipped with jacking screws) until all the knives protrude about $\frac{1}{8}$ in. from the cutterhead. As you do the final tightening, each knife will scoot up a bit, but they'll all move a similar amount if everything is clean. Make sure the cutterhead will rotate without hitting anything and check that it is parallel to the bed, as described above.

If the knives aren't set correctly, the high knife will collect more residue and dull faster than the others. As it dulls, it'll heat up and melted resins from the lumber will stick to it. As soon as you notice this buildup, correct the problem. If you wait, the heat might actually anneal the cutting edge, reducing its edge-holding ability.

Operating a planer—The planer is a relatively safe machine to use, but a few words of caution are in order. Thickness planers can only remove so much material in one pass, usually between ¹⁄₁₆ in and ¼ in. Attempting to remove more will result in either a jammed or broken machine. If chips jam the feed works, don't lower the bed to remove the stock until the cutterhead has stopped turning. Never reach into a planer that's running. Never plane a board that's shorter than the distance between the feed rolls. Otherwise, the piece could lodge in the planer, only to be shattered as it bounces into the cutterhead. No matter what happens, never look into the infeed end of a running planer; a board might be kicked back by the force of the cutterhead. And always wear eye, ear and breathing protection, even when running the planer for just a few minutes at a time.

There's more to planing than just feeding boards into the machine. By itself, a planer will not make warped stock flat: One side of the wood must first be flattened on the jointer or with a handplane. If you feed a twisted, winding board into a planer, the feed rolls will flatten it out as they move it past the cutterhead, but once the roll pressure is gone, the twist will reappear in the freshly planed board. Joint each piece flat but not necessarily clean on one face; low spots that remain rough will be cleaned up by the planer. Check the board's grain direction and feed it into the planer, jointed side down, with the grain oriented as shown in figure 1. If the grain doesn't clearly run in only one direction, feed it in the most prominent grain direction, angling the board slightly through the planer. Flip the boards end for end to reverse grain direction and then plane the opposite face of each board. Removing equal amounts of material from both faces will minimize warping if the board is case hardened from kiln drying.

Knots, splits, checks—When possible, cut defects out before planing the board. Also, you can cut down on planing time by cutting parts for a project to rough length, then planing the shorter pieces flat and smooth, rather than trying to flatten a long plank along its length and cutting it later. Thin stock, especially with erratic grain, might shatter as it's being planed unless it's supported underneath by a backing board. Smaller boards can be temporarily stuck to a scrap piece of plywood with double-stick tape. Without a backing board, it's usually not possible to plane stock less than ⅛ in. thick to ¼ in. thick.

Planer problems—One of the most common planing problems is end sniping, which results in a board that's thinner at the ends than in the middle. Sniping usually occurs because the board is not held flat on the planer bed and it rises into the cut-

---

Adjusting a planer with a dial indicator

by Robert M. Vaughan

When a machinist assembles a stationary woodshop machine like a planer, he often relies on a dial indicator to check alignments and part sizes. It makes sense for woodworkers to use the same tool when adjusting machines. A dial indicator is more suited to fine work than a ruler or tape measure. My eyes find it a lot easier, for example, to see a difference of 0.016 in. as 16 divisions on the face of a dial than to see a ¹⁄₆₄-in. difference on a tape measure. The indicator quantifies adjustments that might otherwise be a matter of "feel," and thus makes them quicker to perform with more predictable results.

The dial indicator I've found best for most planer work has a range of ¼ in., though indicators with a range of anywhere from ⅛ in. to 1 in. are available. The end of the shaft on most indicators has a removable tip; I keep both rounded and flat tips on hand. The ball tip is ideal for feed-roll work, while the convex tip is best for knife setting.

While of limited use on a thickness planer, a magnetic base is the most commonly used means of mounting the dial indicator and temporarily fixing it to the work area. It has an on-off switch that engages or disengages a magnetic field that holds it to any iron or steel object. An adjustable arm and swivel arrangement allows the indicator to be rigidly held in any position relative to

The cutterhead gauge base allows a dial indicator to be used for setting the depth of the knives in the cutterhead. While the base rides on the head itself, the indicator's tip rides on the blade's edge and registers its height on the dial.

the base. With the base attached to the side of the planer and the indicator shaft pressed against the planer's bed (perpendicular to the surface), I can crank the planer's thickness-adjusting wheel back and forth a few times to see if it raises and lowers the bed (or head) with consistent accuracy. I also can use a magnetic-base mounted indicator to quickly check the straightness of

shafts, the roundness of pulleys or sheaves or the amount of free play between any two moving parts.

Besides the magnetic base, two other bases make the dial indicator a particularly useful tool for planer adjustments. The cutterhead gauge base rests on the cutterhead and allows the end of the indicator shaft to ride directly on the edge of a planer knife. With it, you can quickly check how far each knife protrudes from the cutterhead, making sure all the knives are set at exactly the same height. The bed- and feed-roll base is a three-footed base that holds the dial indicator precisely perpendicular to a flat surface, allowing quick checks of cutterhead parallelism and feed- and bed-roll adjustment.

You can make your own cutterhead gauge base and feed-roll gauge base, as I did, from some scrap pieces of steel or aluminum and a few machine screws and nuts. The photos show how they are constructed. If you do make your own bases, make them for the particular dial indicator you plan to use, because the dimensions of various indicators are not all the same. You can also purchase commercially made bases from Powermatic Corp., Morrison Rd., McMinnville, TN 37110. They sell both a feed-roll gauge base (#2230002) and a cutterhead gauge base (#2230007) that will work on Powermatic, as well terhead. Lowering the pressure bar to eliminate freeplay between the stock and the bed, dropping the bed rolls flush to the bed or increasing the downward pressure of the feed rolls should eliminate sniping. Also, long stock can lever itself into the cutterhead and cause sniping, so always support long boards with infeed and outfeed tables or by hand.

Occasionally, a board with significant variations in thickness will jam in the planer. It can sometimes be freed without shutting the planer off by butting another board against its end (or side, if skewed) and pushing the stuck piece through. Sometimes a large chip lodged between the bed and bed rolls will cause a board to stick or leave a long rut on the bottom of the board. Shut off the planer and clear the chips and any gunk that may have accumulated on the bed rolls before it ruins your lumber or your patience.

If you're not getting surfaces as smooth as you'd like from your planer, chatter may be the problem. It could be caused by an uneven knife setting and/or dull knives, too fast a feed rate or the oscillation of thin stock between the bed and cutterhead. A high knife will cut deeper and leave dozens of little troughs along the board, and as the knife dulls, it will compress the board's fibers and burnish the surface rather than slice it clean. The compressed fibers are nearly impossible to sand out.

The rate at which a board passes by the cutterhead greatly influences the quality of the planed surface: Lower feed rates will produce more closely spaced knife cuts and thus smoother surfaces. But if slow feeding doesn't agree with your production schedule, take the first passes on rough boards at a high feed rate, then slow the feed down for the finish passes. Watch it with woods that have a high resin or sugar content, such as rosewood or cherry, because they tend to burn at slower feed rates—especially if the knives are getting dull. If you can't change the feed speed, take lighter cuts on each pass.

Surfacing any type of wood with ribbon or fiddleback grain, crotch swirls and medullary ray flakes can be challenging. Just remember that a slow feed rate, thin cuts and sharp knives all help conquer wicked grain. If you take too much in a single pass or feed the board against its grain, you'll end up listening to chunks of wood tearing out and clattering through the dust collection system or bouncing off the ceiling. And, the surfaced board will look just as bad as it sounded. □

Alfred E. Holland, Jr. is a woodworker in Orangevale, Calif. David Kinter is a self-employed woodworker in Boise, Ida.

The height of the bed rolls can be set with a dial indicator mounted in a magnetic base, but a three-footed feed-roll gauge base, right, will do the job quicker. The indicator can also be flipped in the feed-roll gauge base to check the alignment of all the parts of the planer's head assembly, including the cutterhead and feed rolls.

as other, machines. Each comes with its own dial indicator and sells for about $90.

To use a cutterhead base, first mount the indicator in the base and position it so the tip touches a smooth section of the cutterhead cylinder. Rotate the indicator's movable outer dial to zero the needle. Now set it over the knife as shown in the photo on the facing page and move it back and forth slightly, perpendicular to the edge, until the dial shows its highest reading, which should be about ⅛ in. Check the knife at both ends as well as at several places along its length before locking it down and checking the next knife.

To check cutterhead parallelism, install the indicator in the feed-roll base with the tip projecting upwards. With the base positioned on the bed, rotate the cutterhead so a smooth section contacts the tip, then take readings at several spots along the cutterhead length. The feed rolls can be checked for parallel this way too, as well as to determine if they've worn more in the middle than at the ends. If the wear is great enough, the feed rolls, or even the planer bed, may need to be re-machined. Use the indicator to check the alignment and straightness of the chip breaker and pressure bar and to recheck them after the final tightening of their locking screws to make sure they haven't shifted.

Reverse the dial indicator in the base so its shaft points down to check the bed rolls for proper adjustment and uneven wear. Zero the indicator by positioning all three base feet on the bed. Then, place the base so its feet bridge the bed-roll gap, the tip contacting the roll at its highest point. The indicator will directly measure the roll's projection above the bed. If you're getting erratic readings, examine the surface of the roll for large dips, rough spots or gunk that could cause the hand to move unpredictably. □

Robert Vaughan is a professional woodworker, with his own shop in Roanoke, Va. Other sources of dial indicators and magnetic bases include Enco Manufacturing Co., 5000 W. Bloomingdale Ave., Chicago, Ill. 60639, and L.S. Starrett Co., 121 Crescent St., Athol, Mass. 01331.

Small Thickness Planers
We test six machines

by David Sloan

A thickness planer can make life in the small workshop a lot easier. Most woodworking begins with a straight, flat, uniformly thick board, and while it's nice to know how to dimension a board with hand planes, it's also nice to have a machine that can do it for you. A planer can do the job in seconds, and since you can make boards any thickness you want, it frees you from having to design around the standard commercial thicknesses. In a busy production shop, a planer will soon pay for itself because it saves time and expands the range of work your shop can handle.

My first choice for a production-shop machine would be a big, heavy planer with an 18-in. to 24-in. wide bed. The massive cast-iron frame damps vibration, and a big heavy-duty machine can stand up to the hardest continuous use. Most important, the wide bed can accommodate glued-up carcase panels. But large production planers can cost and weigh more than a new car. A new 24-in. Powermatic with a 10-HP motor, for example, sells for about $15,000 and weighs in at almost 3,000 lb.

As an alternative, machine manufacturers have come up with much smaller, less expensive planers that are appropriate for the pro and hobbyist alike. There are a dozen or so of these small planers on the market—enough choices to give the potential buyer a headache. Since the average woodworker can't take a new planer out for a pre-purchase spin to see if he likes it, we chose six small machines with price tags under $2,000 and tested them in the *Fine Woodworking* shop. We already owned a 13-in. Delta (formerly Rockwell) RC-33 and a 15-in. Makita 2040. We borrowed the other four—the 12-in. Parks 95, 15-in. Grizzly G1021, 7-in. Williams & Hussey, and 12-in. Foley-Belsaw 985— from the manufacturers, and I put them to work on pine, poplar, red oak and hard maple. The ultimate test was bird's-eye maple, which is notorious for tearout.

Before reading on, take a moment to look at the box on the facing page, which explains the parts of a generic planer. The planer evaluations that follow refer frequently to the parts.

Prior to planing wood, I sharpened the knives of each planer on a Hitachi watercooled 1,000-grit knife grinder and set up the knives and rollers following the instructions in each respective manual. Then I surfaced roughsawn boards of different widths and lengths, taking heavy cuts to see how much the machines could take and light cuts to see how smooth a surface they could produce. I planed a few boards down as far as possible to see how thin each planer could go. To really strain the motors, I surfaced a hard-maple panel the full width of the bed, taking the heaviest cut possible.

Needless to say, none of these small machines has all the fea-

The 12-in. Parks 95 planer, with optional sheet-steel base and magnetic starter, is a comfortable 37½ in. floor to table.

tures of the big production planers. To keep the price down, the manufacturers had to make compromises. None of the small planers is wide enough to be much use surfacing glued-up panels. No machine has variable-speed feed, although optional sprockets will change the feed rates of the Makita and Foley-Belsaw.

All six of the small planers performed adequately. Each was capable of surfacing 10-ft. long, roughsawn 8/4 hard-maple boards, although it isn't practical on the Williams & Hussey machine. All six planers produced a surface ready for hand-planing or sanding on every wood except the bird's-eye maple. Even on the lightest cut, with freshly sharpened knives, all but the Williams & Hussey tore out little chunks of bird's-eye. That said, there were significant differences between the machines in both design and convenience. Some duplicated features found on larger, more expensive machines, while others were designed from scratch to be relatively portable and as inexpensive as possible. In this article I'll describe the planers and mention any noteworthy characteristics—good or bad. Detailed specifications for each machine are given in the chart on p. 104.

Parks 95 12-in.—Cast iron is the first thing you notice about this planer—lots of it. The Parks comes closest to being a scaled-down version of a heavy-duty planer. The 95 was designed in 1935 and hasn't changed since. It's a well-crafted machine, solid and straightforward. The cutterhead, for example, has been carefully drilled for balance. None of the other machines showed any evidence of cutterhead balancing.

Our Parks 95 was mounted on a sheet-steel stand which houses the motor. The cast-iron cutterhead cover functions, in the closed position, as a chipbreaker. Instead of springs, its weight holds it against the board. The steel bed and feed rollers are all adjustable. The infeed roller is corrugated and there's also a pressure bar—standard features on the expensive planers. Rollers and pressure bar are easily adjusted with big nuts right on top

How a thickness planer works

A planer simultaneously reduces the thickness of a board and makes opposite faces parallel. The drawing shows the workings of a standard design. The powered infeed roller grips the board, flattens it down against the planer bed and pushes it into the rotating cutterhead. The spring-loaded chipbreaker helps hold the board flat against the table and minimizes tearout by breaking the chips lifted up by the knives, similar to the action of the cap iron on a hand plane. As the newly planed surface emerges from under the cutterhead, the pressure bar and outfeed roller keep the board flat against the table. The powered outfeed roller propels the board past the cutterhead and out of the machine.

A planer won't remove warp, twist or cup, so one face of a board must first be flattened on a jointer. If you feed a

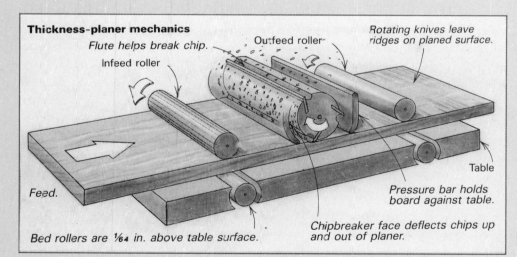

Thickness-planer mechanics

Flute helps break chip.

Infeed roller

Outfeed roller

Rotating knives leave ridges on planed surface.

Feed.

Bed rollers are ¹⁄₆₄ in. above table surface.

Chipbreaker face deflects chips up and out of planer.

Pressure bar holds board against table.

Table

warped or cupped board through a planer, the feed roller will just flatten it out against the table. When the board comes out the other end, it will spring back—thinner, but still warped or cupped.

The surface produced by a planer appears flat, but is actually made up of tiny ridges—although they aren't actually true

arcs. The larger the diameter of the cutterhead, the larger the arc that the knives traverse and the shallower these ridges will be. The number of cuts per inch, however, is the most significant factor in producing a smooth surface. The more cuts per inch, the smoother the surface, and this is achieved with a slow feed rate combined with a high cutter RPM. —D.S.

The only difference between our two-year-old Rockwell and the new Delta RC-33 is the knob that cuts power to the feed rollers. On the older machine (shown), the knob protrudes from the right side; on the new Delta, it's on the top. Table and cutterhead assembly are cast iron. The cutterhead assembly moves up and down on four steel columns.

Three flat steel springs bear down on the Delta chipbreaker to hold it tight against the stock. The chipbreaker adjusts with setscrews that rest on the steel bar shown.

of the machine. The knives were easy to install and adjust. While I could install the knives standing up, I had to squat on the floor to set them accurately. Two V-belts power the cutterhead, which drives the feed rollers through a network of massive gears. A panic lever on the top of the machine can stop power to the feed rollers if necessary.

Because of its height—37½ in. to the table in its highest position—the Parks 95 was the most comfortable to use of all the machines. To change depth-of-cut, the table travels on two vertical screws, one at the center of each long side. The planer's thickness capacity is only 4⅜ in.—the smallest of all the machines.

Except on the very lightest cuts, the Parks I tested didn't feed perfectly. When the infeed roller grabbed a short board, the tail end of the board lifted up in the air, causing the bottom front edge to catch in the bed-roller slot and stop. I had to hold down the tail end to keep the board from hanging up. No adjustment to the infeed roller or the bed roller seemed to help. Perhaps a larger-diameter bed roller would solve the problem. I soon became accustomed to this little quirk, and kept a hand on the tail end of the board until the front end was well under the infeed roller. Other than that, the Parks performed admirably. With a 2-HP motor it had plenty of power and planed both thick and thin stock well.

Delta RC-33 13-in.—The Delta is a well-made, heavy-duty, cast-iron machine. To keep costs down, Delta makes this, its smallest planer, in Brazil. The machine I tested is two years old and carries the Rockwell label, but the Delta planers being sold today are identical, with one exception: a knob that cuts power to the feed rollers has been moved from the side to the top of the planer. In the 16 months that I've worked with this planer, I've never found a need to cut power, so I can't say whether the relocation is an improvement.

The motor is mounted on top, instead of in the base. When you adjust the depth of cut, the cutterhead assembly, not the table, moves up and down on four screws, one in each of the steel columns. There's a lot of cast iron in this assembly, plus the weight of the motor, so it takes some muscle to turn that handle. I like this arrangement. Because the table height doesn't change, you can support long stock with outboard rollers without resetting them for every cut. Three V-belts drive the three-knife cutterhead, which in turn drives a roller chain to power the feed rollers. A phalanx of anti-kickback fingers in front of the infeed roller eliminates any possibility of kickback.

The chipbreaker is a sheet-steel fabrication held down against the stock by three flat springs. There is no pressure bar. Knives are spring-loaded and very easy to set with the new bridge-type gauge supplied with the machine, although my sliced-up fingers can attest to the fact that the edges of the cutterhead are almost as sharp as the knives.

It isn't easy to adjust the height of the feed rollers. First you have to make a beveled wooden gauge block, which you then place under the cutterhead with a feeler gauge between the block and a knife. It's hard to maneuver the block, the feeler gauge, your fingers and your eyes in a very confined space in close proximity to very sharp knives—all this while kneeling on the floor. The adjusting screws themselves are in an awkward place on the underside of the frame.

In use, the Delta atones for the agony of set-up. Feeding was consistently smooth and effortless. The machine hogged through rough stock with ease, yet left a respectable finish on fine cuts. Neither thick nor thin stock posed a problem.

From *Fine Woodworking* magazine (May 1985) 52:72-78

Grizzly G1021 15-in.—The success of the Delta design spawned this Taiwanese knockoff, which sells for about half the list price of the Delta planer. Place these two machines side by side, and the only obvious differences are the elevating wheel and the color: Grizzly green vs. battleship gray. A closer look reveals that the Grizzly isn't quite a carbon copy. Its bed is 15 in. wide instead of 13 in.—a definite improvement. When you turn the wheel, the table, not the head, moves on four screws. The Grizzly also sports extension rollers that bolt onto the cast-iron table. In most other features it duplicates the Delta. Even the pulley covers are interchangeable, though the bolt holes don't quite line up. The amusing similarity was the owners' manual. The Grizzly manual is the Delta manual practically verbatim. The paragraph that refers to the Delta's moving head had just been whited out.

All right, so the Taiwanese copied the Delta, but is it as good? Based on the two days I spent with this machine, I'd say no, but it's close. The castings are excellent. The Grizzly has a cast-iron base assembly that the Delta doesn't have. This machine is heavy—480 lb. with stand and motor, outweighing the complete Delta by nearly 200 lb. Where the Delta has sheet-steel gears to drive the feed rollers, the Grizzly has nicely machined castings—no great improvement functionally, but a nice touch. A dust hood for collection-system hookup is standard. The Grizzly has the same set-up virtues and vices as the Delta since the cutterhead and feed-roller designs are the same. On the other hand, the Grizzly I tested had only one weak, flat spring holding down the chipbreaker, while the Delta has three strong springs.

There was a problem. When I was setting up the machine, I found that the chipbreaker couldn't be adjusted anywhere near specifications. Closer examination showed that the fabricated sheet-steel chipbreaker was warped, possibly from the heat of welding. This meant that when the chipbreaker was mounted in the machine, the left side could bear down against a board, but the right side was about $\frac{1}{16}$ in. above the surface. Boards would catch on the left side, slew over to the right, and go through the planer at an angle. Boards as thin as $\frac{1}{4}$ in. disintegrated because they could lift off the table, but the quality of the cut on thicker stock didn't seem to be affected. I probably could have fixed the chipbreaker with a day's worth of filing, hammering and fiddling, but I ordered a replacement chipbreaker over the phone. It arrived within a few days, and took about 45 minutes to install and adjust. Boards no longer slewed to one side. Thin boards still disintegrated, but only about 40% of the time, with the worst damage occurring to the last few inches of the board. Stronger springs on the chipbreaker would probably solve this problem.

Although the design is the same as the Delta, feeding the Grizzly wasn't as easy. Boards needed a push to get started. The Delta hogged off more wood—$\frac{3}{16}$ in. vs. $\frac{1}{8}$ in. for the Grizzly. The Grizzly is beefy enough that it could probably handle a much heavier cut, but the frame interferes and the stock won't feed if you try to cut more than $\frac{1}{8}$ in. This is a major nuisance when you're rough-planing. Several boards that were thicker at the back end than at the front jammed against the frame halfway through. I had to stop and lower the table to finish the cut.

Since I spent only a few days with this planer, durability is something I can't predict. The Grizzly *looks* good and planed adequately on all but thin stock, but it's hard to judge the quality of motors or bearings from only a few hours of use. Its three-month warranty is the shortest of any of the planers. The importer says that replacement parts are available, and Grizzly says that defective parts will be replaced free, including shipping, during the warranty period.

The Grizzly as shown weighs in at 480 lb.—the heaviest of all the small planers. Extension bed rollers are standard equipment, front and back. The table moves up and down on the four steel columns. Base, table and cutterhead assembly are cast iron.

Almost identical to the Delta in design, the Grizzly sports one chipbreaker spring, where as the Delta has three.

Makita 2040 15-in.—Like the Delta, the Makita I tested is one that we've had for about two years. The 2040 bears little resemblance to an industrial machine, although it does have a pressure bar. Its castings are aluminum instead of iron. The cutterhead has only two knives, and changing them was a snap. A shaft lock holds the cutterhead in position when you're unbolting and setting the knives—a nice feature. A plastic handwheel turns a central screw that elevates the table from underneath, and the table corners ride on four steel columns.

The 2040 is designed to take light cuts. It's the only machine that comes with a 110V motor, which is a small, 2-HP, high-RPM, universal type similar to those found in routers and electric drills. The motor slows noticeably on hardwood, especially when taking the maximum cut on wide stock. All the other planers have induction motors—the type common on tablesaws and other woodworking machines.

The bed rollers are steel, but the feed rollers are rubber. All are adjustable, but the current owners' manual doesn't explain how to adjust feed-roller height (our old manual did). This omission is due to Makita's concern that misadjustment might overstress the cast-aluminum frame of the machine. Anyone who uses the 2040 seriously will need to know how to adjust the feed rollers. Roller height is set by means of screws on the top of the planer at the ends of each roller, and is adjusted with a slotted, threaded ring that surrounds the spring-tension screw. This arrangement could be improved upon. Trying to turn the large out-

The Makita 2040 needs a boost. Without blocks, the table is only 20¼ in. from the floor in its highest position. A small, high-RPM, 110-volt, universal-type motor is concealed in the base.

The Williams & Hussey is a benchtop machine. The motor pivots on a special mount and its weight tensions the V-belt. The add-on power-feed kit bolts on the side of the cutterhead assembly.

side ring is impossible with a regular screwdriver, and I finally resorted to using a big cold chisel as a screwdriver.

The Makita has the fastest feed rate of the small machines—25 FPM, which works out to a very low 37 cuts per inch (CPI). According to accepted planer theory, the more cuts per inch, the smoother the planed surface. The Makita, however, with the lowest CPI of all the planers, gave a smoother cut than any of the other power-feed machines. This *shouldn't* be possible, but it is. So much for theory. A feed-speed reduction kit is available, although this couldn't improve much on the smooth finish that our Makita produced, except perhaps on highly figured wood.

There were some things I didn't like about the Makita. It's loud—by far the loudest of the small planers. Ear protection is a must. The table, at its highest, is only 20¼ in. from the floor—far too low for comfort. Our 2040 rests on 4¾-in. wooden runners, but it's still too low. More than once, I found myself kneeling on the floor to view the depth-of-cut gauge. The machine won't take a cut heavier than ⅛ in. on narrow stock or 1/25 in. on wide stock. As with the Grizzly, the frame interferes and prevents stock from feeding if you try to take a heavier cut. A board that's thicker at the tail end will jam against the planer frame halfway through the cut.

In spite of these problems, I liked this machine because of its smooth cut and wide, 15-in. capacity. I also liked the depth-of-cut gauge that lets you preview the amount of stock the planer will remove. The 2040 can't do fast, heavy hogging on roughsawn stock. It can handle big stock, but a little at a time. Its small size makes it a good choice for a cramped shop and it's light enough that you can slide it across the floor without breaking your back.

Williams & Hussey 7-in. molder/planer—This is a small, benchtop machine that doubles as a molder (I didn't test its molding capabilities). The basic machine comes in three models: W-7, which is a hand-feed model; W-7PF, which has a powered infeed roller; and W-7S, which has powered infeed and outfeed rollers like the larger planers. An add-on kit converts the hand-feed machine to either of the power-feed models. For the test, we got the W-7 hand-feed model and converted it to the W-7S.

This is a very nicely made planer. The bed and cutterhead assembly are cast iron, and machining is of the highest quality. Two ¼-in. thick knives, the thickest of any of the machines, are mounted on the square cutterhead. The heavy cast-iron cutterhead cover also serves as a chip deflector. (It's set too far in front of the cutterhead—2½ in.—to function as a chipbreaker.) There is an unpowered steel outfeed roller on the hand-feed model, but no infeed roller of any kind. The W-7S power-feed model has both rubber infeed and outfeed rollers. There are no bed rollers on any of the models.

Stock up to 7½ in. thick will fit through the planer. You have to remove the chip deflector to raise the head past 6 in., however, because the handle bangs into it.

I set up the planer on a table of 2x4s and particleboard. A 3450-RPM, 1½-HP Sears motor provided the power. Williams & Hussey sells an optional motor mount, which I recommend. With this setup, the weight of the motor keeps tension on the V-belt.

The knives don't require adjustment, as the knives on all the other machines do. You simply butt each knife against a shoulder in the cutterhead and tighten the bolts. This always sets the knives to the same height, even after sharpening, because the bevels aren't supposed to be ground unless they're badly nicked. To sharpen, you're supposed to simply stone the flat back of each knife. If you do grind the bevels, it's easy to set the knives by placing a shim between the knife and the cutterhead shoulder. Don't look for any help from the owners' manual—it's the worst I've ever seen with a woodworking machine. I frequently found myself winging it as I set up and used the W&H.

The hand-feed model is just that—fed by hand. You push the board into the planer with your hands and/or a push stick and pull it out the other end. It takes a little more effort than ripping on a tablesaw. The chip deflector and outfeed roller help hold the board down on the table, but since there's no infeed roller, it's easy to inadvertently lift up the tail end of the board and badly snipe the front end.

One side of the planer is open, so by flipping a board end-for-end and running it through again, you can plane boards up to 14 in. wide on the hand-feed model. Reversing a board means cutting against the grain, which may cause tearout. This method is okay for rough work, but the two cuts never match up and the resulting ridge must be hand-planed. The little machine seems most comfortable with narrower stock. The manufacturer sells optional steel guide bars that clamp to the table and prevent stock from wandering out the open side. I didn't test these, but they're probably a worthwhile investment. For cutting moldings, they're essential. The open side is a boon for molding because you can mold up to 7 in. from the edge of any size board or panel.

The hand-feed model gave the best cut of any of the small planers. Because you can feed the board at a snail's pace, the number of cuts per inch is extremely high. The surface feels as if it's been hand-planed. The Williams & Hussey hand-feed model was the only planer that didn't tear up the bird's-eye, no matter in what direction I fed the board. While the W-7 can plane boards as thin as $\frac{3}{32}$ in., I also managed to hog off $\frac{3}{8}$ in. in one cut on a 4-in. wide pine board by feeding very slowly—though the machine bucked and groaned in protest.

The power-feed kit takes about 30 minutes to install. Off comes the steel outfeed roller and on go the rubber rollers, roller chains and an oil-bath gearbox. The power-feed model has a 15-FPM feed rate.

The power-feed was disappointing. Roller tension is adjustable, but roller height isn't. The rubber feed roller just didn't bite hard enough. I had to push and cajole, and sometimes the board would just slow down and stop in midcut. No longer could I take a heavy cut—$\frac{1}{8}$ in. was the maximum on a 4-in. yellow-pine board. I tried taking $\frac{3}{16}$ in., but the motor jumped back on its mount, the belt slipped and the planer ground to a halt. The power-feed could handle cuts $\frac{1}{8}$ in. or thinner on 7 in. of hard maple, but I no longer got that hand-planed surface and the bird's-eye occasionally misbehaved. For a hefty $340 extra, the power conversion kit raises the price of the W&H almost as high as one of the larger, more powerful planers, but doesn't deliver the same capacity.

The W&H is not well suited for long, wide boards. For small-scale work or highly figured woods, however, the hand-feed model is excellent. The molding capability will appeal to frame-makers or contractors who need custom moldings. In addition to carrying stock molding knives, the manufacturer will make custom knives. If you're so inclined, you could also make your own.

Foley-Belsaw 985 12-in. planer/molder—This dual-purpose machine not only planes, but also can make an impressive variety of moldings. A fancier model, 984, even comes with a built-in ripsaw so you can both rip and plane or mold at the same time.

Compared to the Parks, Delta and Grizzly, the 985 is a lightweight, lacking almost all of the features of what I consider to be the ideal planer. While the table is cast iron, the rest of the

The Foley-Belsaw 985 planer/molder has a beefy 3-HP motor tucked under its sheet-steel frame. The top hinges up to expose the working parts.

frame is made of $\frac{1}{8}$-in. thick sheet steel. Tension can be adjusted on the rubber feed rollers, but roller height can't. When the rollers wear, they must be replaced, but at less than $20, this is no great expense. The cutterhead turns on ball bearings, while the feed rollers turn in lubricant-impregnated bronze bushings. The three knives are held in the cutterhead by wedge-shaped gibs, and it takes a hefty whack to break the grip of the cast-aluminum gibs. There are no bed rollers or pressure bar, and the chip-breaker is not adjustable. The table elevates on four screws.

Our test planer came with a beefy 3-HP motor that lives down in the sheet metal base and drives the cutterhead with two V-belts. This monster caused the sheet-metal 985 to rumble and shake like an old flivver when I threw the switch, but on wide maple boards it was nice to have all that power. Foley-Belsaw offers a 5-HP motor as an option, but I don't think the machine's lightweight construction warrants it.

The owners' manual was the best of the lot, and the optional knife-setting gauge is the best design I've ever come across—a real pleasure to use. Another nice feature is the elevation handle: one turn moves the table exactly $\frac{1}{16}$ in.

Just by eyeballing, it was hard to judge the depth of cut. With most of the small planers, you can tell roughly how much of a cut you're taking just by glancing at the space between the board and the frame. Not so on the 985. With the cutterhead touching the board, there's still a big gap between board and frame. On the other hand, the frame couldn't interfere with boards that were thicker at the tail end, as it did on the Makita and the Grizzly.

As planers go, this is a no-frills machine. For example, the table had the roughest surface of any of the small planers and the edges of the casting were sharp enough to cut. I can't fault the 985 on short-term performance—it planed well on both thin and

Planer characteristics

	Parks 95 (United States)	Delta RC-33 (Brazil)	Grizzly G1021 (Taiwan)	Makita 2040 (Japan)	Williams & Hussey W-7 and W-7S (United States)	Foley-Belsaw 985 (United States)
List price: Complete as shown; planer only	$1620; $1050	$1802; $1445	$844.95;	$1780;	$470 Hand-feed (W-7)* $740 Power infeed and outfeed (W-7S)	$1095; $825
Weight (pounds): Complete; planer only	410; 244	295; 260	480;	254;	; 73	370; 252
Table size (inches)	12⅛ x 20⅛	13 x 19¾	15 x 20⅛	15½ x 23⅝	8½ x 14⅛	12¼ x 27
Minimum stock thickness	³⁄₃₂ in.	³⁄₁₆ in.	³⁄₁₆ in.	³⁄₁₆ in.	³⁄₃₂ in.	⁵⁄₃₂ in.
Heaviest cut possible: 4-in. board; full width	³⁄₁₆ in.; ³⁄₁₆ in.	³⁄₁₆ in.; ³⁄₁₆ in.	⅛ in.; ⅛ in.	⅛ in.; ¹⁄₂₅ in.	³⁄₁₆ in.; ³⁄₁₆ in. (W-7) ⅛ in.; ⅛ in. (W-7S)	⅜ in.; ¼ in.
Maximum stock width	12 in.	13 in.	14⅞ in.	15⅜ in.	14 in. (W-7)** 7 in. (W-7S)	12¼ in.
1-PH motor included in complete price	1½-HP, 220V ***	2-HP, 220V ***	2-HP, 220V	2-HP, 110V, universal type	None ***	3-HP, 220V ***
Switch included in complete price	Magnetic	Magnetic	Magnetic	Mechanical	None	Magnetic
Cutterhead dia.; no. of knives; RPM	3 in.; 3; 4200	3 in.; 3; 4500	3 in.; 3; 4500	3⁵⁄₁₆ in.; 2; 6500	1⅛ in. square; 2; 7000	3¼ in.; 3; 4500
Feed rollers	1½ in.; steel; corrugated infeed	2 in.; steel; corrugated infeed	2 in.; steel; corrugated infeed	2½ in.; rubber	1½ in.; steel; unpowered outfeed (W-7) 1½ in.; rubber; height not adjustable (W-7S)	1½ in.; rubber; height not adjustable
Bed rollers	1 in.; steel	1 in.; steel	1 in.; steel	1⅛ in.; steel	None	None
Feed rate	16 FPM	11½ FPM	11½ FPM	29½ FPM (reduction kit available)	Infinitely variable (W-7) 15 FPM (W-7S)	12 FPM (optional sprocket increases speed)
Cuts per minute; inch	12,600; 66	13,500; 97	13,500; 97	13,000; 37	14,000; infinitely variable (W-7) 14,000; 78 (W-7S)	13,500; 94
Hood for dust-collection attachment	Optional, $70	Optional, $44	Included	None	None	Optional, $25
Warranty	1 yr. parts & labor	1 yr. parts & labor	3 mo. parts/labor	1 yr. parts & labor	1 yr. parts & labor	1 yr. parts & labor
Miscellaneous	Cast-iron frame; pressure bar	Cast-iron frame; anti-kickback fingers	Cast-iron frame; anti-kickback fingers	Cast-aluminum frame; pressure bar; segmented chipbreaker	Cast-iron frame; doubles as molder; bench-mounted. Power conversion kits avail- able, $235 and $340.	Sheet-steel frame; doubles as molder

* $645 power infeed (W-7PF); ** by reversing board; *** other motors available.

thick stock for the few hours I used it. It can also take a bigger cut than the other power-fed machines. The Foley-Belsaw's sheet-metal design, however, cuts too many corners to suit me. But if you can make use of the machine's extensive molding capabilities, it's worth a closer look. The price is right, and it can do things no spindle shaper can. Foley-Belsaw stocks a number of knife patterns and will make custom knives to order.

Conclusions—No machine was perfect. So, weighing the good against the bad, here's how I'd rate the planers:

My first choice for an all-around planer would be the Delta RC-33. Adjusting the rollers was a nuisance, but it's a well-made, smooth-operating, reliable planer for both heavy and light work.

The Parks 95 is a close second. The feeding problem was the only thing that kept it out of a tie for first place. Its ease of adjustment and simple, solid construction were unmatched. It's a hard-working planer that will probably outlast several owners.

The Makita 2040 isn't built for the ages, but it should give years of service. It isn't fast at removing stock, but if a smooth surface is more important than a heavy cut, the Makita may be for

you. Often heavily discounted, it is a good value for the money.

The Williams & Hussey W-7 hand-feed planer would be my choice for small-scale work. It's expensive for its size and weight, but it's very well made. Forget the power-feed models—the cost outweighs the convenience.

The Foley-Belsaw works very well, but I'd consider it only if I wanted the molding capability. Because it skimps on mass and conventional planer design, I wouldn't buy it as a planer alone unless I couldn't afford one of the cast-iron machines.

The Grizzly appears to be made well but assembled without much fine-tuning. It has all the adjustment hassles of the Delta, without the same smooth performance. It is, however, a usable planer at a very low price. Long-term durability is a gamble, but you can wear out two Grizzlys for the price of one Delta. □

David Sloan is an associate editor at FWW. *Since this article was published, Williams and Hussey has fitted its planer with a serrated-steel infeed roller and a rubber outfeed roller, thus improving feed problems. Also, Grizzly added two springs to its planer's chipbreaker.*

Eye Safety

How to treat and prevent eye injuries

by Dr. Paul F. Vinger

Some woodworkers don't wear eye protection. I do. As an ophthalmologist, I've seen woodworkers who've been blinded, lost an eye or suffered for days after having even just a tiny wood sliver removed from an eye. Eyes are among the most vulnerable parts of the body: They are easily punctured, lacerated, perforated or chemically burned. They should be protected at all times in the shop. The eyelid offers protection from dust, but it is no match for the hazards woodworkers encounter every day. A chip, for example, can fly from a 10-in. tablesaw at 103 MPH. That's 2 ft. in $^{13}/_{1,000}$ of a second. If the object hits your arm, it might sting or even cut it. The same chip could puncture your eye.

When I treat injured woodworkers, I often think the safety glasses, goggles and face shield hanging in my shop might just be among the best woodworking tools I own. These three kinds of eye protection will prevent almost any eye injury a woodworker is likely to encounter. Sometimes you only need to wear safety glasses; other times, especially if you've already suffered a serious eye injury, you need to wear two forms of eye protection.

Protection options—Each woodworker must decide what form of protection to wear, but here are some guidelines to follow. If you're using high-horsepower machinery, especially machines that rotate blades at high speeds and are capable of hurling large objects, it's wise to wear maximum eye protection. Machines that deliver less energy at slower speeds may call for less eye protection. For example, you might wear safety glasses or goggles plus a face shield when using a tablesaw, shaper or other tool where there is a danger of a large piece of wood being kicked back and damaging both the eyes and other parts of the face. I always recommend both safety glasses and a face shield for lathe work. Incidentally, protective eyeglasses or goggles should always be worn under face shields, because woodworkers frequently raise the shield to examine a workpiece or to provide ventilation, thus temporarily exposing their eyes to a potential injury. Safety glasses with side shields may be adequate when using drill presses; slow-speed, electric hand tools; or hammers and screwdrivers. Side shields should be worn with safety glasses, because the effectiveness of the safety glasses is reduced by 25% if the shields are removed. Goggles should be worn over street-wear (non-safety) glasses when there is a risk of many fine flying particles, and for use with chemicals and for welding that doesn't require a full face shield. If you have any doubts, wear more eye protection than less.

Hand tools hurt eyes more often than power tools, so don't neglect safety glasses for even simple jobs. The Consumer Product Safety Commission has reported that 6,719 people suffered eye injuries in 1986 while working with hand tools at home. Most of those injuries came from hammers and screwdrivers. For example, one of my patients, a young carpenter, once hit a ten-penny nail with a glancing blow. The nail rocketed from the wood into his left eye, destroying the eye's lens. The contact lens I gave him to replace his natural lens restored the vision in his eye, but he can no longer focus on close objects without bifocals.

Safety glasses are the first line of defense against eye injuries. If you're a woodworking hobbyist, reaching for your safety glasses should be the first thing you do in any woodworking project. If you're a woodworking professional, think of yourself as a person who wears glasses most of the time. Put on your safety glasses before you enter the shop, and don't take them off until you leave at the end of the day. If you wear vision-correcting glasses already, don't be fooled into thinking regular prescription glasses offer protection: They're not designed to withstand heavy impacts. Get a pair of prescription safety glasses with side shields from a quality eye-care professional. There's no excuse not to, given the wide variety of protective equipment available today. Even designer-type safety glasses have been available for some time now (see the sidebar on p. 107).

Years ago, safety glasses were made of just that—glass. Today, virtually all nonprescription safety lenses are made of super-tough polycarbonate, and prescription safety glasses come with polycarbonate, glass or CR-39 plastic lenses. Tests show that a polycarbonate lens is at least five times stronger than a glass lens and more than twice as strong as a CR-39 plastic lens.

Sometimes even safety glasses or goggles are not enough to stop the power of a flying object. A face shield needs to be added. You may be thinking: "No one wears safety glasses and a face shield at the same time." But, this double protection is often advisable. I once treated a man who worked at the same shop for 30 years. He lost both eyes and severely fractured several bones in his face when a planer shot an oak board at him. The pliable sides of a good pair of safety goggles would have dissipated some of the power in that flying piece of lumber, but much of its damaging force would have been transferred to the bones surrounding the eye. Even so, the lenses of the safety glasses or goggles would probably have prevented cuts and punctures to the eyeball. I have no doubt that wearing both safety glasses and a face shield would have lessened this man's injuries enough that his sight could have been saved and his disfigurement reduced or eliminated. Remember, eye injuries are not predictable; they happen in an instant. Many woodworkers who ordinarily wear eye and face protection have paid dearly when the unexpected happened after the protective device was removed while doing "a little touch-up."

Chemicals and irritants—Acids and alkalies such as those used in bleaches, stains and dyes can cause permanent, blinding eye

Safety eye wear

Safety eye wear is available in many types and styles. In nonprescription safety glasses, you can still get the good old "Buddy Holly" model (1), but they are rapidly being replaced by more modern versions that have integral side and top shields (2). Prescription safety glasses are available in a wide variety of styles with clip-on or permanent side shields, and if you need them, bifocal or trifocal lenses (3). Many makers now offer goggles with fog-proof lenses (4). Goggles with rigid lens holders and soft face frames (5) are often worn by people who've lost vision in one eye and want to provide maximum protection for their good eye. Because they have individual lens holders, these goggles can be fitted with prescription safety lenses.

This integral face shield, hard hat and hearing protection system (6), made by Bilsom International, offers a full range of protection when doing heavy noisy jobs such as chainsawing or lumber milling. For more on makers and suppliers of safety eye wear, see the sources of supply box on p. 107.

injuries. In sufficient strength, these chemicals can rapidly eat through the cornea and into the iris and lens; this can damage the eye beyond repair. It may surprise you to find that solvents such as lacquer thinner, acetone and turpentine normally cause only topical (surface) damage to the eye and rarely cause sight-threatening injuries if they can be completely and quickly flushed from the eyes. Even so, many chemicals that woodworkers use can cause extreme pain if they get into the eye. Whenever you work with chemicals, wear goggles. The goggles should have hooded vents that allow ventilation but prevent liquids from getting into the eyes. If any chemical gets into an eye, treat it as a medical emergency; never delay treatment.

Thermal burns to the lids and eyes from exposure to excess heat are rare among woodworkers. However, if you're going to be exposed to high-heat operations, heat-absorbing or -reflecting protective eye wear is available.

I've seen more than one woodworking patient who's had bad experiences working with cyanoacrylate (instantly adhering) glue. They either walk into my office with an eyelid glued shut or a finger stuck fast to an upper or lower eyelid. Repair involves minor surgery. Goggles or safety glasses would probably have prevented the problem.

Contact lenses and woodworking don't mix, especially if you're working with acids or alkalies. If a chemical splashes in an eye, it gets trapped underneath the contact lens. It's hard enough to get a woodworker's eyelid open when acid or alkali is in the eye, and the time needed to pluck out the contact lens just gives these chemicals more time to do their damage. Sawdust and other par-

ticles also constantly get under contact lenses, causing pain and scratches to the eye's cornea.

I suspect that every woodworker has had to remove sawdust from an eye from time to time. I've had to do it myself. Most woodworkers know that flushing the eye with water will remove most particles, and many know the old trick of pulling an upper eyelid over a lower one to remove a spec of sawdust. What many woodworkers fail to do, however, is brush away the additional sawdust that has accumulated on the eyelashes, and they end up with more sawdust in their eyes than they started with.

Even if you do a fine job of removing a foreign particle from an eye, the particle may scratch the cornea, and the scratch will make you think the particle is still in the eye. If that feeling persists, seek medical attention, because the particle may in fact still be there, but invisible. This is often a problem with pine sawdust. When pine sawdust is saturated with water, or tears, it becomes transparent. Ophthalmologists use a special dye that makes invisible particles instantly visible, and therefore, much easier to remove.

There's nothing like the natural beauty of wood, especially when viewed up close with the naked eye. But the time for doing such viewing is only after a project has been completed and is out of the shop. Then you can take your safety glasses off, lean over and take a good, close look. At all other times, some form of protection should rest firmly between the work you are doing and that most sensitive part of the human anatomy—your eyes. □

Dr. Paul F. Vinger is a woodworker and ophthalmologist. He lives in Lexington, Mass.

Buying eye protection

by John Decker

A good pair of nonprescription safety glasses only costs about $5, goggles cost about $4 and face shields cost less than $15. Paying for eye protection is not a problem, but knowing how and where to buy it might be.

First, any safety eye wear you buy should have a "Z87.1" logo on it. This logo tells you the eye wear meets a minimum standard for safety set forth by the American National Standards Institute. On safety glasses, look for the Z87.1 logo on the inside of the temples and frames. On goggles and face shields, look for it near the perimeter of the lens or on the lens holder.

You can buy nonprescription safety glasses, goggles and face shields from hardware stores and building supply outlets, but their selection may be limited. Many cities have safety supply outlets that stock a full line of eye safety wear. For one in your area, check the Yellow Pages under safety equipment. Another way to buy eye safety equipment is through mail-order houses such as those listed at the end of this article.

If you wear prescription glasses, buy

prescription safety glasses from an eye-care professional. When I visited my doctor, he showed me several pairs of designer-style safety frames, all of which were nearly indistinguishable from regular eyeglasses, save the slightly heavier bridge piece around the nose and the Z87.1 logo stamped clearly on the frame and temples I found a pair of frames to my liking that cost $56. All of the frames came with permanent or clip-on side shields. Because I planned on making the safety glasses my full-time eye wear, I chose clip-on shields.

Regular safety lenses for my glasses cost $24 each. I assumed my lenses would be made of polycarbonate plastic, but the doctor told me they were regular plastic. "Polycarbonate lenses are for people who play racquetball and other high-impact sports," he said. After explaining to him about tablesaws, lathes and shapers, he readily agreed that polycarbonate lenses would be better. Polycarbonate lenses added $20 to the original $24 price.

Because the frames and lenses both had to be ordered from the factory, it

took about four weeks to get my new glasses. The bill came to $130.40, extra side shields included. Quite reasonable, I think, for a pair of glasses I'll wear in the shop and on the street. □

John Decker is an amateur woodworker in Katonah, N.Y.

Sources of supply

Companies making safety eye wear:

American Optical Corp., 14 Mechanic St., Southbridge, MA 01550; (617) 765-9711.

Bilsom International, 109 Carpenter Drive, Sterling, VA 22170; (703) 834-1070.

Titmus Optical, 1015 Commerce St., Petersburg, VA 23803; (804) 732-6121.

Willson Safety Products, P.O. Box 622, Reading, PA 19603; (215) 376-6161.

Mail-order suppliers of safety eye wear:

Direct Safety Company, 7815 S. 46th St., Phoenix, AZ 85044; (602) 968-7009.

Industrial Safety & Security, 1390 Neubrecht Road, Lima, OH 45801; (419) 227-6030.

Kenco Safety Products, 70 Rock City Road, Woodstock, NY 12498; (914) 679-5246.

Lab Safety Supply, 3430 Palmer Drive, Janesville, WI 53546; (608) 754-2345.

Workshop Noise

Are machines damaging your hearing?

by Joy O'Neal

Hearing protectors

Hearing protectors come in many shapes and colors but they're all muffs or plugs under the skin. Plugs on a cord (1 and 2) or headband (6) can be worn around the neck so they're handy when needed. Disposable plugs (3) are cheap enough to wear and toss after use. Foam plugs (4) expand inside the ear canal to block out noise. One type of plug (5) requires a plastic tube to stiffen the shaft during insertion. Foam-filled muffs (7) cover the entire ear while canal caps (8) seal off only the ear canal.

D o you wonder whether the noise from your woodworking machines is damaging your hearing? As an audiologist, I often evaluate the hearing of people—woodworkers included—whose work or hobby exposes them to high noise levels. I have found that noise-induced hearing loss is widespread, despite the fact that it's so simple to prevent. Unfortunately, once hearing has been damaged by noise, the loss is permanent and irreversible.

In this article, I will explain what steps you can take to protect your hearing from noise damage. I am particularly concerned about loud woodworking machines because my husband, Michael, is a woodworker who suffers from noise-induced hearing loss. Curious about the noise levels in his shop, I used a sound level meter to measure the intensity of noise at ear level from Michael's machines, as well as some in other shops. Every machine produced sound levels high enough to cause hearing damage after long-term exposure.

Sound is the result of vibrations set up in the air by a mechanical force, which could be anything from rustling leaves to a pounding hammer. The intensity of a sound, which we perceive as loudness, is a measure of the pressure of the sound waves, and the unit of measure is the decibel (dB). The higher the decibel reading, the louder the sound. It's important to remember that the decibel is logarithmic and, therefore, nonlinear. In other words, if the intensity of a sound wave is doubled, the decibel level doesn't double, rather it increases by 3 dB. The reason this is important to you is that if you're in a shop where a router is producing 105 dB, and someone starts another router as loud as the first one, the intensity isn't doubled to 210 dB, but increases only 3 dB to 108 dB.

Frequency, which we perceive as pitch, is a measure of sound vibration in cycles per second (cps or, more commonly, Hz). The more cycles of vibration that occur per second, the higher the frequency of the sound. Most woodworking machinery noise is in the mid- to high-frequency range, but a saw or router cutter turning at a very high rate of speed will produce a higher-pitched sound than a drill press or lathe which turns more slowly. These high-frequency sounds are more likely to cause hearing damage than low-frequency sounds of the same intensity.

Noise levels from the woodworking machines I measured varied from 90 to 108 dB, as shown in the chart on p. 110. Because of its huge high-speed blade, the noisiest machine was a

From *Fine Woodworking* magazine (July 1986) 59:62-65

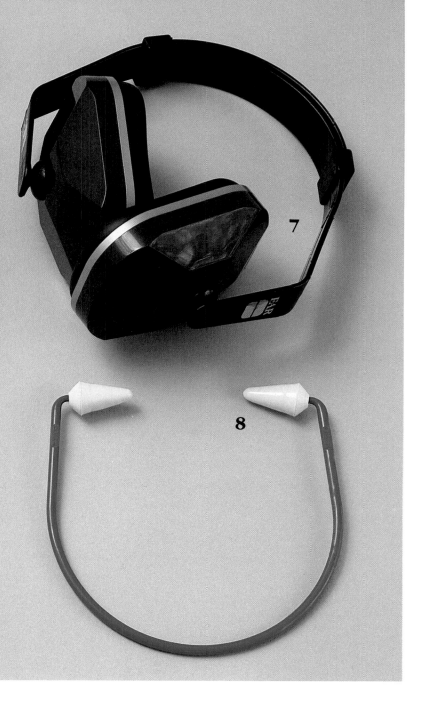

7

8

chines all day, everyday, and the noise levels are quite high.

OSHA's guidelines should be considered a minimum standard. The best way to protect your hearing from damage is to wear hearing protection whenever noise levels exceed 85 dB—even for a short period of time. There are many varieties of hearing protection devices in the form of ear muffs or plugs. Most devices provide adequate protection in the frequency range produced by woodworking machines, but muffs or foam ear plugs provide the best protection.

Hearing protection devices are rated by the amount of noise they block out, referred to as the noise reduction rating (NRR). If you're wearing earmuffs rated at NRR 25 dB, the sound that reaches your ears is reduced by approximately 25 dB. The NRR is derived by a calculation based on the measured effectiveness of the protection device at nine specific frequencies between 125 and 8,000 cps. Catalogs usually list only the NRR of a device, but manufacturers are required to print more complete test information on the package. In reality, the calculated NRR has a lot in common with the miles-per-gallon figures touted in new car ads. Measurements are taken under controlled lab conditions that might be very different from those encountered by real ears subjected to real noise. While it's true that a higher NRR generally means more effective protection, small differences in the NRR aren't substantial. Comfort and convenience are more significant factors in choosing a device than a 5 or 6 dB difference in the NRR. If the difference is greater than that, choose the higher rated device, providing it is comfortable.

Ear plugs are relatively comfortable in hot weather and easy to carry around. There are many different types—custom earmolds, foam plugs, wax plugs, rubber plugs, air-cushioned plugs, plugs with or without cords or headbands. Plugs are much less expensive than muffs and they neither restrict head movement nor interfere with eyeglasses, headgear, or hair. The disadvantages are that some types of plugs require more effort to fit properly than do muffs, and dirt, stain and sawdust from the hands can be transferred to the ear canal if the plugs are inserted with dirty hands. If you have any type of chronic ear problems, such as drainage, plugs are inadvisable. The plugs you choose should be appropriate for the type of noise in which you work. For example, there is a type of plug, often used by shooters, that has a valve that closes when an impact noise, such as a gunshot, occurs. Because most shop noises are not impact noises, these plugs could fail to protect you from most machinery noise.

Foam ear plugs have the highest NRR (29 to 35 dB) of any type of hearing protection. You insert them by rolling the plug between your fingers to compress it into a narrow cylinder. When inserted in the ear canal, the plug slowly expands to conform to the shape of the canal. Foam plugs are inexpensive—less than 50¢ a pair if bought in quantity—and they can be washed and reused several times or discarded after use.

The device called a canal cap consists of soft pads (usually foam) fitted on a headband. It reduces the intensity of sound by sealing off the outside of the ear canal. While these are comfortable and easy to use, it is possible that an effective seal might not be maintained and loud sounds could enter the ears. Canal caps cost more than earplugs but less than muffs.

The final category of hearing protectors is the ear muff, which tends to reduce noise more than any device except foam plugs. There are special muffs with deep cups for low-frequency protection, muffs with foam or glycerin-filled cushions (foam is lighter and cheaper) and muffs made to be worn with hard hats. Expensive muffs usually have metal headbands and fancier cups,

14-in., 5-HP De Walt radial-arm saw at 110 dB. The quietest piece of equipment was a Delta/Rockwell drill press at 87 dB. An air-powered nail gun probably produced a higher intensity level, but my meter could not measure the burst of impact noise.

To provide a meaningful reference point for the intensity levels of the machines, a just-audible sound would be 0 dB, a whisper at four feet would be 20 dB, normal conversation at three feet would be 60 to 70 dB, a pneumatic drill at ten feet would be 90 dB, and hammering on a steel plate at two feet would be 115 dB.

The U.S. Occupational Safety and Health Administration (OSHA) recommends that hearing protection should be worn in industry when a person's exposure to noise equals or exceeds an eight hour average of 85 dB. It is important to keep in mind that the louder (more intense) the sound, the shorter the safe exposure time. OSHA's limits for noise exposure without hearing protection, illustrated in the chart, show that even slight increases in sound intensity dramatically reduce the safe exposure time. Notice that for every 5 dB increase in intensity, the amount of safe exposure time without hearing protection is decreased by half. Most woodworkers don't run machines eight hours a day, but many woodworkers work in shops where others are using ma-but foam-filled muffs with a plastic headband are fine for the workshop. If possible, try on the muffs before you buy them to make sure they are comfortable. Another thing to check is the durability of the attachment between the cup and the headband—some designs are flimsy and liable to break. Unfortunately, muffs may restrict head movement in close quarters, they are uncomfortable in hot weather, eyeglasses may prevent the cups from sealing completely, and they are not as easy to carry around as the plugs. Ear muffs are also the most expensive hearing protection device, starting at about $12.

All of these protective devices are easy to use and once you have become accustomed to thinking in terms of protecting your ears, it becomes an automatic reflex to reach for the muffs or plugs prior to starting noisy equipment. The key to selecting the most appropriate hearing protection device for yourself is to choose the one that you'll use. If you dislike the confining feeling of ear muffs and that's all you have in your shop, chances are you won't wear them. Assess your likes and dislikes and purchase the device that suits your needs. Muffs or plugs can be obtained from sporting goods stores, mail-order woodworking suppliers and safety-equipment supply companies, such as Direct Safety Co., 7815 South 46th Street, Phoenix, Ariz. 85044, or Belmar Safety

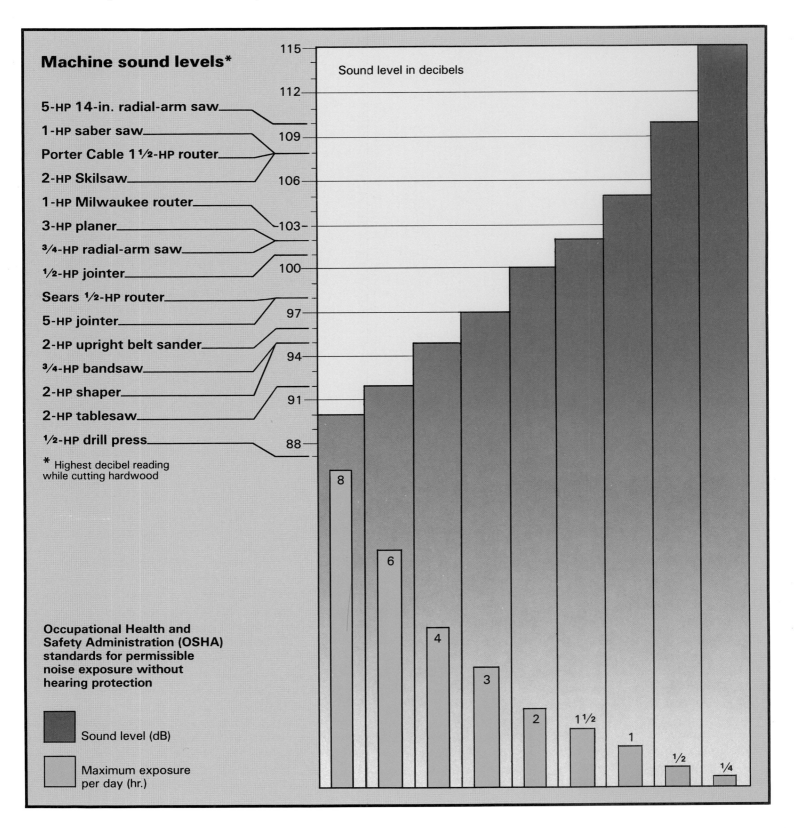

Machine sound levels*

Sound level in decibels

115
112
5-HP 14-in. radial-arm saw
1-HP saber saw
109
Porter Cable 1½-HP router
2-HP Skilsaw
106
1-HP Milwaukee router
3-HP planer
103
¾-HP radial-arm saw
½-HP jointer
100
Sears ½-HP router
5-HP jointer
97
2-HP upright belt sander
¾-HP bandsaw
94
2-HP shaper
2-HP tablesaw
91
½-HP drill press
88

* Highest decibel reading while cutting hardwood

Occupational Health and Safety Administration (OSHA) standards for permissible noise exposure without hearing protection

Sound level (dB)

Maximum exposure per day (hr.)

8
6
4
3
2
1½
1
½
¼

How noise destroys hearing

The hearing mechanism can be divided into three parts: the outer, middle and inner ear. The outer ear includes the part attached to the head (the pinna) and the ear canal as far as the eardrum. The middle ear includes an air-filled cavity behind the eardrum and three tiny bones, called ossicles, as well as the eustachian tube. The inner ear includes the cochlea, a snail-shaped, fluid-filled structure that converts the energy of sound waves into the electrical impulses that our brains perceive as sound, as well as the semicircular canals that are our balance mechanisms.

When a sound wave reaches the ear, it is gathered in by the external part of the ear and sent down the ear canal to the eardrum, where it vibrates across the ossicles and on into the cochlea.

The cochlea is lined with tiny hair cells imbedded in a very thin membrane. Sound waves set up motion in the fluid inside the cochlea which moves the tiny hairs back and forth. The moving hair cells generate nerve impulses which are sent along the auditory nerve to the brain. Different frequencies of sound (perceived by us as pitches) are received in specific locations along the membrane of the cochlea. The cells that respond to higher frequencies are located at the beginning of the structure, while those that respond to lower frequencies are found toward the end of the membrane. It is this specific location of frequency-sensitive receptor cells that is of interest to those who work in high noise areas. When loud noises of any fre-

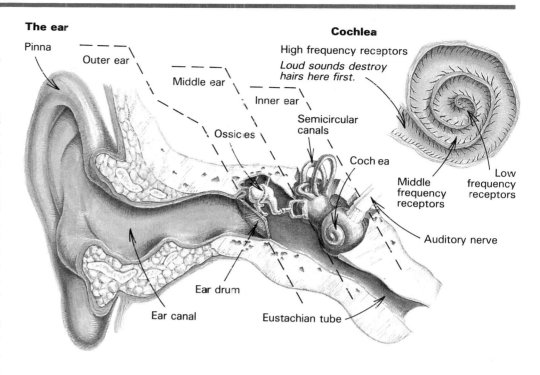

The ear
Pinna
Outer ear
Middle ear
Inner ear
Ossicles
Ear drum
Ear canal
Eustachian tube

Cochlea
High frequency receptors
Loud sounds destroy hairs here first.
Semicircular canals
Cochlea
Middle frequency receptors
Low frequency receptors
Auditory nerve

quency enter the cochlea, they hit with the most force in the first bend of the structure, where the high-frequency receptor cells are found. This area becomes eroded, much like the mud in the bend in a river is eroded when high water rushes along it. The hairs are bent, broken or blown away by the force of the loud sounds, and high-frequency hearing is eventually damaged. This type of hearing loss is called a sensorineural loss

A person with this type of sensorineural loss can have normal hearing in the low frequencies and a severe loss in the higher frequencies. This type of loss causes persons to miss parts of words because they can't hear some of the high-frequency consonants, such as s, sh or f. Because they miss these consonants, words may

sound garbled to them, especially in the presence of noise, while the loudness of the words may not seem affected at all.

Another clue, other than hearing loss, that noise may be damaging your hearing is tinnitus, which is a noise in the ear, generally described as a ringing, buzzing or hissing. Tinnitus often occurs after exposure to very loud noise. It is also an indicator of an already damaged hearing mechanism, although tinnitus which occurs intermittently and lasts for only a few seconds is not uncommon. One explanation for tinnitus among people whose hearing has been damaged by high noise levels, is that when the hair cells in the cochlea are damaged, they no longer wait to be stimulated to send signals, rather, the damaged structure continuously sends signals. —*J.O.*

Equipment, Inc., 212 Clements Bridge Rd., Barrington, N.J. 08007.

When you're standing next to a noisy machine, most of the sound travels directly from the cutterhead to your ears. But in a multi-person shop where others are running machinery, reflected sound levels can be high. Anyone who has spent time in various shops knows that all are not equally noisy. The harder the floor, wall and ceiling surfaces, the more sound will reverberate. The softer, more irregular the surfaces, the more sound will be absorbed. If you were going to build a new shop, the quietest one you could build would have acoustical tile on the ceiling, acoustical board or another soft wallboard for walls, and thick carpeting or thick rubber mats on the floors. In reality this doesn't often occur—people don't want plush carpet on the floors of their shops.

It's not always possible to dictate the specifications of the space in which you work. You can, however, improve things in a multi-person shop by putting acoustical tile on the ceiling, and arranging your equipment so that the noisest machines are away from hard, sound-reflective walls and corners.

When you have purchased hearing protection and taken steps to reduce noise levels in your shop, your next step is to find out whether your hearing has already been damaged. To do this, contact an audiologist in your area and arrange to have your hearing sensitivity evaluated. Audiologists can be found in speech and hearing centers, hospitals, rehabilitation centers, ear, nose and throat physicians' offices or in private practice.

I recommend that all woodworkers have their hearing evaluated immediately to establish a baseline audiogram (a graph of hearing sensitivity) and that they keep copies of the test results and monitor their hearing annually. Although noise-induced hearing loss is irreversible, it's not too late to protect your remaining hearing. Remember to reach for that hearing protector before you reach for the "on" switch of your machine, regardless of how short a time you will be working. □

Joy O'Neal is audiology supervisor at the University of Texas Speech and Hearing Center in Austin, Texas.

Low-Cost Dust Collection
Cleans out your shop, not your wallet

by William S. Harrison III

I used to snicker every time some new fangled safety device hit the market. I'd give up woodworking, I told my wife, before strapping myself into gear more appropriate for moonwalking than woodworking. Then two years ago, I found myself cutting up redwood for hours each day in a closed, two-car garage. I began to feel a bit choked up, but that was only the beginning. I contracted a sore throat (from other causes) and kept on working. Despite all kinds of prescribed medicine, my throat got worse.

When my condition improved after five days away from the shop, it finally hit me that the fine sawdust was doing a number on my throat—and probably on my lungs, too. Donning a paint spray mask in the shop cleared my throat and confirmed my suspicions, so I immediately started work on a dust-collection system.

How serious is any sawdust problem? My gut feeling is that if you machine wood in an enclosed area more than one hour per day, you could be in trouble. The American Society of Heating, Refrigeration and Air Conditioning Engineers (ASHRAE) and the National Institute for Occupational Safety and Health (NIOSH) have standards for allowable dust concentration, but the level of exposure that is unsafe depends on the wood, particle size and so on. The ASHRAE *Handbooks* (which you can find in major-city libraries, or ask an engineer friend) are crammed with information on dust control. If you're still uncertain about your dust-collection needs, ask an industrial-ventilation specialist or a sheet-metal contractor, many of whom fabricate exhaust systems.

I had eight machines that needed dust collecton: radial-arm saw, planer, jointer, tablesaw, bandsaw, stationary belt sander, drill press and shaper. I do quite a bit of industrial fume-collection design, so I dabbled with the thought of hooking all the machines up to a cyclone system with a bag on the outlet. (A cyclone separator creates two concentric helical air currents inside a cone-shaped collector. Centrifugal force separates dust and shavings from the airstream, and these settle out into a bin.) But a commercial cyclone system can cost $1500 and up, so I continued dabbling.

I surveyed my shop layout and my salvage collection, and decided that a single system would require too much piping and a larger blower than I had. So my best bet was to build three collectors: one for the planer, one for the radial-arm saw (these two machines share a separate room) and a multiple-port system for the rest of the machines. The multiple-port system (facing page) is the most complicated, so I'll describe it first.

My model was a dust-collection system designed by Doyle Johnson, comprising PVC drainage pipe (watch for static buildup), a ½-HP industrial collector and a 55-gal. drum. My system had to move enough air to handle two ports on the tablesaw at once, and I wanted to be able to hook up a machine quickly. A used 1-HP Cincinnati Fan #10 (a centrifugal fan) that I bought for $40 fit the bill for a blower. I replaced its three-phase motor with a single-phase (a $65 unclaimed rebuild at my friendly motor-rebuilding shop) and mounted it on a 55-gal. drum. I reinforced the thin metal drum lid with ¾-in. plywood to support the ductwork, which enters on the perimeter at an angle, creating a cyclone effect inside the drum. The heavier particles drop into the drum; lighter dust is caught by a bag on the blower's exhaust.

For the ductwork, I used Schedule 40 PVC pipe. (The name designates wall thickness—the higher the number, the greater the thickness. S-40 walls are about ⅛-in. thick.) S-40 pipe is readily available and isn't too expensive, and its inherent rigidity makes suspension easy. S-30 pipe is cheaper, but harder to find and the fitting selection isn't as great. (The box on p. 115 will help you figure the size blower and diameter and length of pipe you'll need.) PVC pipe glues together easily, and joints used for changing connections may be left unglued since they fit tightly. Where a machine joins the main pipe, I used an angled fitting called a sanitary-T (which is actually Y-shaped). These fittings restrict the airflow by friction losses less than right-angle fittings. You'll have to shape the pipe ends to fit some of the nozzles. PVC molds nicely when heated carefully over a gas burner, but be sure to clamp it while it cools.

Flexible tube is required for difficult connections under and around machines, but it's quite expensive, so I tried to use as little as possible. Industrial-grade runs about $1 per foot per inch of diameter in the 2-in. to 5-in. diameter range (2-in. pipe costs $2/ft. and so on). An adequate flexible tube called Ductall Vinyl costs about half as much and may be obtained from U.S. Plastics, 1390 Neubrecht Rd., Lima, Ohio 45801. It comes in sizes that fit snugly inside S-40 pipe of the same nominal diameter. You force the hose in the pipe with a screwing action, assisted by any vinyl tub-and-tile sealer to lubricate and seal the interface. I didn't bother with shutoffs or "blastgates" to block off machines not in use. I simply plugged the unused ports with bandsawn wooden plugs—cheap and effective.

Each machine required a different sort of nozzle. I made a few experimental nozzles before I reverted to my trusty *Industrial Ventilation, A Manual of Practice* for its tried and true solutions. (The book is published by the Committee on Industrial Ventilation, Box 16153, Lansing, Mich. 48902, and costs about $15.)

Two tablesaw nozzles—one above, one below the blade—may seem like overkill, but they do a super job. Depending on the number of blade teeth, depth of cut and so on, at least half the

From *Fine Woodworking* magazine (May 1985) 52:42-45

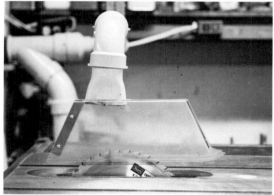

Harrison made his home-shop dust-collection system with PVC pipe, salvaged blowers and some ingenuity. The tablesaw (top) has nozzles above and below the blade. A modified vacuum-cleaner nozzle serves the jointer. The top tablesaw nozzle (middle left) is 2-in. PVC pipe shaped and bolted to a stock blade guard. The bandsaw nozzle (middle right) is PVC cut around the bottom blade guides. At the 55-gal. drum collector (bottom left), 3-in. and 2-in. trunk lines join a 4-in. PVC fitting, angled to create a cyclone in the drum.

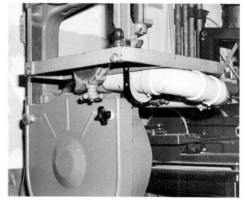

Dust-collection layout

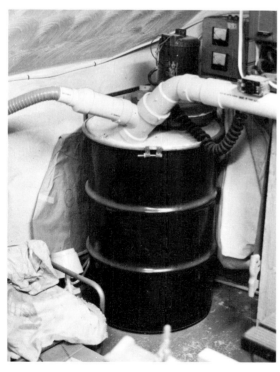

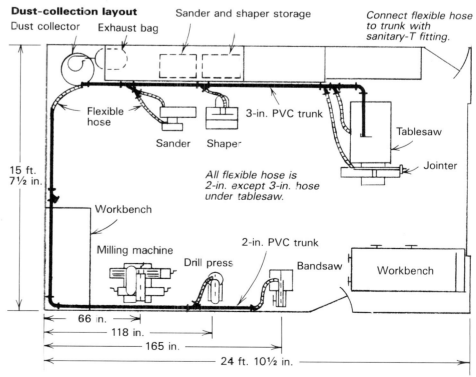

Dust collector   Exhaust bag   Sander and shaper storage   Connect flexible hose to trunk with sanitary-T fitting.

Flexible hose   3-in. PVC trunk   Tablesaw   Jointer

All flexible hose is 2-in. except 3-in. hose under tablesaw.

Sander   Shaper

15 ft. 7½ in.

Workbench

Milling machine   Drill press   2-in. PVC trunk   Bandsaw   Workbench

66 in.
118 in.
165 in.
24 ft. 10½ in.

Four-inch metal duct, a 30-gal. drum and blower service Harrison's planer (above and left). The metal nozzle is extended under the planer's cover with ¼-in. plywood. A powerful vacuum cleaner collects from the two nozzles attached to the radial-arm saw's blade guard (below). An inner tube suspends the flexible hose from the ceiling, permitting the saw to travel easily.

sawdust is thrown down, the remainder up—and in your face if you don't have a top nozzle. Mine fits into a plastic Sears saw guard, which I shortened behind the blade to reduce the volume of air exhausted. The pipe is suspended from the garage-door track (the ceiling would do, too, of course) and the height of the guard can be easily adjusted by sliding the hanger along the pipe; the joints swivel since they aren't glued.

The bottom tablesaw nozzle consists of various bits of plywood and redwood fastened to each other and to the casting around the blade. Your saw, like mine, will probably require a trial-and-error nozzle design. The important thing is to make the nozzle as compact and leakproof as possible, otherwise your blower will be doing extra duty. Remember that the nozzle shouldn't interfere with tilting the arbor or changing the blade.

Nozzles for the remaining machines on the multiple-port system were fairly simple. My 6-in. Delta jointer has an outlet in the base to which I adapted an old vacuum-cleaner nozzle. The die casting on my Sears shaper fence has a hole right behind the spindle, into which I jammed the flattened end of some 2-in. PVC pipe. Some chips escape upward, so I intend to alter the

fence to accept a larger nozzle. The Sears belt and disc sanders come with nozzle attachments which work well. For the drill press, I used 2-in. PVC pipe held in place by a magnet bolted through the pipe. For the bandsaw, I cut 2-in. PVC to fit tightly around the bottom blade guides, then connected this pipe nozzle to the trunk with 2-in. flexible tube and a sanitary-T fitting.

As you can see, I kept my nozzles simple. Your machines may require different configurations. Just remember a couple of things. Try to take the shortest route from nozzle to dust storage. Make the nozzle as leakproof as possible, and position it to take advantage of the velocity of the particles imparted by the cutterhead or blade. At a distance of only one diameter from the intake pipe, the capture velocity (suction as measured by the velocity imparted to the particles by the exhaust system) drops to only 10% of its value at the intake mouth.

When you operate a multiple-port system, remember that blowers work best at rated capacity. Starving a centrifugal-type blower of air makes it work much harder than it needs to. My 1-HP Cincinnati Fan #10 simultaneously captures dust very nicely from the 2-in. and 3-in. inlets on the tablesaw and the 2-in. inlet on the bandsaw. If I'm working on any of the smaller machines, I still leave both tablesaw ports open to feed air to the blower. An air-starved blower will whine about its problem; if your blower sounds shrill, try opening another port.

For my Sears (Belsaw) thickness planer, I mounted an old ⅓-HP Brown and Sharpe blower on a used 30-gal. drum. A piece of S-40 PVC pressed into the ¾-in. plywood lid with tub sealer connects with 4-in. metal elbows and clothes-dryer duct. I enlarged and extended an 8-in. metal Cincinnati nozzle with ¼-in. thick birch plywood. The conventional top location didn't work well because the blower isn't quite powerful enough. Mounted behind the cutterhead, the system picks up about 80% of the particles—abysmal by industry standards, but okay for my purposes.

Serving the radial-arm saw is an old Douglas (Scott and Fetzer) wet-and-dry vacuum cleaner, well made and powerful. I made the bin-type collector suggested by Sears, but it didn't work out, so I cribbed the rig shown in the bottom photo at left from the Industrial Ventilation manual, and it works great. For ductwork to the plywood nozzle, I used the vacuum cleaner's original 2½-in. rigid wand and flexible hose. An old Electrolux hose connects the nozzle on the front of the guard to a brush nozzle (without the bristles) carefully cut into the wand. Here, the shortest route from nozzle to dust storage isn't the best. You need the suspended loop and slack for minimum drag on the saw movement. The hose is hung from an old bicycle inner tube.

How much did it all cost? Forty-plus feet of S-40 pipe with a couple dozen fittings ran about $175; add flex at $40, motor, blower and drum at $120, a dustbag for $35 and miscellaneous stuff at $25, and that totals about $395. A commercial installation using 22-gauge metal duct with the same blower capacity would run about $2,000. I had most of the components for the radial-arm-saw unit, but a good estimate is about $110. The planer unit cost me about $120.

How efficient are these systems? Because of OSHA and NIOSH regulation, industry would strive for 99% capture of all airborne particles. The system shown here captures, on average, about 90% of all particles. This is sufficient to yield a very livable atmosphere in my two-car garage shop. When I plan a multi-hour ripping session, I add my face mask for insurance. □

Bill Harrison is an engineering director for a major company and has been an off-and-on serious woodworker for 30 years.

Of pipe runs and pressure drops

Adequate dust-collection design depends essentially on matching your needs to a blower and correctly dimensioned pipe. Though expensive industrial-standard systems require elaborate calculations to achieve this, an effective small-shop setup needn't strain your wallet or your mathematics. The information here is simplified, but coupled with common sense and some trial and error in the shop, it should get you on the right track.

Start with a shop layout (like the one on p. 113), showing the position of the dust storage, blower and machines. Note which machines need one nozzle and which need two, and determine how many machines you want to collect from at one time. Check the chart at right for the cubic-feet-per-minute (CFM) extraction requirements for each machine.

The most important variables in the system are the blower capacity, the pipe diameter and length, and the losses to the system caused by friction in the pipe and other factors. A blower is generally rated by the volume of air in CFM it will move at a certain static pressure (SP), measured in inches of water. Pressure of 1 lb./sq. in. will raise water in a tube 27.5 in., and so on. (If the CFM and SP ratings aren't given on the blower, ask the manufacturer for them.) You can determine whether a blower is powerful enough by comparing its SP rating with the system losses, which are explained below If the total losses don't exceed the blower's rated SP, it will move its rated CFM.

Velocity is as important as volume for our purposes. The recommended velocity for wood dust and chips is 3500 feet per minute (FPM). Too much below this speed and chips will settle out in the pipes. Knowing velocity and volume, you can calculate the pipe diameter you need using the formula $Q = AV$, where Q is volume in CFM, A is the square-foot area of a cross section of pipe, and V is the velocity in FPM. Reducing the pipe diameter raises velocity, but also raises friction losses in the pipe. (Obviously, the formula can also be used to determine blower capacity for given diameters of pipe.)

Let's figure a simple system with a two-nozzle tablesaw and a one-nozzle bandsaw hooked up to a blower rated 700 CFM at $4\frac{1}{2}$ in. SP. Fourteen feet of 3-in. PVC pipe will run from the collector to a sanitary-T; a 3-in. flexible hose connects the T to the bottom tablesaw nozzle. The bandsaw will be hooked into the 3-in. PVC somewhere along the 14-ft. run.

First, pipe diameters. Plugging in the CFM figure from the chart for the top tablesaw nozzle and the recommended velocity gives $150 = A \times 3500$; $A = 0.0428$ sq. ft., or about $2\frac{3}{4}$-in. dia. pipe. I would push the lower limit and save some money by using 2-in. pipe. For the bottom nozzle, $200 = A(3500)$; $A = 0.0571$ sq. ft., about $3\frac{1}{2}$-in. pipe. I'd use 3-in. The bandsaw calculation also yields $3\frac{1}{2}$ in., but the bandsaw is a long way from the blower and big pipe is costly, so I'll settle for 2-in. pipe and live with its high friction losses. Adding the airflow requirements for each machine, you get a collection system total of 550 CFM ($150 + 200 + 200 = 550$).

Knowing the pipe diameters and run, let's estimate the system losses and see if the blower is up to the job. Friction losses for straight pipe and fittings are shown in the chart, expressed as a loss in inches per foot of water SP. Losses for fittings are rated by equivalent losses for run of straight pipe of the same diameter. The figures are acceptable for a small shop, but they wouldn't meet industry standards.

Industrial-system designers figure losses for every component of a system—a terrifically complicated task. You can get a good idea of a small system's capacity, however, by calculating only the branch with the highest losses, which is usually the branch with a large nozzle located farthest from the collector; in this instance, the bottom tablesaw nozzle. Using friction loss figures

Friction losses at 3500 FPM:
Straight pipe
4-in. pipe at 700 CFM will lose 0.14 in./ft. SP
3-in. pipe at 400 CFM will lose 0.16 in./ft. SP
2-in. pipe at 200 CFM will lose 0.16 in./ft. SP

Fittings
(SP loss equivalents in linear feet of straight pipe)
2-in. S-40 elbow = 4 ft. of pipe
3-in. S-40 elbow = 5 ft. of pipe
4-in. S-40 elbow = 6 ft. of pipe
2-in. or 3-in. sanitary-T outlet with 3-in. run (2x3 or 3x3) = 6 ft. of pipe
2-in. or 3-in. sanitary-T outlet with 4-in. run (2x4 or 3x4) = 8 ft. of pipe

Pipe and blower matchups:
2-HP blower, 1200 CFM at 6 in. to 7 in. SP—5-in. to 6-in. main pipe
1-HP blower, 700 CFM at 4 in. to 5 in. SP—4-in. to 5-in. main pipe
½-HP blower, 400 CFM at 5 in. to 6 in. SP—3-in to 4-in. main pipe
⅓-HP blower, 250 CFM at 4 in. to 5 in. SP—3-in. main pipe

Typical exhaust volumes, CFM

Machine	Recommended industrial std.	Home-shop compromise
Tablesaw, top	300	150
Tablesaw, bottom	350-400	200
Radial-arm saw, blade guard	75-100	50
Radial-arm saw, blade back	350-400	150-200
Bandsaw, under table	350	150-200
Disc sander, to 12 in.	300	150
Belt sander, to 8 in.	400	200
Jointer planer, to 8 in.	400	200
Planer, to 18 in.	750	350
Shaper, small, ½-in. spindle	400	250
Shaper, large, 1-in. spindle	800-1,000	400-500
Drill press	300	150

from the chart, and given nozzle and collector losses, you get this simplified calculation of losses in inches of water:

Bottom nozzle	(given)	1.20 in.
Bottom hose, 6 ft.	6(0.16 in./ft.)	0.96 in.
3x3 sanitary-T outlet	6(0.16 in./ft.)	0.96 in.
3-in. main pipe, 14 ft.	14(0.16 in./ft.)	2.20 in.
Collector	(given)	1.30 in.
Total		6.62 in.

Determining nozzle and collector losses is complicated. The figures above are rough approximations for my own bottom tablesaw nozzle—a tight, 2-in. by 12-in. plywood funnel—and my collector—a 55-gal. drum, 4-in. intake fitting and blower. A smaller drum would lose less. If your nozzle and collector are different, a sheet-metal contractor might be able to help you with the calculations.

As it turns out, the blower's 4.5-in. SP rating is lower than the estimated losses. But because we're not aiming for high efficiency and the blower is rated 200 CFM greater than the load, I think it will be adequate. At worst, some dust will settle in the pipes, and the blower won't operate at peak efficiency. Increasing the pipe size will bring the system losses down. I use 4-in. pipe on my planer, but only a ⅓-HP motor, so the tradeoff there is the other way around. (The chart also gives some rough rules of thumb for matching pipe diameter and blower capacity.)

A final example will demonstrate the tradeoffs between blower capacity, system losses and expediency. My 1-HP Cincinnati Fan #10 is rated at 700 CFM at 4½-in. SP. It captures dust nicely from two 2-in. and one 3-in. inlet simultaneously. These openings correspond to a velocity of 7551 FPM, much in excess of the 3500 FPM recommended for wood dust. But numbers are deceiving. The actual velocity is much lower due to the numerous losses in the system. My sanitary-T inlets, for example, are far from ideal. Good practice would increase pipe size at every inlet and would assume how many inlets would be in use or just open drawing air only. But then, everything in life represents a compromise.   —W.S.H.

Small-shop dust collection needn't be elaborate, as Claude Graham, owner of Masterworks in Wood of Jacksonville, Fla., demonstrates. Graham wheels a large Grizzly portable dust collector around the shop, connecting it where needed with a length of flexible hose. The same collector can be used in conjunction with ductwork as a central system.

Clearing the Air
Selecting and sizing a small-shop dust collector

by Roy Berendsohn

The advent of portable dust collectors during the past five years has made dust collection both affordable and practical for the small shop. Although portable dust collectors have been manufactured here for over 30 years, many find their way into the U.S. market from Europe, where small-shop dust collection has been more the rule than the exception for years. Most of these collectors consist of a motor-driven blower that sucks dust and chips into a cloth bag or a drum.

The main purpose of dust collection is safety—chips and dust on the floor are slippery underfoot and pose a danger during operations when you need firm footing, such as ripping on a tablesaw. With the system permanently connected to your worst dust-making equipment, to capture dust and wood chips at their source, your shop will be cleaner and safer. And, at the end of a tiring day, you won't have to shovel planer shavings into plastic bags.

Then there's the health issue. Wood dust has been implicated as a cause of sinonasal cancer, so it stands to reason that, at best, a dust-collection system might reduce the risk of cancer; at the least, it will remove some of the eye-irritating, sneeze-provoking particles from the air. Also, insurance companies like to see dust collectors in woodworking shops—whether home shop or commercial—and installing one may reduce your fire rates.

The smallest portable collector on the market, Makita's Model 410, is light enough to be carried from machine to machine. The larger portables are usually mounted on dollies, so if you're not up to building a full-blown central collection system with ductwork and hoses, you could simply wheel the machine around the shop and connect it as needed. In this case, estimating the size of the collector is easy: it simply needs to have slightly more capacity than that required for the heaviest collection task, which

From *Fine Woodworking* magazine (November 1987) 67:70-75

is usually a planer or a shaper. However, in interviewing owners of various collection systems, I learned that all but a few of the dolly-mounted dust collectors available are, in fact, powerful enough to operate small central dust-collection systems. If I were setting up a shop, I'd buy one with a central system in mind. Though centralized dust collection is more expensive to install, it's much more convenient and efficient than a portable system.

Designing a central system—To set up a central dust-collection system, you'll need to design the ductwork that connects your machines to the collector, then calculate the size of collector you'll need. Start with plan and elevation drawings of the shop, each showing the proposed location of the collector, as well as the ducts and the various woodworking machines. The drawing on p. 118 shows a typical duct setup, and the accompanying text explains the steps necessary to calculate collector capacity. As the drawing shows, a typical dust system consists of a main duct from which branch ducts sprout, connecting each machine. As a general rule, duct runs should be as short as possible, with a minimum number of bends. Flexible hose lengths should also be minimized to reduce friction losses. Each branch duct will need a metal or plastic blast gate (see "Sources of Supply," p. 121) that disconnects the machine from the system when another one is in use.

In researching this article, I discovered some disagreement over the best type of duct to use. I've seen a number of systems constructed of either Schedule 40 plastic plumbing pipe or a thin-walled variety of plastic used for sewers and drains. From what I've seen, plastic is easier to assemble than metal, and it works quite well. However, because plastic pipe is an insulator, air moving through the pipe builds up a static electricity charge that can discharge with disastrous results. One reader reported that a static discharge shattered a section of plastic pipe in his shopmade system, and it seems possible that suspended dust could explode or catch fire. It's possible to ground a plastic pipe with copper wire routed inside the pipe or around its outside diameter, but the safer choice is metal duct, which also happens to be more resistant to cracks from sharp-edged scraps hurtling along at 3,500 feet per minute inside the pipe.

The usual choice in metal duct is 22-gauge or 24-gauge round spiral duct, but other types and wall thicknesses will do the job adequately. For the example shown on p. 118, we used 24-gauge spiral duct and connectors. The cost of outfitting a system like the one shown wouldn't be cheap—the example calls for about $1,000 worth of spiral metal duct, elbows, hose and blast gates (minus freight costs). In any case, shop aggressively. I was quoted wide differences in prices for metal duct and, surprisingly enough, one supplier I contacted quoted higher prices for Schedule 40 plastic pipe than for 24-gauge spiral duct. Before buying duct, check with the local building inspector or fire marshal. Local codes may require a certain type of metal duct for dust-collection systems.

If you're collecting from only one machine at a time, the branch ducts (or, if you prefer, flexible hoses) to each machine can be 4 in. or 5 in. in diameter, connecting to a main branch that is also constructed of 4-in. or 5-in. duct. If you plan to operate all the machines at once, or if your shop is equipped with industrial equipment, you may need to increase the diameter of the main duct where each branch enters, but this isn't a job to be taken lightly. In complex systems, where there are multiple connections being made to the main duct run, you may want to have an air-movement-system engineer check your calculations. It's a tricky job to balance duct diameters and connections so the system

works properly regardless of how many machines are running. If one or more machines are shut off, then the duct diameter may be too large for the amount of air moving through it. Though you may expect the air velocity to increase in these situations, just the reverse is true. Air velocity will be slowed enough to allow dust to settle out and plug the duct.

Once you've determined the layout of your duct system, calculate the size collector you'll need to operate it. Dust collectors are rated for their ability to move a certain number of cubic feet of air per minute (cfm) at a certain static pressure. Simply stated, static pressure is a measure of the friction the air encounters as it moves through the duct. If there's too much resistance, the collector won't be able to move its rated cfm. As a result, the velocity inside the main duct may fall too far below the 3,500 feet per minute velocity recommended as the minimum for wood dust and chips, and the waste will settle out, clogging the system. Generally speaking, the higher the static pressure rating a collector has, the more powerful it is, given equal cfm ratings.

Engineers who design industrial dust systems calculate volume and static pressure requirements with all machines running, but the typical small shop won't require that kind of capacity. You can easily figure your maximum volume requirements by referring to chart A on the following page and determining the need of the largest machine. A tablesaw or planer, for example, will require a collector with a minimum capacity of 300 or 400 cfm.

Similarly, use charts B, C and D to calculate static pressure losses on the worst branch of the system, which is usually the one most distant from the collector and containing the most bends and connections. Note that chart D is calculated to give the static pressure loss per foot of pipe at the 3,500 fpm or 4,000 fpm minimum velocity, based on the required cfm of volume. Recommended duct diameters are also included. As the chart shows, each section of straight duct accounts for its share of static pressure loss. Furthermore, as illustrated in charts B and C, elbows and branch connectors create turbulence, so the air travels a much longer distance than the actual length of the component. Using your plans, add up the linear feet of straight runs and equivalent duct lengths for elbows and branches (from charts B and C), then multiply this figure by the pressure loss per foot (from chart D) for the cfm capacity you've determined your system will need (from chart A). This figure represents the total system static pressure loss, and you'll need a collector

Fig. 1: Two types of dust collectors

Single-stage collector

Two-stage collector

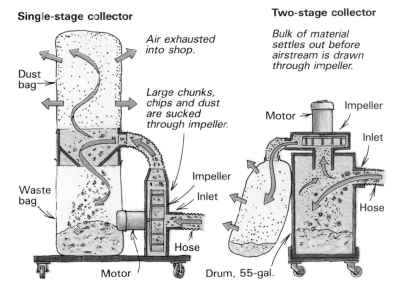

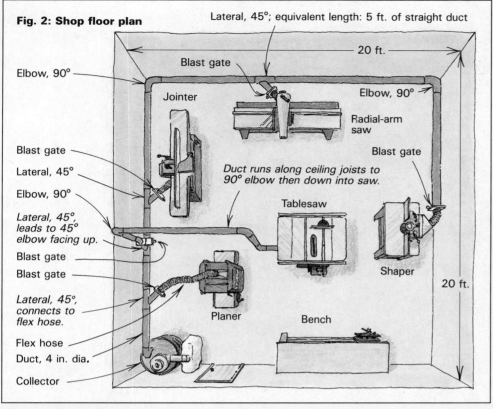

Fig. 2: Shop floor plan

Lateral, 45°; equivalent length: 5 ft. of straight duct

Elbow, 90°

Blast gate

Jointer

20 ft.

Elbow, 90°

Radial-arm saw

Blast gate

Blast gate

Lateral, 45°

Elbow, 90°

Duct runs along ceiling joists to 90° elbow then down into saw.

Lateral, 45°, leads to 45° elbow facing up.

Blast gate

Blast gate

Tablesaw

Shaper

20 ft.

Lateral, 45°, connects to flex hose.

Planer

Bench

Flex hose

Duct, 4 in. dia.

Collector

Figuring dust-collection needs

To calculate the size of collector you need, follow these steps:

1. First, determine how to interconnect the duct to the machines. In the hypothetical shop shown above, the duct runs about 42 in. off the floor from the shaper to the radial-arm saw, where a plywood or sheet-metal hood draws in dust. The duct continues on to the jointer, where the connection is made with flexible hose and a 45° lateral connector. About 20 ft. down the line, another lateral connector runs the duct up to ceiling height, where it makes a turn perpendicular to the main run and continues on to the tablesaw. There, the duct drops down again and into the side of the saw through a cutout in the saw body. Inside the saw, a plywood or sheet-metal hood is positioned below the blade. A lateral connector is also used at the planer, and flexible hose runs from it to a sheet-metal hood atop the machine. Note that lateral connectors are specified throughout. These Y-shaped connectors impose a fraction of the friction loss imposed by T-shaped connectors.

2. Next, determine the duct diameter needed, based on the cfm requirements of the machine. (In this example, calculations are based on the use of 4-in.-dia. duct.) Chart D shows the relationship between the velocity you want the airstream to move at and the static pressure loss the airstream will experience at that

A. Exhaust volume requirements for industrial (I) machines and home-shop (H) machines* in cubic feet per minute (cfm)

Machine	I	H
Jointer, 4-12 in.	350	300
Disc sander, to 12 in.	350	300
Vertical belt sander, to 12 in.	440	300
Bandsaw, 2-in. blade	700	400
Tablesaw, up to 16 in.	350	300
Radial-arm saw	500	350
Planer, to 20 in.	785	400
Shaper, ½-in. spindle (see note)	400-1,400	300
Shaper, 1-in. spindle (see note)	350-1,400	500
Lathe (see note)	350-1,400	500
Floor sweep	800	350

* Figures courtesy of Delta International Machinery Corp., Cincinnati Fan and Ventilator Co., Manual of Industrial Ventilation. Exhaust requirements for shapers and lathes can vary greatly depending on operation. The larger the cutter on the shaper, or the more complex a cutter's shape, the greater the exhaust requirement. Lathes also require more exhaust volume during heavy cutting as opposed to light sanding.

B. Equivalent resistance in feet of straight pipe for 90° elbow, center-line radius*

Duct dia.	1.5 D.	2.0 D.
3 in.	5 ft.	3 ft.
4 in.	6 ft.	4 ft.
5 in.	9 ft.	6 ft.
6 in.	12 ft.	7 ft.
7 in.	13 ft.	9 ft.
8 in.	15 ft.	10 ft.
10 in.	20 ft.	14 ft.
12 in.	25 ft.	17 ft.

1.5 D. and 2.0 D. describe the radius of the elbow's bend. An elbow with a 1.5 D. bend has a radius 1.5 times the diameter of the pipe. Note: For 60° elbows, loss equals .67 × loss for 90° elbow; loss for 45° elbows equals .50 × loss for 90° elbow; loss for 30° elbows equals .33 × loss for 90° elbows.

* *Industrial Ventilation, A Manual of Recommended Practice,* 19th edition, Edward Brothers, Inc., 2500 South State St., Ann Arbor, Mich. 48104. Also, Ductilator slide rule, Manufacturers' Service Co. (See "Sources of Supply," p. 121).

C. Equivalent lengths for lateral branch connectors

Duct dia.	30° branch	45° branch
3 in.	2 ft.	3 ft.
4 in.	3 ft.	5 ft.
5 in.	4 ft.	6 ft.
6 in.	5 ft.	7 ft.
7 in.	6 ft.	9 ft.
8 in.	7 ft.	11 ft.
10 in.	9 ft.	14 ft.
12 in.	11 ft.	17 ft.

speed while moving through a recommended duct diameter. If you want the airstream to move faster through the duct, you'll experience greater static pressure losses. These losses are compensated for by buying a more powerful dust collector that has the ability to pull in air against greater static pressure losses. A machine that requires 300 or 350 cfm exhaust volume needs 4-in.-dia. duct to permit the airstream to move at the required speed. At 3,500 fpm, you can expect a static pressure loss of .05 in. per ft. of duct. *(Note that static pressure losses are described at two different air speeds—3,500 fpm and 4,000 fpm. Make calculations based on 3,500 fpm for the main duct and 4,000 fpm for branches leading to the main duct.)*

3. Calculate straight and equivalent lengths of duct along the ductwork branch that will have the greatest static

pressure loss. In this example, only one machine is typically used at a time. Thus, the duct length likely to have the highest losses would be either the one leading to the tablesaw or the one to the shaper.

There are 50 straight ft. of duct running from the shaper to the collector, plus the equivalent length of 12 ft. in the two elbows. Multiply the static pressure loss per ft. (.05—see chart D) experienced when moving 300 cfm of air volume at 3,500 fpm by 62. The static pressure loss for this run of duct was about 3.1 in. There is the equivalent of 46 ft. of straight duct (three straight sections, three 90° elbows, a 45° elbow and a 45° lateral connector) leading to the tablesaw. Multiply 46 by the static pressure loss for a 300 cfm airstream you want to move at 4,000 fpm through 4-in. dia. duct (.07). This equals a static pressure loss of 3.2 in. Thus, the static pressure loss for the tablesaw is the greatest of any in the dust-collection system and should be used in all subsequent calculations.

4. Add to the total static pressure loss another 1 in. of loss due to dirty filter bags, plus 1 in. for other system losses. The total system loss is about 5.2 in.

5. The collector should have sufficient cfm capacity to draw from either the tablesaw and or shaper. The minimum collector that this shop would need would have a 300 cfm rating at 5.2 in. of static pressure. A better collector would be oversized by 20 percent, with a 360 cfm rating at about 6.2 inches of static pressure. Several collectors on the chart, p. 120, would fit the bill.   —R.B.

A plastic pipe pulls dust away from a radial-arm saw. More elaborate hoods can be made from solid wood, plywood, plastic sheet or sheet metal.

Above left, Verner Peer of Summit, N.J., turned a handful of plugs on his lathe to act as blast gates. Commercial blast gates, right, shut off duct leading to an industrial Torit dust collector at Coastal Woodworking of Bridgeport, Conn.

Below, left: Peer's homemade setup is made from white pine and combines a fence and built-in guard made from clear plastic laminate. The hood/fence is fastened to a home-made shaper with quick-action clamps. Below, right: An interchangeable flexible hose leads to a high-volume dust hood for a shaper at Coastal Woodworking. The hose can be pulled off the shaper and plugged on to a hood at another smaller shaper.

D. Static pressure loss per foot of pipe at 3,500 FPM and 4,000 FPM			
CFM	**Duct dia.**	**3,500 FPM**	**4,000 FPM**
300	4 in.	.05	.07
350	4 in.	.05	.07
400	4 in.	.05	.06
500	5 in.	.04	.06
600	5 in.	.04	.05
700	6 in.	.04	.024
800	6 in.	.03	.04
900	6 in.	NA	.04
900	7 in.	.03	NA
1,000	7 in.	.03	.04
1,100	7 in.	NA	.035
1,100	8 in.	.025	NA
1,200	7 in.	NA	.035
1,200	8 in.	.025	NA
1,300	8 in.	.022	.03
1,400	8 in.	.022	.03
1,500	8 in.	NA	.03
1,500	9 in.	.02	NA

Manufacturers' specifications

Make-Model	CFM	Static pressure (in. of water)	Motor (HP)	Volts	Storage capacity (gal.)	Impeller type	Inlet dia. (inches)	Casters
AGET 11T-51	1,000	3.2	1.5 or 3	220	55	cast alum.	6	opt.
Cincinnati 200S	1,100	8.5	2	220	55	cast alum.	6	opt.
Delta 50-181	1,100	8.5	2	220	55	cast alum.	6	opt.
Dustking 750-4	1,100	8	2	110,220,440	55	cast alum.	6	yes
Elektra Beckum SPA-1000	765	4.7	3,4	110,220	40	ABS plastic	4	yes
Grizzly G-1029	1,182	9	2	110,220	30	welded steel	4	yes
Holz 910	1,030	8.5	1	220	35	cast alum.	4.9	yes
Inca 910	840	8.5	6,10	110	25	welded steel	4	yes
Jet DC-1182	1,182	9	2	110,220	40	welded steel	5 or 4	yes
Kraemer S2	1,011	5	2	110,220,550	52	cast alum.	7	yes
Makita 410	300	20	1.3	110	52	welded steel	3	NA
Moldow MF	1,000	5	3	110,220,440	52	welded steel	6	opt.
Murphy-Rodgers MRT-5B	804	7	2	110,220,440	55	welded steel	5	opt.
Rees 211C	900	5	2	110,220	55	cast alum.	6	opt.
Sen Kong UFO-101	1,182	9	2	110,220	30	welded steel	4	yes
Scheppach HA 261	1,780	5	3,4	220	30	welded steel	4	yes
Shopsmith DC3300	368	5	1,2	110	30	plastic	2.5	wheels
Torit 19FM	1,200	4.6	2	220	55	welded steel	6	opt.
Ulmia DCAG	700	5.5	1.25	110	35	cast alum.	4	yes

Standard equipment: 1. Vacuum cleaner or floor-cleaning attachments; 2. Barrel or cabinet storage; 3. Starter switch; 4. Inlet hose; 5. Multi-branch inlet.

Optional equipment: 1. Vacuum cleaner or floor-cleaning attachments; 2. Starter switch; 3. Industrial options (explosion vents, bag-house covers, dust bag shaker, etc.); 4. Aluminum impeller; 5. Multi-branch inlet.

with at least that much static pressure capacity to do the job.

A word to the wise here: Allow generous excess capacity in determining the size of collector you need. A collector that's at least 20 percent larger than the demands placed upon it by the collection system, both in cfm capacity and static pressure loss, should be sufficient. The collector won't be overworked and will probably last longer. It'll also be adequate to handle an additional hook up, should you add a machine in the future.

Picking a system—I discovered some 30 portable dust collectors made by 19 manufacturers, and I'm sure there are a few that escaped my search. Practically all of the dust-collector owners I interviewed bought their machines on price, and I came to understand why: As far as light-duty collectors are concerned, there's not much to distinguish one machine from another, apart from physical size, minor features and capacities. In fact, two Taiwan-made brands, Jet and Grizzly, look identical.

Besides allowing for expansion, there's another reason for buying a slightly larger collector than you need immediately: cfm and static pressure figures can be misleading, even inflated. The cfm rating for any dust collector can be arrived at in two ways. One way is to measure what's called "free air movement"—the air moved only by the collector's fan. This figure is determined by the fan manufacturer (not necessarily the same company that makes the collector), based on standards established by the Air Movement and Control Association, an industry trade group. The second method is more realistic. It involves measuring the volume the collector will actually deliver with the resistance of its dust bag and hose accounted for.

Determining which manufacturers use what calculation method can be difficult. AGET, a maker of industrial systems, employs a test lab complete with ductwork and baffles to test their collectors,

while Dustking performs some of its tests with collectors hooked up to a thickness planer. I had to pry the static pressure ratings out of one importer, who insisted he didn't want to provide them because his competition was simply pulling numbers out of thin air. My research suggests that makers of industrial collectors—AGET, Murphy-Rodgers and Torit, to name a few—provide more realistic or, at least, more consistent ratings than do makers of inexpensive home-shop portables. The issue isn't super critical for the small shop; just remember to oversize the collector slightly.

Portable collectors are manufactured in two basic design types: single stage and two stage. Single-stage collectors pull dust and large chips through an impeller, right along with the air. A cyclone action deposits heavy debris in a lower waste bag while lighter dust rides the center of the cyclone up into a dust bag, usually mounted on top of the waste bag. The airstream moves through the dust bag and back into the shop, keeping heated air inside the building. Most industrial-commercial dust-collection units—the type you see installed on the roof of a factory, for example—are just gigantic, heavy-duty, single-stage collectors.

In a two-stage collector, the impeller is positioned so that heavy debris and scraps are first deposited in a barrel or waste bag, so only light dust moves through the impeller. This translates into less wear and tear on the impeller, as well as on the motor and the arbor attached to it. As in a single-stage collector, the airstream passes through a bag, filtering out the remaining dust before the air re-enters the shop.

Single-stage collectors like the Grizzly, Jet and Shopsmith have one advantage over two-stage designs: The waste is collected in an easily detachable bag, so they're easier to empty out. A two-stage collector is likely to be mounted atop a drum, requiring you to disconnect and remove the drum to empty out the waste. Also, some two-stage collectors come without a barrel or bag: you supply

Standard equipment	Accessories	Type	Suggested retail price
2	2,3,4	single stage	$2,200
None	5	two stage	$ 750
3,4	5	two stage	$ 731
2,3,4,5	1	two stage	$ 459
2,4	1,2,3	single stage	$ 495
2,3,5	None	single stage	$ 355
1,2,3,5	None	single stage	$ 905
3,4	5	single stage	$ 695
3,5	2,5	single stage	$ 561
2,3	1,2,4,5	single stage	$1,090
2,3,4	None	single stage	$ 410
2	None	single stage	$ 850 (3-phase)
None	1,2,3,4,5	single stage	$ 860 (West Coast)
None	None	single stage	$1,125
2,3,5	None	single stage	$ 325
1,2,3,4	None	single stage	$ 499
1,2,3,4,5	None	single stage	$ 449
2	3,4	single stage	$1,598
2,3	1,5	single stage	$1,250

Sources of supply

Dust-collector manufacturers:

AGET Manufacturing Co., P.O. Box 248, Adrian, MI 49221-0248.

Cincinnati Fan & Ventilator Co., Inc., 5345 Creek Rd., Cincinnati, OH 45242-3999.

Delta Machinery Corp., 246 Alpha Dr., Pittsburgh, PA 15238.

Dustking, BEC Industries, Box 368, Sunman, IN 47041.

Elektra Beckum USA Corp., 401-403 Kennedy Blvd., P.O. Box 24, Somerdale, NJ 08083.

Grizzly Imports, Inc., P.O. Box 2069, Bellingham, WA 98227.

Holz Machinery Corp., 45 Halladay St., Jersey City, NJ 07304.

Inca, Garrett Wade Co., 161 Ave. of the Americas, New York, NY 10013.

Jet Equipment & Tools, P.O. Box 1477. Tacoma, WA 98401.

Kraemer Tool and Mfg. Co. Ltd., 190 Milvan Dr., Weston, Ont., Canada M9L 1Z9.

Makita USA, Inc., 12950 E. Aldondra Blvd., Cerritos, CA 95701.

Moldow, EAC Engineering, 322 Edwardia Dr., Greensboro, NC 27409.

Murphy-Rodgers, Inc., 2301 Belgrave Ave., Huntington Park, CA 90255.

Rees-Memphis, Inc., Memphis Machinery & Supply Co., Inc., P.O. Box 13225, Memphis, TN 38113.

Sen Kong (Pit Bull), A.J. Tool Company, Inc., 15250 Texaco Ave., Paramount, CA 90723.

Scheppach, ABBA International, Inc., Box 135, N. Miami Beach, FL 33163.

Shopsmith Inc., 3931 Image Dr., Dayton, OH 45414-2591.

Torit (a division of the Donaldson Co. Inc.), P.O. Box 1299, Minneapolis, MN 55440.

Ulmia, Mahogany Masterpieces, Inc., RFD 1, Wing Rd., Suncook, NH 03275.

Manufacturers and distributors of dust-collection hardware:

AGET Manufacturing Co.—see address above (duct, hoppers, bins, bag houses).

AIN Plastics, Inc., P.O. Box 151, Mt. Vernon, NY 10550 (plastics for forming hoods and connectors).

Cincinnati Fan & Ventilator Co.—see address above (dolly bases, dust bags, hose extension arms, hose, nozzles, related hardware).

Duravent, Dayco Corp., Dayflex Co., 333 W. First St., Dayton, OH 45402 (flexible hose).

Dustex Corp., P.O. Box 7368, 3139 Westinghouse Blvd., Charlotte, NC 28217 (valves, filters, cyclones, hoppers).

Manufacturers' Service Co., Inc., Air Handling Systems, 358 Bishop Ave., Bridgeport, CT 06610 (duct, duct-calculating aids, hose, connectors, nozzles, blast gates, duct-related hardware, filter bags).

Murphy-Rodgers, Inc.—see address above (duct, hoods, connectors. fittings, blast gates, dust bags, hose).

Northfab Systems, Inc., Box 429, Thomasville, NC 27361 (duct connector clamps).

Wyndon Inc., P.O. Box 1359, Hillsboro, NH 03244 (blast gates wired to function as on/off switches, Sen Kong distributor, hose).

your own. Two-stage collectors are, on the other hand, generally quieter running and will probably hold up better if your system draws in large chunks of waste.

Another consideration is how the collector's impeller is constructed. There are two common designs: cast aluminum or welded sheet steel. A cast impeller is less likely to spark and ignite wood waste if metal debris is sucked into the impeller, or if the impeller itself runs out of balance, scraping against its housing. Local fire codes or your insurance company may require an aluminum impeller in your collector; check before you install.

A collector's waste capacity is tied directly to its physical size. Smaller portables, like the Inca 910 and the Shopsmith DC3300, will hold 25 and 30 gallons of waste, respectively. Because of their small size, portability and limited capacity, these machines are ideal for a home shop having only a few stationary tools. They can be connected as needed, without bothering with a central system. A busy commercial shop, on the other hand, will require more capacity, particularly if a thickness planer is often running. Unless you want to empty the collector bag or drum more than once a day—or rework the collector so it has greater capacity—buy at least enough capacity to contain what you'd sweep up off the floor in a typical day.

A dust collector won't be able to hold its advertised capacity, either. Several woodworkers told me what happens if you allow a collector's waste container to fill up right to the top; the air back-up pops the dust bag off the collector, raising great clouds of dust. String or cord tied tightly around the bag solves this problem, but you should empty the bag before it's too full. An overfilled collector is inefficient and defeats the purpose of having dust collection in the first place.

The chart above lists portable dust collectors and the accessories available for them. With the right attachments, you can press some portable collectors into service as large shop vacuums. Check the chart to see which manufacturers offer vacuum attachments. Elektra Beckum, Holz, Scheppach, Shopsmith and Ulmia, for instance, offer floor-cleaning attachments.

Hoods and nozzles that funnel chips and dust from the machine into the duct need not be elaborate. One shop I visited simply tied a portable dust collector's hose to a shaper that hadn't been hooked into the main system. Granted, it was far from the most efficient setup I've seen, but it was still better than letting the machine throw chips all over the shop floor, and it served its purpose until they could fashion a more elaborate setup. Hoods can be made from solid wood, plywood, plastic sheet (see "Sources of supply," above) or sheet metal. □

Roy Berendsohn is an assistant editor of Fine Woodworking.

Tablesaw Safety Devices

A survey of blade guards, hold-downs and push sticks

by Charley Robinson

Many woodworkers don't use guards on their tablesaws, and they're quick to offer various reasons why: the guards have a reputation for getting in the way during some rabbeting, ripping and molding-head operations; they decrease visibility during a cut or setup; they create a safety hazard because stock hangs up on the guard; and they can damage the stock, reduce control and be a real hassle when you try to switch from one operation to another. And in many shops there can be some peer pressure against guards—use one and brace yourself for an afternoon of assorted ridicule.

Even though none of the commonly cited reasons can make up for the loss of a finger or hand in an accident that might have been prevented by a guard or other safety device, few woodworkers invest much time or thought in improving the guards that came with their saws or in developing their own safety devices. Fortunately, some manufacturers now offer devices designed to overcome most of the standard complaints about stock guards. In this article, I'll examine a couple of these alternatives, as well as several available hold-down devices, that can make the tablesaw a safer tool and give you more control over your work. First, let's consider how accidents happen.

Kickback's the key—*Fine Woodworking*'s 1983 survey of hand injuries showed the tablesaw caused more injuries than any other tool in the shop: 42% of the accidents reported by the more than 1,000 woodworkers who responded to our survey. The jointer was second at 18%. Most of the accidents occurred when operators tried to rip short, narrow or thin pieces of wood, although ripping knotty or warped lumber, plunge-cutting and using accessories such as molding, dado or planer attachments were also cited.

Tablesaw accidents are generally caused by one of two factors: the first is kickback, which frequently leads to the second—the operator hitting the rotating blade. Kickback generally occurs when the work binds against the back of the blade. The force lifts the wood until it hits the top of the blade and is hurled with great velocity toward the operator. This can happen when the kerf in the workpiece closes enough to grab the back of the blade, when the work is pinched between the back of the blade and a misaligned fence, or when the workpiece is moved away from the fence or twisted so it binds the sides of the blade. Kickback can also happen when cutoffs left on the table vibrate into the blade or are caught between the throat plate and the blade. Kickback happens so quickly that the operator has no time to react, and often a finger or hand is pulled into the blade, or the projectile hits the operator.

Safety devices can go a long way to protecting the operator. In the previously cited survey, reports of accidents to woodworkers using a blade guard, anti-kickback pawls and a splitter were practically non-existent. The American National Standards Institute (ANSI), composed of representatives of manufacturers and labor, established guidelines for safe operation of woodworking equipment in shops under the jurisdiction of the federal Occupational Safety and Health Administration (OSHA). These guidelines state that the blade on a tablesaw must be covered on the top and sides down to the table. Also, ripping operations must be done with a splitter and anti-kickback pawls in place, but there is no requirement that these devices be attached to the guard itself. And, there are no standards regulating guard manufacturers, so they have freedom in designing shields that provide the visibility, easy adjustability, versatility and anti-kickback features that would most benefit woodworkers. With this in mind, let's take a look at some of the safety devices currently available.

Blade guards—*Biesemeyer Manufacturing's BladeGuard*, shown in the left photo on the facing page, is a metal-and-Plexiglas assembly suspended over the saw table on the end of a 50-in. arm. I found this arrangement provides good visibility and the guard is wide enough to work with the blade set at any angle for miter or compound miter cuts without interference. The guard will protect hands from side or top access to the blade, but a hand slid along the table will raise the guard out of the way just as easily as a piece of wood will, and there are no anti-kickback pawls or splitters attached to the guard.

I experienced no problems with stock being fed through the saw hanging up on the guard, until stock was more than 2 in. thick. When the blade is centered in the guard, there is potential for kickback of scraps in production crosscutting-type situations where small scraps accumulate on the table. Cut-offs trapped between the guard and blade are thrown toward the operator with potential for injury. Adjusting the guard close to the cut-off side of the blade helped keep scraps away from the blade and all but eliminated this problem.

The 2-in.-square tubular steel arm that's mounted at the end of an extension table to support the guard gives 50 in. of clear cutting to the right of the blade and unlimited cutting to the left of the blade or behind the saw. This system was designed to work with an extended table and installs in about 15 minutes; there is also a floor mount model available. An adjustable counterweight lets you balance the guard so there is very little added resistance when feeding stock. The *BladeGuard* is easily raised and locked out of the way, about 8¼ in. above the table, for making fence setups or using a sliding table. Because the guard is suspended above the table, it can be left in place for dado or rabbet cuts or most operations that usually require removing a stock guard. The overhead arm that supports the guard slides inside the support arm that is bolted to the table. Turning a crank on the support arm positions the movable arm over the blade. While this procedure is fairly slow, it does provide safe and accurate adjusting and you normally would not have to move the setup more than a couple of inches.

In addition, the guard also has an alarm system that can be

From *Fine Woodworking* magazine (March 1990) 81:84-88

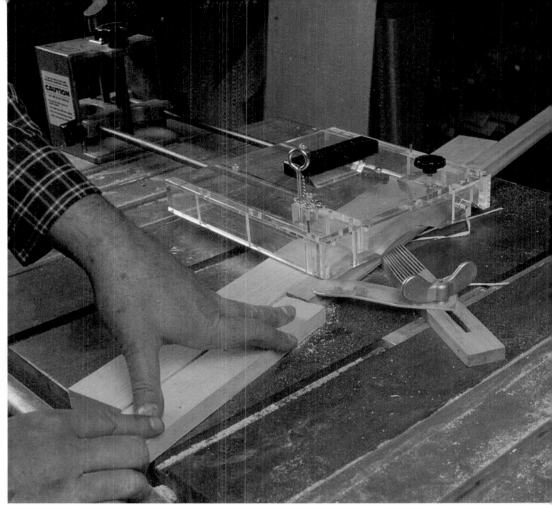

The large, clear Brett-Guard offers good visibility of the blade and the workpiece, and holes through the guard allow you to easily attach a fence for coving or other operations. The guard must be adjusted to stock thickness, however, and the inflexible mounting and large area covered can make it difficult to push the work past the blade.

The Biesemeyer BladeGuard, which is suspended over the table at the end of a 50-in. arm, allows operations, such as dadoing large panels with the guard in place, that are impossible with other guards. Although the unit is convenient and easy to use, a separate splitter and anti-kickback device are also needed.

switched on or off with a key. A loud and obtrusive warning, equal in intensity to a smoke alarm, sounds the second the guard is locked into the raised position. This alarm system was primarily designed for high school shop situations so the shop monitor would be more aware of students' guard usage. Commercial shops may consider the alarm to be strong evidence of their commitment to safety when the OSHA inspector makes a visit, but I doubt it will be used at other times. One minor complaint is that with the guard down, the knob that releases it from the raised position is just about where I want my nose to be when I'm lining up my cutting mark with the blade.

At $385, the *BladeGuard* may show up more in commercial production shops than the home market and that's where it will be most appreciated. This is the most convenient guard I've used: Once it's on the saw, it seems to do its job without needing readjustments and creates minimal interference with the work at hand. It is easily raised to a locked position, to adjust jigs or fences or to clear cut-off tables or other special operations, and then is just as easily returned to the working position. Although the lack of anti-kickback pawls and a splitter will require additional devices to meet OSHA requirements, the guard is so convenient that it will probably be used.

The *Brett-Guard,* manufactured by *HTC Products, Inc.,* is an 11-in. by 11-in. Plexiglas box that is suspended over the sawblade on steel rods attached to a control unit, as shown in the right photo above. The control unit is in turn secured by a locking rod and knob assembly to auxiliary plates bolted to the sides and back of the saw table. Although moving the guard to a new mounting plate is easily accomplished by unscrewing the locking knob, it did take an inordinate number of turns. Tim Hewitt, president of *HTC,* said that on newer models the thread length has been reduced by half and the knob will now lock down in about a turn and a half. The hardest part of installing the *Brett-Guard* is drilling holes in the saw table. One problem on saws like the Delta Contractor's model, to which I mounted it, is that the back mounting plate interferes with motor movement when the blade is tilted for bevel cuts. However, an

optional mount is available that provides clearance for the motor.

The large, clear box that serves as the guard provides the best blade and work visibility of any of the guards I used. However, for precise alignment of the rip fence, I still found it easier to set up the fence before positioning the guard. As with all the guards I tried, static electricity attracted dust particles to the plastic box, but that was more of a nuisance than a real problem. The adjustable anti-kickback plate of the *Brett-Guard* works only when the guard is mounted on the left side of the saw and I found this device tended to scratch the work when adjusted to a position that would prevent kickback. A crank on the control unit raises and lowers the guard; and loosening a couple of thumbscrews allows it to be moved toward or away from the control unit. It is necessary to manually readjust the guard each time you work with material of a different thickness. The manufacturer recommends that the guard be adjusted to rest lightly on top of the work and in this position, it helps hold down the stock being cut. If the work is too high to fit under the guard, adjust the guard to form a channel between it and the fence through which the work can be passed. Although this leaves the blade uncovered, it does offer more protection than no guard. I also found a potentially dangerous situation might occur when ripping long boards or cutting large panels. Without some means of support on the outfeed side of the saw, a long board can lever up the guard, possibly exposing or jamming the blade and damaging the guard.

A stop pin included with the guard is handy for repetitive cuts, and a series of holes in the guard can be used for mounting accessories, such as an angled fence when making cove cuts. In theory this has some interesting possibilities, but in practice I found there was too much play in the suspended guard to yield consistent results when coving a piece of stock. Clamping the fence to the saw table would eliminate the play, but then why bother screwing it to the guard if you have to clamp it anyway. There were a few situations when the guard interfered with the saw operation, such as when ripping sheet goods, or limited the capacity, such as when

Above: Ripstrate's hold-down is the most compact of the group and required the fewest adjustments, although it did not hold boards against the fence as well as the others.

Left: The flexibility of Leichtung's Anti-Kickback Hold-Down Guide System and the superior grip of its soft rubber wheels give it an advantage over similar systems.

crosscutting. The *Brett-Guard* retails for $214, but the manufacturer advises that for $379 you can order a cantilevered system that mounts at the end of a 50-in. extended side table that solves these problems. Also, an overhead mounting system and a floor mounting system have been developed, but these are probably most suited for larger shops and industrial applications.

Hold-down devices—Most commercial hold-downs rely on a series of rollers to force stock snugly down on the saw table. This setup protects operators in two main ways: it allows them to feed stock through the saw without putting their hands near the blade and it reduces the likelihood of kickback because the stock cannot lift off the table enough to be thrown by the blade. Many hold-down devices also have additional anti-kickback features, which the manufacturers say allow operators to stop feeding stock in the middle of the cut, walk to the back of the saw and pull the work through. In all cases, make sure the motor pulley and belt guards are in place if you are going to be working behind the saw. Also, this technique can be dangerous and, at best, requires a little practice before you are able to produce perfect results. Many operators working on the back of the saw tend to pull the work away from the fence on the outfeed side, which in turn can wedge the stock between the blade and fence on the infeed side. Not only does this ruin the workpiece, it can cause kickback and possibly pull you into the blade. One problem I encountered with most of the hold-downs I tried is that they interfere with push sticks and with the normal function of the guards when trying to rip pieces narrower than 3 in. Sometimes the guards can be removed and the hold-down device positioned over the blade in its place. This does not protect the side of the blade, however, so be careful when using this setup. All of these devices should be used in conjunction with guards, safe practices and common sense, not in place of them.

The *Anti-Kickback Hold-Down Guide System,* shown in the left photo above, is available only from *Leichtung Work Shops* for $49.99. It was the best of the hold-downs I tried, although it took about 30 minutes to assemble the pieces. Two spring-loaded hold-down arms equipped with rubber wheels are independently mounted to an auxiliary fence and can be adjusted to hold the work firmly to the table and to the fence. I like the adjustability of these units the most. The wheels can either move freely or be set to lock in either

direction. By adjusting the angle of the wheels to the fence up to 15°, the operator can fine-tune the amount of pull to the fence required by each job. Reversing the wheels on the arm allows you to rip very narrow stock with the wheels close to the fence, which contributes to one of the nicest features of this unit: When ripping very narrow stock, the wheels can be set parallel to the fence so they span the sawkerf. Pushing the stock through and past the blade from the left side causes the wheels to turn, acting like a power feed and driving the cut-off stock out the back side of the blade without a push stick. I was unable to duplicate this trick with any of the other hold-downs. Hold-down pressure is adjustable, as is the control arm for stock thickness. The anti-kickback feature also performed quite well. The soft rubber of the wheels was able to grip the workpiece firmly enough to prevent my pulling the board out from under the unit, although it did allow the board to back up about ¾ in.—enough to prevent a kickback from jamming the blade and possibly burning out your saw motor. As icing on the cake, all of this performance comes without having to buy any optional accessories.

The *Ripstrate* from *Fisher Hill Products,* shown in the right photo above, is $69 and consists of a pair of wheels mounted via spring-loaded arms to a cast-iron carriage. A built-in clamp on the carriage holds the auxiliary fence, as well as the unit itself, to your stock saw fence. Mounting the carriage at about a 5° angle helps direct any stock pushed under the wheels toward the fence. It took about 10 to 15 minutes to set up the first time, but then the auxiliary fence and hold-down could be removed or installed in just minutes. The *Ripstrate* is self-adjusting to the thickness of stock, and it requires fewer adjustments than any of the other devices. When ripping narrow stock, the small size of this unit left more room for push sticks than the other units.

I found the *Ripstrate* to work fairly well as a hold-down, but I was disappointed with its ability to pull and hold material to the fence, particularly when ripping large panels, a situation where hold-downs can be most helpful. Also, the hard rubber wheels didn't grip the workpiece as well as some of the other devices. Although I was unable to generate a kickback with any of these hold-downs, I could, without difficulty, pull the board back out of the *Ripstrate* in spite of the wheels locking up as they were designed to do. The manufacturer assured me that the *Ripstrate* will eliminate kickback under most circumstances, but in the rare in-

Above: Shophelper's yellow wheels hold the work to the fence, but gaining the adjustability of other systems requires a considerable investment in accessory tracks and wheels.

Right: The simply designed Vega Stock Feeder can be stored in place on top of Vega fence, but it would interfere with the company's push stick, which rides in the same track.

stance that it does occur, the wheels will stop the board.

At $69.95, the *Shophelper,* by *Western Commercial Products,* is a pair of wheels individually mounted on levered axles, as shown in the left photo above. The wheel-and-axle housing slips into a mounting bracket that is screwed to an auxiliary fence. Rather than relying on a canted position to hold stock to the fence, the spring action of the axle arms directly pulls the work to the fence. This results in the workpiece being held more firmly against the fence than all of the canted wheel designs except the *Leichtung* system, which has an adjustable cant. Anti-kickback is provided by single-direction bearings in the wheels that limit stock feed to a right-to-left direction. While the bearings stopped the hard composition wheels, the wheels themselves were less effective at gripping the workpiece. Again, although I wasn't able to induce kickback, the board could be pulled back out of the *Shophelper.* Optional wheels ($19.90) are available for reverse-direction feeding and an optional 24-in. mounting track ($29.95) will allow front-to-back adjustability. The long mounting brackets that are standard with the *Shophelper* allow the wheels to be adjusted between ⅝ in. and 5 in. of the fence.

Vega Enterprises' new entry in the wheeled hold-down market is the *Stock Feeder,* which mounts directly onto a *Vega* fence, as shown in the right photo above. The unit is $59 and optional mounting rails, 12 in. long for $7 and 24 in. long for $12, are available for mounting the Stock Feeder to other fences. Immediately evident is that this device has a single wheel that rides on the stock in front of the blade combined with a spring steel hold-down finger in the back. The wheel, canted at 4° to pull stock toward the fence, can be adjusted to ride directly in front of the blade for stock up to 10 in. wide and is adjustable fore and aft along the length of the *Vega* fence or of the optional mounting rails. Both the front and rear hold-downs must be adjusted each time stock thickness changes, and setting the hold-down wheel as directed by the manufacturer greatly increases resistance to feeding stock through the saw. Although the wheel is easily adjustable to stock thickness, by itself it doesn't offer much resistance to kickback. The spring steel rear finger, held at 40° to the stock, provides the real means for preventing kickback, and its end is ground and polished to prevent scratching stock. By adjusting the hold-down to the extreme right, the unit can be stored out of the way on top of the fence. In this position, however, it will interfere with *Vega's Finger Saver,* a push stick that also rides on top of its fence.

Fingerboards—In general, fingerboards operate in much the same manner as hold-down devices. As shown in the bottom photo on the following page, they can be homemade or commercial, clamped to the saw table or clamped in the miter slot to hold work tight to the fence, or clamped to the fence to act as a hold-down. Their slanted, flexible fingers also help control kickback.

The *Universal Clamp,* shown in the top photo on the following page, is one of those devices that makes you wonder "Why didn't I think of that?". It's a simple fingerboard that mounts in the miter gauge slot of your tablesaw. When the large, comfortable wing nut on top is tightened, it clamps the fingerboard in position and expands a split aluminum bar in the miter gauge slot to lock the unit to the table. An aluminum finger that serves as a hold-down for ¾-in. stock can be easily moved out of the way when it's not needed. Because the clamp mounts in the miter gauge slot, its capacity is limited, but it is so easy to use and effective that I want one; and at $24.95 it's not worth the trouble to try to make something like this in your shop. The *Universal Clamp* is available from a number of mail order sup-

Sources of supply

Biesemeyer Manufacturing, 216 S. Alma School Road #3, Mesa, AZ 85210; (602) 835-9300.

Fisher Hill Products, Fisher Hill, Fitzwilliam, NH 03447; (603) 585-6883.

Garrett Wade Co. Inc., 161 Ave. of the Americas, New York, NY 10013; (800) 221-2942, (212) 807-1757.

HTC Products, Inc., 120 E. Hudson, Box 839, Royal Oak, MI 48067; (313) 399-6185.

Leichtung Work Shops, 4944 Commerce Parkway, Cleveland, OH 44128; (216) 831-6191.

The Original Wall-Marker Co., Box 436045, Louisville, KY 40243-6045; (502) 245-5930.

Shopsmith Inc., 3931 Image Drive, Dayton, OH 45414-2591; (800) 543-7586, (513) 898-6070.

Vega Enterprises, Inc., R.R. #3, Box 193, Decatur, IL 62526; (217) 963-2232.

Western Commercial Products, Box 1202, Tulare, CA 93275; (800) 344-7455, in CA (800) 828-8833.

Woodcraft, 210 Wood County Industrial Park, Parkersburg, WV 26102; (800) 225-1153.

Woodworker's Supply of New Mexico, 5604 Alameda Place N.E., Albuquerque, NM 87113; (800) 645-9292, (505)821-0500.

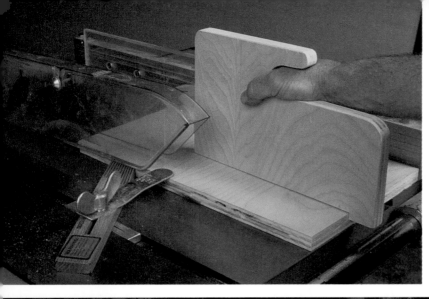

A variety of push sticks and hold-downs that can help save your fingers are clockwise from the left front of the saw table: the Universal Clamp, the Shopsmith Safety Kit, a shopmade featherboard, a shopmade push stick, the Saw-Aid (manufactured by The Original Wall-Marker Co.), two shopmade push sticks and a Biesemeyer push stick.

pliers, including Woodworker's Supply, Woodcraft and Garrett Wade (see sources of supply on previous page).

For $23 the *Shopsmith Safety Kit,* shown in the bottom photo above, offers a variety of push sticks, blocks and a featherboard, all made of a plastic that is designed to powder if hit by a blade. The conventionally designed push stick has a nice heft and a molded handle that feels good. The fence straddler is a push stick designed specifically for narrow rip cuts on the Shopsmith tablesaw fence. It could, however, be adapted for use on other machines and offers more stability than a regular narrow push stick would for these cuts. A pair of push blocks that could be used for rip cuts over 4 in. wide are also included with the kit. The tilted handles keep your hands away from the fence while the substantial feel and the excellent grip of the soft rubber base make them a pleasure to use. I found them far superior to any other push blocks I've used, particularly for face-jointing boards. The final item in the package is a featherboard designed to mount in the miter gauge slot. Tightening the lock knobs not only fastens the featherboard to the miter bar, but also expands the miter bar in the miter gauge slot to hold it in place. This unit worked well on the Shopsmith, but tended to slide in the miter slot on my Delta Contractor's saw. I found a piece of 100-grit sandpaper glued to one edge tightened the fit in the slot and provided the grip needed to keep it in place. Although these tools were designed with the Shopsmith in mind, they are readily adaptable to other machines and they keep your hands out of harm's way.

Common sense—All the best safety equipment in the world can't replace common sense when working with hazardous equipment. You should always be aware of where your fingers are and where they might go if the board you are working on should suddenly disappear. Use a push stick, like those shown in the bottom photo above, to keep your fingers away from sawblades. My favorite design, which is shown in use in the top photo above, came from Todd Randall, a Cupertino, Cal., woodworker. Randall, who lost four fingers to a molding head cutter in a tablesaw, designed this push stick to be gripped between his thumb and the first knuckle of his index finger. Maintain good balance and don't overextend yourself or push too hard toward the blade. A smooth and well-waxed work surface and fence will reduce the effort needed. Take a second look at your procedures, even if you've been doing the same thing for a long time; there may be a safer way of doing it. Many operations can be done more safely on the bandsaw, especially with small pieces and knotty or warped boards. Heed the premonitions you have as you're about to perform a dangerous operation and ignore the less informed who would have you believe you're less of a woodworker for using guards. As Randall says, "If you like woodworking enough, take the steps necessary to protect your ability to do it." □

Charley Robinson is an Assistant Editor at FWW.

Index